THE COMBINED ANGLO-SAXON CHRONICLES:

A READY-REFERENCE ABRIDGED CHRONOLOGY

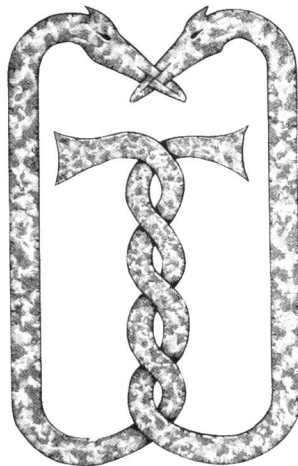

GUY POINTS

The Combined Anglo-Saxon Chronicles:
A Ready-Reference Abridged Chronology

First Published in Great Britain in 2013 by the author as
RIHTSPELL PUBLISHING

ISBN 978-0-9557679-2-0

By the same Author:
A Gazetteer of Anglo-Saxon & Viking Sites: County Durham & Northumberland (2012)
Yorkshire: A Gazetteer of Anglo-Saxon & Viking Sites (2007)
A Concise Guide to Historic Northumberland and Tyne & Wear (1987)
A Concise Guide to Historic Shetland (1984)
A Concise Guide to Historic Orkney (1981)

Marketed and Distributed in the UK and Rest of World by:
Oxbow Books Ltd,
10 Hythe Bridge Street,
Oxford,
OX1 2EW
www.oxbowbooks.com
General Enquiries: oxbow@oxbowbooks.com

Marketed and Distributed in North America by:
The David Brown Book Company,
PO Box 511 (20 Main Street),
Oakville CT 06779, USA.
queries@dbbconline.com

Printed by Binfield Print & Design Ltd.
www.binfieldprint.com

PREFACE

This book provides a narrative in chronological order of the information provided by the extant manuscripts of the Anglo-Saxon Chronicle using as its principal source "The Anglo-Saxon Chronicle", translated by G N Garmonsway first published in 1953. I have further developed and abridged the Garmonsway version to produce one continuous text using different print fonts to identify each of the source manuscripts. This removes the necessity for cross-referencing by paragraph, page and year. The font index is supplied at the foot of every single page of the narrative. Direct quotes from the Garmonsway text are punctuated by quotation marks. I set our below my omissions, additions, the problems arising from the dating of some entries, and what I have termed "irreconcilable inconsistencies" because of the spellings used in different manuscripts or the difficulty now in identifying the places or individuals named.

Omissions
To assist the narrative of events I have excluded prefaces and genealogies, poems about people or events, eulogies extolling the Christian virtues of individuals, most references to the relationship of individuals (often kings) to their predecessors or successors. The number of years a king reigned or a bishop held his post has been omitted. Entries commence where Britain and its peoples are specifically mentioned.

The full title of a king or person and the identification of their kingdom, bishopric, abbey, earldom, place of residence etc are included on the first occasion they are mentioned in an entry in a single year and are not repeated in full again in the same year.

The Manuscripts are listed in alphabetical order A to H. Information provided in any one is not repeated when it is also included in whole or part in another. Only new and additional information provided in the different manuscripts is added.

Additions
In some entries I have inserted additional information enclosed in standard brackets ( ) and in the same font as the relevant manuscripts, to assist understanding the context of the information.

Where possible, to assist geographical location, places are identified by their modern county name unless the town or city provides the name for their shire: London, Durham, Peterborough and Canterbury are exceptions to this addition. The modern name for the appropriate country has been added to places located on the Continent: Normandy, Flanders, Rome and Jerusalem are exceptions to this addition.

When recording people I have tried to add some clarity by attempting to identify who they are. Where the manuscripts themselves simply give the title of a person with no name, or give their title and name, with no indication of the geographical location where they "ruled" or lived, I have added information to the narrative. Thus the entry for 807 reads: "King Cuthred of Kent, Abbess Ceolburh of Berkley, Gloucestershire, and Ealdorman Heahberht of Kent die." Where it has not been possible to easily identify the individual mentioned in an entry by title or location I have put in brackets "(no further information readily available)".

When recording events I have also tried to add some clarity by attempting to identify where they took place especially when the manuscripts themselves simply refer to a place, river or battle with or without a name, I have added information in the narrative. Thus my entry for 885 reads: "King Alfred of Wessex sends a fleet to East Anglia where it defeats at the mouth of the River Stour (on the border between Essex and Suffolk) a fleet of sixteen ships of pirates and kills all their crews." Where it has not been possible to easily identify the location referred to in the events mentioned I have put in brackets: "(this site has not been confidently identified)".

Problems of Dating
Dates shown in different manuscripts for the same or similar events can vary and can contradict each other. The dates indicated in Manuscript "A" are those generally quoted. After the cessation of Manuscript "A" the dates in Manuscript "E" are quoted. The date at the start of each entry and any cross references to annual entries elsewhere in the text, are shown in Arial Black font. Dates which are not included in Manuscript "A" are entered under the Manuscript in which they first appear – "B" to "H".

Manuscripts do not necessarily have entries for every sequential year, and events recorded are not always in strict chronological order. Mostly years begin on 25 December (the festival period, Christmas or Mid-Winter) although sometimes they begin on the preceding 24 September (the entries 866-925 for Manuscript "A" in particular); and sometimes on the succeeding 25 March.

To achieve a more consistent chronology I have quoted the more generally accepted dates, included in square brackets in the "Garmonsway" text. However, it should be noted that the majority of events in entries 754-845 are dated two years early. There are also errors in the dating of events caused by a scribe providing an entry for a sequential year rather than leaving it blank and placing it in the correct year, or omitting a year altogether.

Where manuscripts other than Manuscript "A" provide additional information on the same events, this is placed in the dates indicated in Manuscript "A". Where there is a difference between manuscripts in date attribution, the date quoted in Manuscript "A", or the first manuscript in sequence "B" to "H" in which they appear, I have inserted an annotation: "(Manuscript X attributes these events/specific named event to Y)" in the font of the relevant manuscript identifying the alternative year.

Irreconcilable inconsistencies
Names and their spellings are as used in the manuscripts themselves even if they are not perhaps those by which the individual or place are now known. (Note: Modern English Ae, ae and th are used rather than Old English Æ, æ or þ.) Names may be altered or differently spelled in different entries in the same manuscript, resulting in difficulty in identifying whether the same person or place is being referred to. Some manuscripts, rather than name an individual may simply refer to them as "the wife of, son of, daughter of" or initially mention them by name and then by reference to their relations or their titles. In some of these instances I have been able to add the name. (Emma of Normandy, the widow and second wife of King Aethelred II of England, and the second wife of King Cnut, is known as Aelfgifu because she was considered a replacement for Cnut's first English Queen Aelfgifu.) Entries relating to the eleventh and twelfth centuries mention a number of people named or referred to as "Matilda" and so care has to be taken differentiating the individuals concerned. Now known as "Empress Matilda", the Chronicle initially refers to her as (King Henry's) "his daughter Aethelic, wife of the late emperor of Germany", then "the daughter of king Henry, who had been empress of Germany and was now countess of Anjou" and then more frequently "the empress".

Certain descriptors included in the manuscripts have been retained. Thus, the word "host" and variations such as the "pirate host", the "great host", usually refer to the bands, forces and armies from Scandinavia, sometimes referred to as the "Danes" irrespective of their origin. The "host" may also be referred to collectively as the "heathen" or "ships' companies" "or pirates". The "levies" usually refer to English, Wessex or Mercian troops, forces or armies.

Use of Different Fonts to Identify Manuscripts
For speedy identification and reference the key to these fonts is as follows:

Manuscript "A" (Winchester or Parker): Trebuchet.

Manuscript "B" (Abingdon I) & Manuscript "C" (Abingdon II): 18th Century.

Manuscript "D" (Worcester): Swiss 721 Hv BT.

Manuscript "E" (Peterborough or Laud): Courier New.

Manuscript "F" (Canterbury): Alexa.

Manuscript "H" (Winchester): Calligraphic.

This key to the fonts is set out at the foot of every single page of the narrative.

INTRODUCTION

The Anglo-Saxon Chronicle originally derived from a collection of annals created in the late ninth century, probably in Wessex, during the reign of Alfred the Great (reigned 871-899). Multiple copies were made and sent to monasteries all over England where they were independently updated, amended and copied. Today some nine manuscripts survive to make up what is known as the "Anglo-Saxon Chronicle".

The manuscripts record events, people and places BC 60 to AD 1154 often not recorded elsewhere. Their content is selective, not comprehensive and not always entirely accurate; different manuscripts can contradict each other. The information recorded can be without enlightening explanations and sometimes it is very perfunctory. As the years unfold entries for some years become more detailed and sometimes include commentaries on events and people by individual scribes.

Whilst recognising the inaccuracies and omissions, bias and limitations, any study of the Anglo-Saxon Chronicle, whether in its collective or individual form, can lead to whole new lines of investigation into some hidden gems of history.

MANUSCRIPTS

Written between the end of the ninth century and the middle of the twelfth century, the Chronicles were written in Old English rather than Latin even though it is likely that none of the documents consulted in its compilation was in English. Each manuscript was written by a number of scribes with the exception of manuscript "B" written by a single scribe, and manuscript "E" which appears to have been written by a single scribe until a second made the entries for the years 1132-1154.

The manuscripts evolved from the list-like "Easter Tables" drawn up to determine the dates of church feasts – holy days and saints days – and the seasons. These included astronomical information and notes to distinguish one year from another. As the notes expanded over the years they became more like the records recognisable as forming the Anglo-Saxon Chronicle. The manuscripts of the Anglo-Saxon Chronicle include, selectively and inconsistently between copies, material from Bede's "Ecclesiastical History of the English People", the "Annals of St Neots", the Mercian Register, the "Battle of Brunanburh" and other poems, and extracts from other manuscripts of the Chronicle which have not survived, including the northern manuscripts. Material was also used from earlier annals, genealogies, lists of Episcopal appointments and charters as well as contemporaneous accounts including speech quotations. In addition scribes were not averse to inventing material to fill in the blank pages or amending and deleting entries relating to earlier periods – twelfth century scribes in particular.

Nine manuscripts commonly numbered "A" to "I", survive in whole or in part:

Manuscript "A" is known as "The Winchester" or "Parker" Chronicle (named after Matthew Parker, Archbishop of Canterbury 1559-1575 and Master of Corpus Christi College). It covers the period BC 60 to AD 1070. Writing began sometime in the late ninth century towards the end of the reign of King Alfred the Great. It may well have been written at the Old Minster in Winchester but it is a copy of a copy and so the scriptorium of its origin is uncertain. It was transferred to Canterbury sometime in the eleventh century. It is now housed in the Parker Library in Corpus Christi College, Cambridge.

Manuscript "B" is known as "Abingdon I". It covers the period AD 1 to AD 977. It was probably written at Abingdon sometime in the eleventh century and utilises material from a copy now lost which was sent (source unknown) to Abingdon Abbey sometime in the tenth century; it is a copy of a copy. It is now housed in the British Library.

Manuscript "C" is known as "Abingdon II". It covers the period BC 60 to AD 1066. It was probably written at Abingdon sometime in the eleventh century. It utilises material from Manuscript "B" and a copy now lost which was sent (source unknown) to Abingdon Abbey sometime in the tenth century; it is a copy of a copy. It is now housed in the British Library.

Manuscript "D" is known as "The Worcester Chronicle". It covers the period AD 1 to AD 1080 with an addition for the year 1130. It includes material from the Mercian Register, Bede's "Ecclesiastical History" and from Northumbrian annals dating from the eighth century. It is a copy of a northern manuscript, possibly written at Ripon in North Yorkshire, which no longer survives. It was probably written at Worcester in the middle of the eleventh century. It is now housed in the British Library.

Manuscript "E" is known as the "Peterborough" or "Laud" Chronicle (named after William Laud, Archbishop of Canterbury 1633-1654). It covers the period AD 1 to AD 1153 using similar source material to Manuscript "D" but not including material from the Mercian Register. It was written at Peterborough after the fire in 1116. It was copied from a lost Kentish version of the Chronicle probably originating at Canterbury. The final entry was written in Middle English – one of the earliest examples of this development in the language. It is now housed in the Bodleian Library, Oxford.

Manuscript "F" is known as the "Bilingual Canterbury Epitome". It covers the period AD 1 to AD 1058. It was written around 1100 providing an abridged copy of a lost Kentish version of the Chronicle probably originating at Canterbury also used by the scribe writing Manuscript "E". Each entry in Old English is followed by a Latin translation. It is now housed in the British Library.

Manuscript "G" (sometimes referred to as "A2" or "W"), is a copy of "The Winchester Chronicle". It was probably made at Winchester at around 1013. It was burnt in a fire at Ashburnham House, Little Dean's Yard, Westminster, London in 1731 where it formed part of the Cotton Library (Sir Robert Cotton AD 1571-1631, MP for Huntingdon, antiquarian and bibliophile). As a result only a few leaves survive. A transcript of the original was made by the sixteenth century antiquarian Laurence Nowell which was used by Abraham Wheloc – hence the "W" for Wheloc reference – when it was printed in 1643. It is now housed in the British Library.

Manuscript "H" is known as "The Cottonian Fragment". Only a single leaf survives relating to the years 1113 and 1114. It is a copy of an original thought to have been made at Winchester. It is now housed in the British Library.

Manuscript "I" is not included in this narrative. It is an "Easter Table Chronicle" containing single annual entries for some of the years 988-1268. Its entries written in English end in 1109 with one further entry in English recording the dedication of the cathedral church at Canterbury in 1130; the remaining entries are in Latin recording mostly the deaths of kings, archbishops and bishops and pilgrimages to Rome by bishops. It was written at Canterbury soon after 1073. It is now housed in the British Library.

CONTENT

The Chronicle records events including the first landings of the Angles, Saxons and Jutes in England; the appointment, succession and deaths of kings, churchmen and important lay people; the conversion of England to Christianity; battles between kings and the nascent kingdoms of England; battles against the Picts, Welsh, Irish, Scots, the Vikings, the Normans and the French. There are often inaccuracies and contradictions between the different manuscripts.

PLACES AND PEOPLE

Early entries in particular can be brief, posing many questions impossible to answer. Why were these particular events and people recorded; why were they considered significant; what happened next? As the Chronicle unfolds, events and people are recorded in greater detail inviting further questions; can the places referred to now be identified; are the events commemorated; and are semi-biographical details of the people mentioned available elsewhere? Particular difficulties arise with the varying spellings of the names of people and places, and where these names are spelt differently in the same manuscript or between manuscripts.

GOVERNANCE

The Chronicle also raises questions on the way the country was governed and its taxation. The entry for 1014 records that after King Swein's death the English councillors in England sent for King Aethelred "if only he would govern his kingdom more justly than he had done in the past". King Aethelred agreed to address their concerns and "a complete and friendly agreement was reached and ratified with word and pledge on either side".

Taxation often features and in 1041 "King Harthacnut had all Worcestershire harried on account of his two housecarles who were collecting the heavy tax". The inhabitants killed them inside the minster church. In 1105 there were complaints about "the numerous taxes from which there was no relief". The entry for 1137 records that King Stephen introduced a tax, "tenserie", local protection money paid by villagers to save their homes, livestock and crops from being plundered by armies operating in their area.

FOREIGN AFFAIRS

Foreign affairs are also mentioned in the Chronicle, referring to people and events in Flanders, France, the Holy Roman Empire, Hungary and Norway. The entry for 888 gives details of the division of the Kingdom of the Franks after the death of King Charles while the entry for 1049 provides details of events concerning the Holy Roman Emperor Henry III. The entry for 1073 records that King William leads "an English and French host oversea, and conquered the province of Maine, and the English laid it completely waste; they destroyed the vineyards, burnt down the towns, and completely devastated the countryside, and brought it all into subjection to William".

COMMENTARY BY THE SCRIBE

In some entries the scribe adds a commentary. The entry for 999 records: "Time after time the more urgent a thing was the greater delay from one hour to the next, and all the while they were allowing the strength of their enemies to increase; and as they kept retreating from the sea, so the enemy followed close on their heels. So in the end these naval and land preparations were a complete failure, and succeeded only in adding to the distress of the people, wasting money, and encouraging their enemy." The entry for 1043 records that after Edward the Confessor is crowned king he confiscates from his mother Queen Emma of Normandy all the lands, gold and silver and all that she possessed because "she had been too tight-fisted with him". The entry for 1085 referring to King William and The Domesday Book records: "So very thoroughly did he (William) have the inquiry carried out that there was not a single hide, not one virgate of land, not even – it is shameful to record it, but it did not seem shameful to him to do – not even one ox, nor one cow, nor one pig, which escaped notice in his survey." Many entries appear completely random and unconnected with the adjacent text. These may reflect information received by letter or visitor, indicating that the scriptorium was in touch with the wider world.

NATURAL EVENTS

The Chronicle also records a variety of matters impacting on the population including great famines, the destruction of crops, eclipses of the sun and moon and the arrival of comets, severe winters, storms, dry summers with wildfire, and earthquakes. Some entries are fuller than others, and whilst accepting they may have been within the personal experience of the scribe and his contemporaries rather than simply a record, they do provide a greater insight to the mindset and experience of people living at that time. For example, in 1047 "severe winter with frost and snow and widespread storms: it was so severe that no living man could remember another like it, because of the mortality of both men and cattle; both birds and fish perished because of the hard frost and from hunger"; and in 1114 "an ebb-tide which was everywhere lower than any man remembered before; so people went riding and walking across the Thames to the east of London Bridge".

THE COMBINED ANGLO-SAXON CHRONICLES:

A READY-REFERENCE ABRIDGED CHRONOLOGY

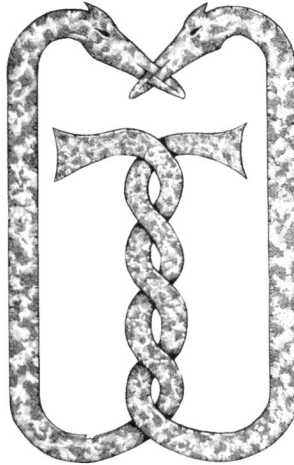

THE NARRATIVE

THE NARRATIVE

THE YEAR - **All numbers identifying year of entry are printed in font Arial Black irrespective of manuscript origin.**

60 years before the birth of Christ, the Roman Emperor Julius Caesar comes to Britain with eighty ships; fierce fighting ensues, much of his host is destroyed. He returns to Gaul and then comes back to Britain with six hundred ships. A great battle takes place where the Britons place stakes at a ford in the River Thames (no further information readily available) to prevent the Romans crossing. The Romans are victorious and the Britons flee to the woods. After strenuous efforts Caesar conquers many strongholds (no further information readily available) but finally returns to Gaul (France).

47 – The Roman Emperor Claudius takes possession of most of Britain. He also makes Orkney subject to Roman Empire.

189 – The Roman Emperor Severus by battle conquers much of Britain (no further information readily available) builds an earthwork in Britain from sea to sea. He dies in York.

283 – St Alban is martyred in St Albans in Hertfordshire. (Manuscript E attributes this event to **286**.)

409 – The Goths take Rome, "never afterwards did the Romans rule in Britain".

418 – The Romans collect all the treasures in Britain, some they bury so that no one can find them, and some they take with them to Gaul (France).

430 – Pope Celestine I sends Patrick to the Scots to "strengthen their faith"/"preach baptism".

443 – Britons send to Rome to ask for troops to fight the Picts. The request is declined because Rome is fighting Attila the Hun. The Britons make the same request of the Angles.

449 – Vortigern, King of the Britons, invites Hengest and Horsa to Britain who come in three ships. He gives them land in the southeast of the country. They land at Ypwinesfleot (Ebbsfleet, Kent) to help the Britons but then fight against them. They fight the Picts and are victorious. *After killing the enemies of King Vortigern they turn against the King and destroy the Britons "by fire and by the edge of the sword". (Manuscript F attributes these events to* **448**.*)* Hengest and Horsa send for more support from three nations of Germany telling them of "the worthlessness of the Britons and the excellence of the land". From the Jutes come

---

Manuscript "A" (Winchester or Parker): Trebuchet.

Manuscript "B" (Abingdon I) & Manuscript "C" (Abingdon II): 18thCentury.

Manuscript "D" (Worcester): Swiss 721 Hv BT.

Manuscript "E" (Peterborough or Laud): Courier New.

Manuscript "F" (Canterbury): Alexa.

Manuscript "H" (Winchester): Calligraphic.

the people of Kent and the people of the Isle of Wight. From the Old Saxons come the East Saxons, South Saxons and West Saxons. From Angel, the land between the Saxons and the Jutes, "which has stood waste ever since", come the East Angles, Middle Angles, Mercians and all the Northumbrians.

455 – Hengest and Horsa fight King Vortigern at Agaelesthrep/`Aegelesthrep` (Aylesford, Kent) and in the battle Horsa is killed. Hengest and his son Aesc succeed to the kingdom.

457 – Hengest and his son Aesc kill four thousand Britons in a battle at Crecganford (Crayford, Kent). As a result the Britons abandon Kent and flee to London. (`Manuscript E attributes these events to` **456**`.`)

465 – Hengest and his son Aesc fight the Welsh near Wippedesfleot (possibly Ebbsfleet in Kent); one of their thanes called Wipped (no further information readily available) is killed. Twelve Welsh nobles are killed.

473 – Hengest and his son Aesc fight the Welsh (no further information readily available) and capture much booty, "the Welsh fled from the English like fire".

477 – Aelle and his sons Cymen, Wlencing and Cissa come to Britain with three ships and land at Cymenesora (to the south of Selsey Bill, West Sussex - now lost to the sea) and defeat the Welsh in battle there. Many Welsh flee into the woods, the Andredesleag (the Sussex Weald).

485 – Aelle fights the Welsh near the bank of the river Mearcraedesburna/`Mearcredesburna` (possibly the River Cuckmere in Sussex).

488 – Aesc becomes King of Kent.

491 – Aelle and one of his sons Cissa besiege the Roman fort at Andredescester/ `Andredesceaster` (Pevensey, East Sussex) and kill all the inhabitants "there was not even one Briton left there".

495 – Cerdic and his son Cynric come to Britain with five ships and on the same day as they land at Cerdicesora/`Certicesora` (in Hampshire - The Solent or Southampton Water) they fight the Welsh.

501 – Port and his two sons Bieda and Maegla come to Portesmutha (Portsmouth, Hampshire) with two ships where they kill a young Briton "a very noble man" (no further information readily available).

508 – Cerdic and Cynric kill five thousand Welsh and their king Natanleod/`Nazaleod` in the district afterwards known as Natanleag/`Nazanleog` (Netley Marsh, Hampshire) which extended to Cerdicesford/`Certicesford` (Charford, Hampshire).

Manuscript "A" (Winchester or Parker): Trebuchet.
Manuscript "B" (Abingdon I) & Manuscript "C" (Abingdon II): 18thCentury.
Manuscript "D" (Worcester): Swiss 721 Hv BT.
Manuscript "E" (Peterborough or Laud): Courier New.
Manuscript "F" (Canterbury): Alexa.
Manuscript "H" (Winchester): Calligraphic.

514 – Stuf and Wihtgar, West Saxons, come to Britain with three ships and land at Cerdicesora/Certicesora (see **495** above). They fight and defeat the Britons (it is not clear whether this took place at or in the vicinity of Cerdicesora or elsewhere).

519 – Cerdic and Cynric (his son) take possession of the kingdom of the West Saxons and fight the Britons at Cerdicesford/Certicesford (see **508** above). (Cerdic is accredited as the founder of the West Saxon royal line.)

527 – Cerdic and Cynric fight the Britons at Cerdicesleag/Certicesford (this site has not been confidently identified.)

530 – Cerdic and Cynric take possession of the Isle of Wight and kill a few men at Wihtgaraesburh/Wihtgarasburh (possibly Carisbrooke on the Isle of Wight).

534 – Cerdic dies. Cynric reigns for twenty-six years (this is the first reference to someone "reigning", implying wider kingship rather than local chieftainship). They had given the Isle of Wight to their grandson and nephew Stuf and Wihtgar (it is unclear in which year this gift took place).

538 – On 16 February there is an eclipse of the sun from early morning until nine o'clock in the morning.

540 – Eclipse of the sun on 20 June; the stars appear for almost half an hour after nine o'clock in the morning.

544 – Wihtgar dies and is buried at Wihtgaraburh/Whitgarasburh (possibly Carisbrooke on the Isle of Wight).

547 – Ida succeeds to the Kingdom of Northumbria. He builds Bamburgh (in Northumberland); the site is first enclosed with a stockade and then a rampart.

552 – King Cynric of Wessex defeats the Britons at a battle at Searoburh (Old Sarum, Wiltshire). *King Aethelberht of Kent is born; he is the first of the kings in Britain to receive a Christian baptism.*

556 – King Cynric of Wessex and Cealwin (his son) fight the Britons at Beranburh (Barbury Castle, Wiltshire).

560 – Cealwin becomes King of Wessex. King Ida of Northumbria dies (in 559). Aelle becomes King of Northumbria (more accurately king of Deira, the southern part of Northumbria. In Bernicia, the northern part of Northumbria, a number of sons rule as kings, among them Adda, Aethelric, Clappa, Frithwold and Theodric – their names and the spellings vary dependent on the source.)

565 – Aethelberht becomes King of Kent. Columba the priest comes from Ireland to Britain

---

Manuscript "A" (Winchester or Parker): Trebuchet.
Manuscript "B" (Abingdon I) & Manuscript "C" (Abingdon II): 18thCentury.
Manuscript "D" (Worcester): Swiss 721 Hv BT.
Manuscript "E" (Peterborough or Laud): Courier New.
Manuscript "F" (Canterbury): Alexa.
Manuscript "H" (Winchester): Calligraphic.

to instruct the Picts "inhabitants along the northern mountains" and establishes a monastery on the island of Iona where he dies. (The scribe records) that the South Picts had been baptised much earlier by Ninian whose church is St Martin's at Whithorn, Dumfriesshire. The scribe also records that Columba was an abbot and not a bishop and that all the bishops of the Scots were subject to him.

568 – King Cealwin of Wessex and Cutha (possibly his son) fight King Aethelberht of Kent and force him back to Kent. Two princes (probably both ealdorman, but possibly a reference to King Cnebba of Mercia) Oslaf/`Oslac` and Cnebba are killed at Wibbandun (possibly Worplesdon in Surrey). (This is the first recorded fighting between Anglo-Saxons rather than the Anglo-Saxons against Britons or others.)

571 – Cuthwulf (probably from the royal line of Wessex, his exact relationship is uncertain) fights the Britons at Bedcanford/`Biedcanford` (possibly Bedford) and captures Limbury, Aylesbury, Benson and Eynsham in the Oxfordshire/Buckinghamshire area. Cuthwulf dies later in the year.

577 – King Ceawlin of Wessex and Cuthwine (son) kill three British kings – Coinmail, Condidan and Farinmail – at the battle of Dyrham, Gloucestershire and capture Gloucester, Cirencester (Gloucestershire) and Bath (Somerset).

584 – King Cealwin of Wessex and Cutha (see **568** above) fight the Britons at Fethanleag/`Fethanlea` (near Stoke Lyne, Oxfordshire). Cutha is killed. King Cealwin captures many villages (no further information readily available) and much booty.

588 – King Aelle of Deira dies and is succeeded by Aethelric.

591 – King Ceol/`Ceolric` of Wessex reigns for five/`six` years.

592 – Many people are killed at Adam's Grave (Alton Priors, Wiltshire). King Cealwin of Wessex is "expelled" (by a rival – no further information readily available).

593 – King Cealwin of Wessex, Cwichelm and Crida die (both Cwichelm and Crida were probably from the royal line of Wessex, but their exact relationship is uncertain). Aethelfrith succeeds to the kingdom of Northumbria.

595 – Pope Gregory sends Augustine to Britain with "very many monks to preach to the English nation". (`Manuscript E attributes their arrival to` **596** *and Manuscript F to* **597**.)

597 – Ceolwulf becomes king of Wessex and is always fighting the Angles, the Welsh, the Picts or the Scots.

601 – Pope Gregory I sends the pallium (vestment of office, a cloak) to Archbishop Augustine

---

Manuscript "A" (Winchester or Parker): Trebuchet.
Manuscript "B" (Abingdon I) & Manuscript "C" (Abingdon II): 18thCentury.
Manuscript "D" (Worcester): Swiss 721 Hv BT.
`Manuscript "E" (Peterborough or Laud): Courier New.`
Manuscript "F" (Canterbury): Alexa.
Manuscript "H" (Winchester): Calligraphic.

of Canterbury, with "very many religious teachers to help him" and Bishop Paulinus who converts King Edwin of Northumbria to Christianity.

603 – King Aedan (Aidan) of the Irish (Dalreidi, the people of the kingdom in the area of Argyll in western Scotland) loses most of his army led by Hering (a Bernician prince who had fled to Dalriada), son of Hussa (King of Bernicia from 585 to 592 or 593. After Hussa's death the kingdom went to Aethelfrith, Hering's cousin) where it is defeated at the battle of Daegstan/Daegsanstan, in Lidderdale, the Borders by the forces of King Aethelfrith of Northumbria. Theodbald, King Aethelfrith's brother, is killed in the battle along with all his retinue. Thereafter "no king of the Scots dared to lead a host against this nation".

604 – Archbishop Augustine of Canterbury consecrates Bishop Mellitus and Bishop Justus (both Mellitus and Justus were among the monks sent to Britain in **595** or **601** by Pope Gregory I). He sends Bishop Mellitus to convert the East Saxons and their King Saeberht to Christianity. King Aethelberht of Kent gives Mellitus the diocese of London and Justus the diocese of Rochester in Kent.

606 – Pope Gregory I dies. (Manuscript E attributes this to **605**.)

607 – King Ceolwulf of Wessex fights the South Saxons. At the battle of Chester, King Aethelfrith of Northumbria defeats a "countless number" of Welsh thus fulfilling the prophecy of Archbishop Augustine of Canterbury, "If the Welsh refuse peace with us, they shall perish at the hands of the Saxons". Two hundred priests are killed who had come to pray for the Welsh. The priests are led by Scrocmail/Brocmail (no further information readily available) who was one of the fifty who was able to escape. (Manuscript E attributes the battle of Chester to **605**.)

611 – Cynegils succeeds to the kingdom of Wessex.

614 – King Cynegils of Wessex and Cwichelm (probably from the royal line of Wessex, but his exact relationship is uncertain) fight at Beandun/Beamdun (possibly near Axmouth in Devon) and kill two thousand and sixty-five/forty-five Welsh. *Laurentius (Laurence, Lawrence) is appointed Archbishop of Canterbury.*

616 – King Aethelberht of Kent dies, *the first of the English kings to receive baptism,* and is succeeded by his son Eadbald who abandons Christianity. Archbishop Laurentius of Canterbury contemplates fleeing the country but is persuaded to stay by a vision of the Apostle Peter who orders him to convert Eadbald back to Christianity, which he does. Archbishop Laurentius (Laurence, Lawrence) of Canterbury dies on 2 February *(Manuscript F attributes this to **619**)* and is buried beside Archbishop Augustine of Canterbury (he died on 25 May in 604 or 605). He is succeeded as Archbishop by Bishop Mellitus of London.

Manuscript "A" (Winchester or Parker): Trebuchet.
Manuscript "B" (Abingdon I) & Manuscript "C" (Abingdon II): 18thCentury.
Manuscript "D" (Worcester): Swiss 721 Hv BT.
Manuscript "E" (Peterborough or Laud): Courier New.
Manuscript "F" (Canterbury): Alexa.
Manuscript "H" (Winchester): Calligraphic.

(The following events relate to future unspecified years, other than "within five years" but are recorded in the entry for **616**.) Archbishop Mellitus of Canterbury dies (Manuscript E attributes this to **624**) and is succeeded by the Bishop Justus of Rochester, Kent. Archbishop Justus consecrates Romanus (it is presumed that he too was sent to Britain in **595** or **601** by Pope Gregory I) as Bishop of Rochester in Kent.

617 – King Raedwald of East Anglia kills King Aethelfrith of Northumbria who is succeeded by his son Aelle who conquers all of Britain apart from Kent.

625 – Paulinus (sent to Britain in **595** or **601** by Pope Gregory I) is consecrated bishop of Northumbria by Archbishop Justus of Canterbury.

626 – Penda becomes King of Mercia at the age of fifty. King Cwichelm of Wessex sends Eomer to kill King Edwin of Northumbria but instead he stabs (and kills) Lilla (Edwin's thane), and stabs Forthhere (no further information readily available), and wounds the king. The same night as this incident, a daughter Eanfled is born to King Edwin who promises Bishop Paulinus of Northumbria to give his daughter to God if he is able, with God's help, to overcome his enemy who had sent the assassin. King Edwin goes to Wessex with his levies and kills five kings (no further information readily available) and many people. **Eanfled, daughter of King Edwin of Northumbria, is baptised** by Bishop Paulinus **on Whit Sunday 6 June** with eleven others (no further information readily available).

627 – King Edwin of Northumbria and his court are baptised at Easter on 12 April in York where King Edwin had built a church in wood and dedicated to St Peter. King Edwin gives Paulinus the Archbishopric of York and afterwards orders a larger church in stone to be built in York. (Manuscript E records this event in the entry for **626** where it first refers to King Edwin's baptism.)

Archbishop Paulinus preaches Christianity in Lindsey (Lincolnshire), and converts the reeve Blecca and all his chief followers (no further information readily available).

Pope Honorius I, who had succeeded Boniface V as Pope, sends the pallium (vestment of office, a cloak) to Archbishop Paulinus.

Archbishop Justus of Canterbury dies on 10 November and is succeeded by Honorius (not to be confused with Pope Honorius I) who is consecrated by Archbishop Paulinus of York at Lincoln. (Archbishop Honorious had sought and received the permission of Pope Honorious I to raise the see of York to that of an archbishopric so that when one archbishop

Manuscript "A" (Winchester or Parker): Trebuchet.
Manuscript "B" (Abingdon I) & Manuscript "C" (Abingdon II): 18thCentury.
Manuscript "D" (Worcester): Swiss 721 Hv BT.
Manuscript "E" (Peterborough or Laud): Courier New.
Manuscript "F" (Canterbury): Alexa.
Manuscript "H" (Winchester): Calligraphic.

in England died the other would be able to consecrate the deceased archbishop's successor.) Pope Honorius I sends Archbishop Honorius his pallium; the Pope also sends a letter to the Scots (no further information readily available) encouraging them to adopt the correct date for Easter.

628 – King Cynegils of Wessex and Cwichelm (probably from the royal line of Wessex, but his exact relationship is uncertain) fight King Penda of Mercia at Cirencester, Gloucestershire and then come to an agreement (no further information readily available).

632 – King Eorpwald of East Anglia is baptised (his conversion to Christianity is brought about by King Edwin of Northumbria).

633 – King Edwin of Northumbria is killed and his son Osfrith on 14 October at the battle of Hatfield Chase in Yorkshire fighting the armies of the Welsh King Cadwallon and the Mercian King Penda. Cadwallon and Penda lay waste the whole of Northumbria (they burn the Royal Palace at Yeavering in Northumberland). Bishop Paulinus leaves Northumbria and returns by ship with King Edwin's widow Aethelburh to Kent where he takes over as Bishop of Rochester in Kent.

634 – Osric, who had been baptised by Bishop Paulinus, succeeds as King of Deira and Eanfrith succeeds as King of Bernicia. Bishop Birinus first preaches Christianity to the West Saxons. Oswald succeeds as King of Northumbria and reigns nine years. (The scribe records) that the ninth year was assigned to him instead of his predecessors the pagans Osric and Eanfrith who had reigned one year between King Oswald and King Edwin.

635 – King Cynegils of Wessex, sponsored by King Oswald of Northumbria, is baptised by Bishop Birinus of Dorchester-on-Thames, Oxfordshire.

636 – King Cwichelm of Wessex is baptised by Bishop Birinus at Dorchester-on-Thames, Oxfordshire; and later in the year he dies. Bishop Felix preaches Christianity to the East Anglians.

639 – Cuthred (presumably a West Saxon, probably from the royal line of Wessex, but his exact relationship is uncertain) is sponsored and baptised by Bishop Birinus at Dorchester-on-Thames, Oxfordshire.

640 – King Eadbald of Kent dies and is succeeded by his son Eorcenberht who puts down all heathen practices in his kingdom and is the first English king to enforce the observance of Lent. Eorcenberht's daughter is Eorcengota, "a holy virgin and a remarkable person": her mother is Seaxburh, daughter of King Anna of the East Anglians. King Eadbald's other son Eormenred

Manuscript "A" (Winchester or Parker): Trebuchet.

Manuscript "B" (Abingdon I) & Manuscript "C" (Abingdon II): 18thCentury.

Manuscript "D" (Worcester): Swiss 721 Hv BT.

Manuscript "E" (Peterborough or Laud): Courier New.

Manuscript "F" (Canterbury): Alexa.

Manuscript "H" (Winchester): Calligraphic.

has two sons who are later "martyred" by Thunor (a royal retainer who had the two brothers murdered to prevent them contesting the succession of the future Ecgberht I of Kent. The two murdered brothers are venerated as saints).

642 – King Oswald of Northumbria is killed on 5 August 641 in battle with King Penda of Mercia at Maserfeld (probably Oswestry, Shropshire). King Oswald is buried at Bardney in Lincolnshire and his uncorrupted hands are taken to Bamburgh, Northumberland; his holiness and miracles are known throughout the country. (Manuscripts B, C and E attribute King Oswald's death to **641**.)

643 – Cenwalh succeeds to the kingdom of Wessex and orders the building of *St Peter's* church at Winchester, Hampshire. (Manuscripts B and C attribute the building of the church at Winchester to **642**. *Manuscript F attributes this to* **648** – *a more likely date, since as a heathen Cenwalh is unlikely to have ordered the building of a church; he was still heathen when he was expelled in* **645**.*) Oswy, King Oswald's brother, succeeds as King of Northumbria (probably initially King of Bernicia only). (Manuscript E attributes these events to **641**.)

644 – Paulinus, former Archbishop of York and later Bishop of Rochester in Kent, dies at Rochester on 10 October. Oswine succeeds as King of Deira. (Manuscript E attributes these events to **643**.)

645 – King Cenwalh of Wessex is "expelled" by King Penda of Mercia. (King Cenwalh initially refused conversion to Christianity and he repudiated his wife who was King Penda's sister – no further information readily available. King Cenwalh later marries Seaxburh – no further information readily available.)

646 – King Cenwalh of Wessex is baptised.

648 – King Cenwalh of Wessex gives his kinsman Cuthred three thousand hides (a hide is the amount of land which could be tilled with one plough in a year to support one family and its dependants) of land by Ashdown (in the area of the Berkshire Downs).

650 – Agilbert of Gaul (France) succeeds Birinus *who dies* as Bishop of the West Saxons (like Birinus the diocese is based at Dorchester-on-Thames, Oxfordshire). (Manuscript E attributes this event to **649**.)

651 – On 20 August King Oswy of Northumbria (Bernicia) orders King Oswine of Deira to be/is killed. Bishop Aidan of Lindisfarne in Northumberland dies on 31 August. (Manuscript E attributes these events to **650**.)

652 – King Cenwalh of Wessex fights at Bradford-on-Avon, Wiltshire (whom he fought is not recorded).

Manuscript "A" (Winchester or Parker): Trebuchet.
Manuscript "B" (Abingdon I) & Manuscript "C" (Abingdon II): 18thCentury.
Manuscript "D" (Worcester): Swiss 721 Hv BT.
Manuscript "E" (Peterborough or Laud): Courier New.
Manuscript "F" (Canterbury): Alexa.
Manuscript "H" (Winchester): Calligraphic.

653 – The Middle Saxons/Angles (the East Midlands) under the Ealdorman Peada (the son of King Penda of Mercia) are converted to Christianity. (Manuscript E attributes these events to **652**.) Archbishop Honorius of Canterbury dies.

654 – King Anna of East Anglia is killed. Botwulf (an Irish monk who is venerated as a saint) begins to build a monastery at Icanhoh in Ireland. On 30 September Archbishop Honorius of Canterbury dies. (Manuscript E attributes these events to **653**.)

King Oswy of Northumbria and King Peada of Mercia establish the monastery dedicated to St Peter at Medeshamstede (now Peterborough) named after the nearby spring called Medeswael. Seaxwulf, nobly born and powerful, is appointed abbot.

655 – King Penda of Mercia is killed along with "thirty princes", "some of them were kings", with him including Aethelhere (brother of King Anna of East Anglia) in battle with King Oswy of Northumbria at Winwidfeld (to the west of the Stanks/Seacroft area of Leeds, West Yorkshire.) Peada, son of Penda, succeeds as King of Mercia but he did not reign long (see **657** below) because he was betrayed by his own queen at Easter (no further information readily available). The Mercians convert to Christianity. (Manuscript E attributes these events to **654**.) On 26 March Bishop Ithamar of Rochester, Kent, consecrates Deusdedit Archbishop of Canterbury.

656 – (This entry records the expansion of the monastery at Medeshamstede (Peterborough), its consecration and its charter.) The monastery of Medeshamstede which King Peada of Mercia founded grows "very wealthy". King Wulfhere of Mercia decides to "honour and reverence" the monastery at Medeshamstede out of love for his late brother King Peada, King Oswy of Northumbria and Abbot Seaxwulf of Medeshamstede, and on the advice of his brothers Aethelred and Merewala (this brother does not attend the consecration or attest its charter), his sisters Cyneburh and Cyneswith, Archbishop Deusdedit of Canterbury, and on the advice of his councillors both spiritual and temporal.

King Wulfhere summons Abbot Seaxwulf and provides him with gold and silver and land and property "and all that is needed" so that the work on the monastery at Medeshamstede can be completed. After a few years work it is finished.

The monastery is consecrated by Archbishop Deusdedit in the presence of King Wulfhere, his brother Aethelred, and his sisters Cyneburh and Cyneswith. Also present are Bishop Ithamar of Rochester, Kent; Bishop

---

Manuscript "A" (Winchester or Parker): Trebuchet.

Manuscript "B" (Abingdon I) & Manuscript "C" (Abingdon II): 18thCentury.

Manuscript "D" (Worcester): Swiss 721 Hv BT.

Manuscript "E" (Peterborough or Laud): Courier New.

Manuscript "F" (Canterbury): Alexa.

Manuscript "H" (Winchester): Calligraphic.

Wine of London; Bishop Jaruman of Mercia; Bishop Tuda of Lindisfarne, Northumberland (he did not become bishop until **664**); Wilfrid the priest who later became bishop (he became a bishop at different times of Northumbria, the Middle Angles and Ripon in North Yorkshire, and was later venerated as a saint); and all the thanes in the kingdom.

King Wulfhere addresses those present. He indicates the extent of the lands he has given to the monastery. He also confirms that the monastery should hold the lands "royally and freely" and that taxes and rents levied should be for the sole benefit of the monks. He confirms that the monastery should be subject only to Rome. "Amongst other matters discussed" Abbot Seaxwulf requests from the king, and is granted, lands on the island of Ancarig (Ancarraig, Donegal, Ireland) so that some of the monks can build a monastery dedicated to St Mary and provide an anchorite cell.

The charter for the monastery at Medeshamstede setting out land holdings, waters and fenland is then witnessed by King Wulfhere; King Oswy; King Sigehere and King Sebbi – a nephew and uncle who were joint kings of Essex; and Aethelred, King Wulfhere's brother and his sisters Cyneburh and Cyneswith; Archbishop Deusdedit; Abbot Seaxwulf; Bishop Ithamar; Bishop Wine; Bishop Jaruman; Bishop Tuda; Wilfrid the priest; and Eoppa the priest who King Wulfhere sent to preach Christianity in the Isle of Wight (see **661** below).(The charter is also attested by the following people on whom there is no further information readily available): Ealdorman Immine, Ealdorman Eadberht, Ealdorman Herefrith, Ealdorman Wilberht, Ealdorman Abo. (No title, occupation or role is mentioned with the following names): Brorda, Wilberht, Ealhmund, Frithugis and many others of the king's retainers.

(Note: In this entry this charter is dated **664**.) The charter is subsequently blessed by Pope Vitalian in Rome who issues a Papal Bull. The monastery at Medeshamstede was afterwards called "Burh" (hence Peterborough – Saint Peter's borough; see **963** below).

Archbishop Theodore of Canterbury holds a synod (at Hertford; this divided the dioceses in England into smaller units) where Bishop Winfrith of Mercia is deprived of his bishopric and replaced as Bishop by Abbot Seaxwulf of Medeshamstede who is in turn replaced as abbot by Cuthbald a monk from Medeshamstede. (Although the entry itself refers to the synod taking place in **673**, see below, it is included in the Manuscript E entry for the year **656**. Theodore of Tarsus is not consecrated Archbishop of Canterbury until 668 – see **668** below.)

Manuscript "A" (Winchester or Parker): Trebuchet.
Manuscript "B" (Abingdon I) & Manuscript "C" (Abingdon II): 18thCentury.
Manuscript "D" (Worcester): Swiss 721 Hv BT.
Manuscript "E" (Peterborough or Laud): Courier New.
Manuscript "F" (Canterbury): Alexa.
Manuscript "H" (Winchester): Calligraphic.

657 – At Easter King Peada of Mercia dies, betrayed by his queen (Alchfleda – this information about Peada's death is included in the entry in Manuscript E for **654** despite his death being recorded in the entry for **656** – the accepted date – in Manuscript E) and is succeeded by Wulfhere.

658 – King Cenwalh of Wessex defeats the Welsh at Penselwood, Somerset where they retreat as far as the River Parret, Somerset. Cenwalh had lived in exile in East Anglia for three years before this battle because King Penda of Mercia had expelled him and deprived him of his kingdom – Cenwalh had "repudiated" Penda's sister (see **645** above).

660 – Bishop Agilbert of the West Saxons leaves England and takes over the diocese of Paris on the Seine in Gaul (France); he is succeeded by Wine. (Agilbert had been invited by King Cenwalh of Mercia to become bishop of the West Saxons at Dorchester-on-Thames, Oxfordshire in 650 – see **650** above. The king became dissatisfied with Agilbert because of his inability to speak West Saxon dialect and so the king split the diocese in two appointing Wine as bishop at Winchester, Hampshire. The action by the king encouraged Agilbert to leave Wessex. His problems over the language resulted in his declining the role of advocate for the case for Roman Christianity at the Synod of Whitby in 664. It was Agilbert who appointed Wilfrid – who became a bishop at different times of Northumbria, the Middle Angles and Ripon in North Yorkshire, and was later venerated as a saint – to speak in his place.)

661 – At Easter time King Cenwalh of Wessex fights at Posentesburh (this site has not been confidently identified and the implication is that he fought the Mercians). King Wulfhere of Mercia ravages the lands as far as/in Ashdown (in the area of the Berkshire Downs). Cuthred and "king" Coenberht die (both were probably from the royal line of Wessex, but their exact relationship is uncertain). King Wulfhere of Mercia ravages the Isle of Wight and gives it to King Aethelwald of Sussex because he had stood sponsor for him at baptism. Eoppa the priest (see **656** above) at the command of Wilfrid (see **660** above) and King Wulfhere of Mercia is the first to bring Christianity to the Isle of Wight.

664 – On 3 May there is an eclipse of the sun. A great pestilence comes to Britain during which Bishop Tuda of Lindisfarne, Northumberland dies; he is buried at Wagele (this site has not been confidently identified). Eorcenberht, King of Kent, dies and is succeeded by his son Egbert. "Colman and his companions went to his native land." (This is the only oblique reference to the Synod of Whitby which determined that the Roman rather than the Celtic form of Christianity would be followed in England. After the Synod of Whitby) two new bishops are consecrated Ceadda (better known as Chad, as Bishop of the Northumbrians) and Wilfrid (see **660** above), as Bishop at York. Deusdedit dies (the first Englishman to be Archbishop of Canterbury).

667 – King Oswy of Northumbria and King Egbert of Kent send Wigheard the priest to Rome to be consecrated Archbishop of Canterbury but he dies as soon as he arrives in Rome.

Manuscript "A" (Winchester or Parker): Trebuchet.

Manuscript "B" (Abingdon I) & Manuscript "C" (Abingdon II): 18thCentury.

Manuscript "D" (Worcester): Swiss 721 Hv BT.

Manuscript "E" (Peterborough or Laud): Courier New.

Manuscript "F" (Canterbury): Alexa.

Manuscript "H" (Winchester): Calligraphic.

668 – Theodore is consecrated Archbishop of Canterbury.

669 – King Egbert of Kent gives Reculver, Kent to Bass the priest (no further information readily available) to build a church there.

670 – King Oswy of Northumbria dies on 15 February and is succeeded by Ecgfrith his son. Hlothhere (Leutherius, Leuthere), nephew of Bishop Agilbert of Paris, Gaul (France), succeeds as bishop to the West Saxons at Winchester, Hampshire and is consecrated by Archbishop Theodore of Canterbury.

671 – A great mortality of birds takes place.

672 – King Cenwalh of Wessex dies and is succeeded by his Queen, Seaxburh who reigns for one year.

673 – King Egbert of Kent dies. Archbishop Theodore of Canterbury summons/ the Synod of Hertford takes place (see **656** above). The monastery at Ely, Cambridgeshire is founded by Saint Aethelthryth (formerly married to King Ecgfrith of Northumbria).

674 – Aescwine becomes king of Wessex.

675 – King Wulfhere of Mercia and King Aescwine of Wessex fight at the battle of Biedanheafod/ Bedanheafod (possibly near Marlborough, Wiltshire). King Wulfhere of Mercia dies and is succeeded by Aethelred. King Aethelred of Mercia sends Bishop Wilfrid (he became a bishop at different times of Northumbria, the Middle Angles and Ripon in North Yorkshire, and was later venerated as a saint) to Rome to Pope Agatho, and asks the Pope to confirm the charter relating to the monastery at Medeshamstede (Peterborough) and issue a "Papal Bull"; this the Pope does. (In this entry the date of the Papal Bull is given as **680**.)

King Aethelred orders Archbishop Theodore of Canterbury to hold an assembly of all the councillors at Hatfield, Hertfordshire (or possibly South Yorkshire), to hear the bull read which the Pope had sent, and to agree and confirm it. King Aethelred also gives to the monastery at Medeshamstede lands at Breedon-on-the-Hill and Lodeshac (Loddington) Leicestershire; Hrepingas (possibly Repton, Derbyshire); Cedenac (this site has not been confidently identified); Bardney and Swineshead in Lincolnshire (possibly Bedfordshire?); Heanbyrig (Henbury, Gloucestershire?); Shifnal, Costesford (Cosford), Stratford (Stretford), Wattlesborough, and Lizard (Lufgeard), in Shropshire; Aethelhuniglond (possibly in Kent?).

His charter granting these additional lands is witnessed by Archbishop

Manuscript "A" (Winchester or Parker): Trebuchet.
Manuscript "B" (Abingdon I) & Manuscript "C" (Abingdon II): 18thCentury.
Manuscript "D" (Worcester): Swiss 721 Hv BT.
Manuscript "E" (Peterborough or Laud): Courier New.
Manuscript "F" (Canterbury): Alexa.
Manuscript "H" (Winchester): Calligraphic.

Theodore, Archbishop Wilfrid of York, Bishop Seaxwulf of Mercia, Queen Osthryth (King Aethelred's queen), Adrian the papal legate, Bishop Putta of Rochester, Kent, Bishop Waldhere of London and Abbot Cuthbald of Medeshamstede (Peterborough).

676 – King Aescwine of Wessex dies and is succeeded by Centwine. Hedde (Haeddi, Haedda) succeeds as Bishop of the West Saxons at Winchester, Hampshire. King Aethelred of Mercia ravages/overran Kent.

678 – A "star" comet appears in August and for three months appears every morning. Bishop Wilfrid of Northumbria is expelled from his post by King Ecgfrith of Northumbria and two bishops are consecrated to replace him, Bishop Bosa of Deira and Bishop Eata of Bernicia. Eadhed is consecrated as the first bishop of Lindsey (Lincolnshire).

679 – King Aelfwine of Deira is killed beside the River Trent (possibly near Marton, Lincolnshire) at the battle between King Ecgfrith of Northumbria and King Aethelred of Mercia. Queen Aethelthryth of Ely, Cambridgeshire dies (venerated as a saint). Coldingham Abbey (Berwickshire) is burnt as a result of lightning.

680 – Synod of Hatfield, Hertfordshire (or possibly South Yorkshire) presided over by Archbishop Theodore "because he wished to amend the doctrines of the Christian faith" - see **675** above. Abbess Hild of Whitby, North Yorkshire, dies (venerated as a saint).

681 – Trumberht is consecrated Bishop of Hexham in Northumberland and Trumwine is consecrated Bishop to the Picts "because then they were subject to us".

682 – King Centwine of Wessex "drove the Britons as far as the sea".

684 – King Ecgfrith of Northumbria sends Ealdorman Beorht (no further information readily available) with a host to Ireland who devastate the country and burn churches.

685 – King Caedwalla of Wessex "began to contend for the kingdom" (of Wessex). His brother Mul is later burned to death in Kent (see **687** below; it is not clear why this event is mentioned here). At York King Ecgfrith of Northumbria has Cuthbert (venerated as a saint) consecrated Bishop of Hexham, Northumberland (Cuthbert swaps the see with Bishop Eata (venerated as a saint) of Lindisfarne) – Bishop Trumberht had been "removed" (he died in **684**?). King Ecgfrith of Northumbria is killed on 20 May with the great host in a battle north of the Firth of Forth. (The battle of Nechtansmere, near Forfar, Angus, Scotland. The army of King Ecgfrith fought the army of

Manuscript "A" (Winchester or Parker): Trebuchet.
Manuscript "B" (Abingdon I) & Manuscript "C" (Abingdon II): 18thCentury.
Manuscript "D" (Worcester): Swiss 721 Hv BT.
Manuscript "E" (Peterborough or Laud): Courier New.
Manuscript "F" (Canterbury): Alexa.
Manuscript "H" (Winchester): Calligraphic.

Bruide, King of the Picts who reigned circa 672-93). King Ecgfrith is succeeded as King of Northumbria by Aldfrith. **King Hlothhere of Kent dies.** John is consecrated Bishop of Hexham in Northumberland (Saint Eata dies as Bishop of Hexham in **685** or **686**, John becomes Bishop of Hexham in **687**) and remains there until the return (in **706**) of Bishop Wilfrid (who is in Sussex and then the Isle of Wight converting the inhabitants to Christianity). John was subsequently appointed Bishop of York after Bishop Bosa dies. Wilfrid (not Saint Wilfrid), Bishop John's priest (a pupil of Abbess Hild of Whitby, venerated as a saint) is consecrated Bishop of York sometime afterwards and John then retires to his monastery at Beverley in East Yorkshire. *"In Britain it rained blood, and milk and butter were turned into blood".*

686 – King Caedwalla of Wessex and his brother Mul lay waste Kent and the Isle of Wight. King Caedwalla gives Hoo on the island of Avery in Kent to the monastery at Medeshamstede (Peterborough) which is under the care of Abbot Egbalth.

687 – Mul (brother of King Caedwalla of Wessex) and twelve other men (no further information readily available) are burnt to death in Kent (Mul's death is also mentioned in the entry for **685** above). King Caedwalla again lays waste Kent.

688 – King Caedwalla of Wessex (abdicates and) goes to Rome where he is baptised by the Pope Sergius I and named "Peter". Caedwalla dies seven days later on 20 April and is buried within St Peter's Church in Rome. Ine succeeds as King of Wessex and has built the monastery at Glastonbury, Somerset. After reigning thirty-seven/twenty-seven years King Ine goes to Rome and remains there until he dies (see **728** below).

690 – Archbishop Theodore of Canterbury dies and is buried inside Canterbury (presumably the cathedral) and is succeeded by Berhtwald (two years later). Until this date all the archbishops appointed had been "Roman", after this date they were English (The scribe overlooks Deusdedit whose death is mentioned in **664** above and who was the first Englishman to be Archbishop of Canterbury.)

692 – Berhtwald, the former abbot at Reculver in Kent, is elected Archbishop of Canterbury on the 1 July. (The scribe comments that) before this time the Archbishops had been Roman and from this date on they were English. At this time there are two kings in Kent, Wihtred and Waebheard (or Swaefheard or Suaebhard, an East Saxon sub king of West Kent).

693 – On 3 July Berhtwald is consecrated Archbishop of Canterbury by Bishop Godun of Gaul (France). Bishop Gifemund of Rochester, Kent dies

---

Manuscript "A" (Winchester or Parker): Trebuchet.
Manuscript "B" (Abingdon I) & Manuscript "C" (Abingdon II): 18thCentury.
Manuscript "D" (Worcester): Swiss 721 Hv BT.
Manuscript "E" (Peterborough or Laud): Courier New.
Manuscript "F" (Canterbury): Alexa.
Manuscript "H" (Winchester): Calligraphic.

and is replaced by Tobias (no further information readily available). Berhthelm dies (also referred to as Drythelm a monk at the monastery at Melrose, Borders).

694 – The Kentishmen come to terms with King Ine of Wessex and pay him thirty thousand (pounds) (Manuscript B says thirty pounds, Manuscript C says thirty thousand pounds; wergild – compensation payment for taking a man's life) because they had burned Mul (brother of King Caedwalla of Wessex) to death (see **687** above). Wihtred succeeds as King of Kent. (Waebheard or Swaefheard or Suaebhard, the East Saxon sub king of West Kent had been expelled.)

697 – Queen Osthryth (King Aethelred of Mercia's queen), sister of King Ecgfrith of Northumbria, is killed by the Mercians (murdered by Mercian nobles).

699 – The Picts kill Ealdorman Beorht of Northumbria.

703 – Bishop Hedde (Haedda, Haeddi) of Winchester, Hampshire, dies.

704 – After reigning twenty-nine years King Aethelred of Mercia becomes a monk at Bardney, Lincolnshire and is succeeded as king by Coenred. (Manuscript E attributes Coenred's succession to **702**.)

705 – King Aldfrith of Northumbria dies on 14 December at (Little) Driffield East Yorkshire and is succeed by his son Osred (I). Bishop Seaxwulf dies. (The date of this entry may be incorrect if this is the known Bishop Seaxwulf who founded the monastery at Medeshamstede - Peterborough - and later became Bishop of Lichfield. He died circa 692.)

709 – Bishop Aldhelm of Wessex dies - he was bishop "to the west of the wood" (Selwood, i.e. the diocese based at Sherborne, Dorset). In the early days of Bishop Daniel (705-44), Wessex was divided into two dioceses: Bishop Daniel (at Winchester, Hampshire) and Bishop Aldhelm (at Sherborne, Dorset). Forthhere succeeds Aldhelm as bishop (at Sherborne, Dorset). Ceolred becomes King of Mercia and Coenred, the former King of Mercia, goes to Rome to become a monk and is accompanied by King Offa of the East Saxons (who abdicates). The former King Coenred of Mercia dies in Rome. Bishop Wilfrid dies (venerated as a saint) at Oundle, Northamptonshire and his body is taken to Ripon, North Yorkshire.

710 – Acca, chaplain to Bishop Wilfrid (venerated as a saint) succeeds as Bishop of Hexham, Northumberland. Ealdorman Beorhtfrith (a high-ranking Northumbrian ealdorman associated with Bamburgh in Northumberland) fights the Picts at a battle between the River Avon in Linlithgow, West Lothian and (to the north-west) the River Carron in Stirlingshire. Ine (no further information readily available) and Nunna (no further information readily available) Beorhtfrith's kinsmen

---

Manuscript "A" (Winchester or Parker): Trebuchet.

Manuscript "B" (Abingdon I) & Manuscript "C" (Abingdon II): 18thCentury.

Manuscript "D" (Worcester): Swiss 721 Hv BT.

Manuscript "E" (Peterborough or Laud): Courier New.

Manuscript "F" (Canterbury): Alexa.

Manuscript "H" (Winchester): Calligraphic.

fight Geraint, King of the Britons (in Cornwall). **Sigbald**/Hygebald is killed (no further information readily available).

714 – Guthlac dies. (Venerated as a saint, he was an aetheling, i.e., a male of royal blood, the heir apparent of the royal house of Mercia who gave up the warrior-life to become a monk at Repton in Derbyshire; then became a hermit at Crowland in Lincolnshire. The Life of St Guthlac is contained in a poem in the "Exeter Book" - a late tenth century anthology of poetry written in Old English. The poem was probably based on an early eighth century life of the saint written in Latin by a monk at Crowland.) *King Pippin (Pepin II Prince of the Franks) dies.*

715 – King Ine of Wessex fights King Ceolred of Mercia at Adam's Grave (Alton Priors, Wiltshire). *King Dagobert II (a French king and Holy Roman Emperor) dies.*

716 – King Osred (I) of Northumbria is killed south of the border (between Northumbria and Mercia) and is succeeded by Coenred who in turn is succeeded by Osric. King Ceolred/Ceolwold of Mercia dies and his body taken to Lichfield, Staffordshire. Aethelred former King of Mercia dies and is buried at the monastery (he founded) at Bardney in Lincolnshire. (He had abdicated and retired as a monk.) Aethelbald succeeds (Ceolred) as King of Mercia. Egbert (Ecgberht, a Northumbrian monk who may have been a bishop and venerated as a saint) "rightly induced the monks on the island of Iona to celebrate Easter at the proper time, and to adopt the Roman tonsure".

718 – Ingeld, brother of King Ine of Wessex, dies; Cwenburh and Cuthburh were their sisters. Cuthburh was married to King Aldfrith of Northumbria (reigned 685-705) but left him (to become a nun at Barking, Essex). (Later) she (and Cwenburh) founded a double-monastery at Wimborne, Dorset.

721 – Bishop Daniel of Winchester, Hampshire goes to Rome. King Ine of Wessex kills Prince Cynewulf (no further information readily available). John of Beverley (East Yorkshire) dies (venerated as a saint) and is buried at Beverley.

722 – Queen Aethelburh destroys Taunton, Somerset which had been built by her husband King Ine of Wessex. Ealdberht (future king of Kent) goes into exile in Surrey and Sussex. King Ine of Wessex fights the South Saxons (no further information readily available).

725 – King Wihtred of Kent dies on 23 April and is succeeded by Ealdberht who had been banished by King Ine of Wessex. When King Ine fights the South Saxons King Ealdberht is killed.

727 – Bishop Tobias of Rochester, Kent dies and Archbishop Berhtwald of Canterbury consecrates Ealdwulf (no further information readily available) as his successor.

728 – King Ine of Wessex goes to Rome (see **688** above) and is succeeded by Aethelheard.

Manuscript "A" (Winchester or Parker): Trebuchet.
Manuscript "B" (Abingdon I) & Manuscript "C" (Abingdon II): 18thCentury.
Manuscript "D" (Worcester): Swiss 721 Hv BT.
Manuscript "E" (Peterborough or Laud): Courier New.
Manuscript "F" (Canterbury): Alexa.
Manuscript "H" (Winchester): Calligraphic.

(Manuscript E attributes these events to **726.**) *King Ine dies in Rome. (Manuscript F attributes this event to 726.)* King Aethelheard of Wessex fights Prince Oswald (presumably a West Saxon, probably from the royal line of Wessex, but his exact relationship is uncertain – see **730** below).

729 – The star comet is seen/two comets are seen. Saint Egbert dies on Iona (Ecgberht, a Northumbrian monk who may have been a bishop and venerated as a saint – see **716** above).

730 – Prince Oswald dies (see **728** above).

731 – King Osric of Northumbria is killed and is succeeded by Ceolwulf (to whom Bede's Ecclesiastical History of the English Nation is dedicated). **(Manuscripts D,** E **and** F **attribute these events to 729 – the accepted date.)** Archbishop Berhtwald of Canterbury dies on 13 January and is succeeded by Abbot Tatwine of the monastery at Breedon-on-the-Hill, Leicestershire. Tatwine is consecrated Archbishop of Canterbury on 10 June by Bishop Daniel of Winchester, Hampshire, Bishop Ingwald of London, Bishop Ealdwine of Lichfield, Staffordshire and Bishop Ealdwulf of Rochester, Kent.

733 – King Aethelbald of Mercia captures Somerton, Oxfordshire. The sun is eclipsed/*"all the circle of the sun became like a black shield"*. Bishop Acca of Hexham, Northumberland is driven from his bishopric (reasons now unknown).

734 – The moon appears as though it were "suffused with blood". Archbishop Tatwine of Canterbury dies. Bede dies (**735** is the accepted date, the Venerable Bede, the theologian, historian, scientist, teacher and poet – author of the Ecclesiastical History of the English Nation – at Wearmouth-Jarrow monastery). Bishop Egbert (he studied under Bede at Wearmouth-Jarrow monastery) is consecrated Archbishop of York.

735 – Archbishop Egbert of York receives the pallium (vestment of office, a cloak) from Rome.

736 – Archbishop Nothhelm of Canterbury receives the pallium (vestment of office, a cloak) from "the bishop of the Romans".

737 – Bishop Forthhere of Sherborne, Dorset and Queen Frithugyth (wife of King Aethelheard of Wessex) journey to Rome. King Ceolwulf of Northumbria becomes a monk/*secular priest* on Lindisfarne, Northumberland and "gave" his kingdom to Eadberht. Bishop Aethelwald (responsible for binding the Lindisfarne Gospels written by his predecessor Eadfrith) of Lindisfarne, Northumberland and Bishop Acca (venerated as a saint) of Hexham, Northumberland die. Cynewulf is consecrated Bishop of Lindisfarne (it is possible that this Cynewulf is the Anglo-Saxon poet Cynewulf who was known to be living

---

Manuscript "A" (Winchester or Parker): Trebuchet.
Manuscript "B" (Abingdon I) & Manuscript "C" (Abingdon II): 18thCentury.
Manuscript "D" (Worcester): Swiss 721 Hv BT.
Manuscript "E" (Peterborough or Laud): Courier New.
Manuscript "F" (Canterbury): Alexa.
Manuscript "H" (Winchester): Calligraphic.

about this time). King Aethelbald of Mercia harries Northumbria.

738 – Eadberht becomes king of Northumbria (the accepted date is **737** as recorded in Manuscript E). His brother is Archbishop Egbert (the first Archbishop of York). On their deaths they were buried in the same chapel in York.

741 – King Aethelheard of Wessex dies and is succeeded by Cuthred who "resolutely made war" against King Aethelbald of Mercia. Cuthbert is consecrated Archbishop of Canterbury and Dunn is consecrated Bishop of Rochester. (Manuscript E attributes these events to **740**.) York is burnt down (no further information readily available).

742 – *A great synod is held at Cloueshoh (this site has not been confidently identified) attended by King Aethelbald of Mercia, Archbishop Cuthbert of Canterbury and "many other learned men".*

743 – King Aethelbald of Mercia and King Cuthred of Wessex fight the Welsh.

744 – Bishop Daniel of Winchester, Hampshire retires and is succeeded by Hunferth (no further information readily available). Many shooting stars are seen in this year. Archbishop Wilfrid the Young (Wilfrid II) of York dies on 29 April.

745 – Daniel, the former Bishop of Winchester, Hampshire, dies.

746 – King Selred (Saelred) of Essex is killed.

748 – Cynric, prince of Wessex, is killed (presumably a West Saxon, probably from the royal line of Wessex, but his exact relationship is uncertain). King Eadberht of Kent dies and is succeeded by Aethelberht.

750 – King Cuthred of Wessex fights Aethelhun "the presumptuous Ealdorman" (no further information readily available).

752 – King Cuthred of Wessex fights/defeats King Aethelbald of Mercia at the battle of Beorgfeord/Beorhford (possibly Burford in Oxfordshire).

753 – King Cuthred of Wessex fights the Welsh (no further information readily available).

756 – King Cuthred of Wessex dies and is succeeded by Sigeberht. Cyneheard (no further information readily available) succeeds Hunferth as Bishop of Winchester, Hampshire. Canterbury is burnt down (no further information readily available).

757 – Cynewulf and the Wessex Witan depose King Sigeberht because of his unlawful actions. Initially he retained Hampshire but lost this when he murdered Ealdorman Cumbra

---

Manuscript "A" (Winchester or Parker): Trebuchet.
Manuscript "B" (Abingdon I) & Manuscript "C" (Abingdon II): 18thCentury.
Manuscript "D" (Worcester): Swiss 721 Hv BT.
Manuscript "E" (Peterborough or Laud): Courier New.
Manuscript "F" (Canterbury): Alexa.
Manuscript "H" (Winchester): Calligraphic.

(of Hampshire) who had stayed loyal to him longer than anyone else. King Sigeberht is killed by a herdsman near the River Privett in Hampshire in the Weald where he had taken refuge. Cynewulf becomes king of Wessex and frequently fights the Welsh (no further information readily available).

King Aethelbald of Mercia is murdered at Seckington, Warwickshire and his body is taken to Repton, Derbyshire. Beornred succeeds as King of Mercia and rules "a short time and unhappily" (he was deposed by Offa). Offa becomes King of Mercia and is succeeded (in **796**, see below) by his son Ecgfrith who then reigns for one hundred and forty-one days.

(Note: although the following events are recorded in the entry for **757** they take place in **786** - see **786** below where there is a shorter reference but with the additional information that Cyneheard was killed with eighty-four of his men.)

King Cynewulf wishes to expel Cyneheard, brother of Sigeberht the former king. Cyneheard learns that King Cynewulf is visiting his mistress at Merantun (Marton in Wiltshire) with a small retinue and so he goes there with his men. In the ensuing fighting King Cynewulf is killed, Cyneheard is severely wounded and all Cynewulf's thanes are killed despite Cyneheard offering them money and their life - a wounded Welsh hostage survives. The following morning those of the king's thanes who had not been with him, Ealdorman Osric (no further information readily available) and Wigfrith his thane, ride to Merantun where Cyneheard offers them "their own choice of money and land" if they will accept him as king; they decline the offer as their loyalty to Cynewulf remains. A fight ensues and Cyneheard is killed along with all those who were with him apart from the Ealdorman's (Cyneheard's) godson who is severely wounded. King Cynewulf is buried at Winchester, Hampshire; Cyneheard is buried at Axminster, Devon. (The recording of these events represents the earliest known piece of English narrative prose.)

758 – King Eadberht of Northumbria becomes a monk and is succeeded by his son Oswulf who reigns for a year and is killed on 24 July 759 by members of his own household.

759 – Aethelwald Moll becomes King of Northumbria and abdicates after six years.

760 – Archbishop Cuthbert of Canterbury dies.

761 – Bregowine is consecrated Archbishop of Canterbury at Michaelmas. On 6 August King Aethelwald Moll of Northumbria kills Oswine (possibly a brother of the former King Oswulf of Northumbria – see **758** above) at the battle of Aedwinesclif (this site has not been confidently identified.

762 – King Aethelberht of Kent dies.

Manuscript "A" (Winchester or Parker): Trebuchet.
Manuscript "B" (Abingdon I) & Manuscript "C" (Abingdon II): 18thCentury.
Manuscript "D" (Worcester): Swiss 721 Hv BT.
Manuscript "E" (Peterborough or Laud): Courier New.
Manuscript "F" (Canterbury): Alexa.
Manuscript "H" (Winchester): Calligraphic.

763 – On 7 May Bishop Frithuwald of Whithorn, Dumfriesshire, who was consecrated at York on 15 August 734, dies and is succeeded by Peohtwine (no further information readily available), who on 17 July is consecrated Bishop of "Whithorn at Elvet".

763-4 – There is a hard winter. (**764**) Ceolwulf, former King of Northumbria who retired to become a monk at Lindisfarne, Northumberland, dies (see **737** above).

765 – *Archbishop Bregowine of Canterbury dies* (and is replaced by) Jaenberht who is consecrated Archbishop forty days after Christmas. Alhred (a member of the royal family) becomes King of Northumbria.

766 – Archbishop Jaenberht of Canterbury receives the pallium (vestment of office, a cloak). On 19 November Archbishop Egbert of York dies. Bishop Frithuberht of Hexham, Northumberland, dies.

767 – Aethelbert is consecrated Archbishop of York, and Ealhmund is consecrated Bishop of Hexham, Northumberland.

768 – On 19/**20 August** Eadberht, former king of Northumbria dies. (He abdicated as king in 758 in favour of his son Oswulf. He became a canon at York where his brother Ecgberht was archbishop. On their deaths they are buried in the same chapel in York – see **738** above.)

774 – Bishop Milred of Worcester dies. At York at Eastertide the Northumbrians replace King Alhred with Aethelred son of the former King of Northumbria Aethelwald Moll (he had probably been forced to abdicate and enter a monastery).

776 – The Mercians and Kentishmen fight at Otford, Kent. A red cross was seen in the sky after sunset (no further information readily available). Strange adders were seen in Sussex (no further information readily available). On 19 September Bishop Peohtwine of "Whithorn at Elvet" dies.

777 – On 15 June at York Aethelberht is consecrated Bishop of Whithorn, (Dumfriesshire or "Whithorn at Elvet").

778 – On 22 March Aethelbald (no further information readily available) and Heardberht (no further information readily available) kill the three "high-reeves" Ealdwulf, son of Bosa (no further information readily available) at Coniscliffe (possibly High Coniscliffe in County Durham), and Cynewulf and Ecga at Helathyrne (this site has not been confidently identified). Aelfwald I (son of King Oswulf of Northumbria)

Manuscript "A" (Winchester or Parker): Trebuchet.
Manuscript "B" (Abingdon I) & Manuscript "C" (Abingdon II): 18thCentury.
Manuscript "D" (Worcester): Swiss 721 Hv BT.
Manuscript "E" (Peterborough or Laud): Courier New.
Manuscript "F" (Canterbury): Alexa.
Manuscript "H" (Winchester): Calligraphic.

succeeds as King of Northumbria and expels the former King Aethelred I (son of the former King Aethelwald Moll of Northumbria). *(Manuscript F attributes the succession of Aelfwald I to* **779***.)*

779 – King Cynewulf of Wessex fights King Offa of Mercia near Benson, Oxfordshire: King Offa takes the village. Abbot Beonna of Medeshamstede (Peterborough) leases to Ealdorman Cuthbert of Mercia (?) ten farms at Swineshead in Lincolnshire on the understanding the Ealdorman provides the Abbot with fifty pounds plus a day's supply of food a year or pay thirty shillings. On the death of the Ealdorman the farms are to revert to the monastery. This lease is attested in the presence of King Offa of Mercia, King Ecgfrith of Mercia (his son who succeeds him – see **757** above and **787** below), Archbishop Hygeberht of Lichfield, Staffordshire, Bishop Ceolwulf of Lindsey (Lincolnshire), Bishop Unwona of Leicester and Abbot Beonna of Medeshamstede (Peterborough) and many other bishops and abbots and prominent men.

Ealdorman Brorda of Surrey (possibly a sub-king) petitions King Offa to free a church at Woking in Surrey from all obligations – to the king, to the bishop, to the earl and all other men – so that it could be given to the monastery at Medeshamstede (Peterborough) now under the care of Abbot Pusa who has succeeded Abbot Beonna. King Offa agrees to the request at his royal manor of Freoricburna (this site has not been confidently identified).

780 – On 8 September Bishop Ealhmund of Hexham, Northumberland, dies and Tilberht (no further information readily available) is consecrated in his place on 2 October. Hygebald (no further information readily available) is consecrated Bishop of Lindisfarne, Northumberland at Sockburn-on-Tees, County Durham. King Aelfwald I of Northumbria sends a man (Alcuin of York the scholar and teacher) to Rome for the pallium (vestment of office, a cloak) for Archbishop Eanbald of York. *(Manuscript F attributes these events to* **782***.)*

On 24 December the Northumbrian high-reeves (no further information readily available) burned to death Ealdorman Beorn (no further information readily available) at Seletun (this site has not been confidently identified). Archbishop Aethelberht of York dies at York and is succeeded by Eanbald who had been consecrated in 778. Bishop Cynewulf of Lindisfarne, Northumberland resigns his office.

782 – The Old Saxons fight the Franks. Queen Waerburh, wife of King Ceolred (of Mercia – is this entry an error? Queen Waerburh who was venerated as a saint died in 699 and King Ceolred of Mercia reigned 709-716).

Manuscript "A" (Winchester or Parker): Trebuchet.
Manuscript "B" (Abingdon I) & Manuscript "C" (Abingdon II): 18thCentury.
Manuscript "D" (Worcester): Swiss 721 Hv BT.
Manuscript "E" (Peterborough or Laud): Courier New.
Manuscript "F" (Canterbury): Alexa.
Manuscript "H" (Winchester): Calligraphic.

Bishop Cynewulf of Lindisfarne, Northumberland dies. A synod is held at Acleah (Aycliffe, County Durham).

785 – Abbot Botwine of Ripon, North Yorkshire, dies.

786 – Both Cyneheard (brother of murdered former King Sigeberht of Wessex) with eighty-four men and King Cynewulf of Wessex are killed in a fight (at Merantun – Marton, Wiltshire. See **757** above.) Beorhtric succeeds as King of Wessex; he is (later) buried at Wareham, Dorset. King Ealhmund reigns in Kent (a sub-king under King Offa of Mercia).

787 – "Contentious" synod at Chelsea in London. Archbishop Jaenberht of Canterbury gives up part of his diocese and Hygeberht is appointed Archbishop of Lichfield (a new archbishopric) by King Offa of Mercia. Ecgfrith (son of King Offa) is consecrated king. Pope Adrian I sends messengers from Rome to "renew the faith and the peace" which St Gregory had sent to us by Bishop Augustine: they were received with ceremony **and sent back in peace.** On 2 September a synod is held at **Wincanheale**/Pincanhalh (this site has not been confidently identified) in Northumbria. Abbot Aldberht (Bishop of Hereford) dies **in Ripon, North Yorkshire.**

788 – On 23 September King Aelfwald I of Northumbria is killed by Sicga (probably a Northumbrian ealdorman). Where King Aelfwald is killed (probably near Chesters, Northumberland), a light is frequently seen in the sky. King Aelfwald is buried in Hexham Abbey, Northumberland. A synod is held at Acleah (Aycliffe, County Durham). Osred II succeeds as King of Northumbria.

789 – King Beorhtric of Wessex marries Eadburgh, daughter of King Offa of Mercia. The reeve (of King Beorhtric of Wessex with a small retinue) tries to compel the crews of three Danish/Norwegian (Manuscripts B, C, **D** and *F* describe them as Norwegian) ships from Hörthaland (around Hardanger Fjord in Norway, who make landfall at Portland, Dorset) to go to the royal manor (at Dorchester, Dorset) and is killed. "These were the first ships of the Danes to come to England."

790 – King Osred II of Northumbria is betrayed (no further information readily available) and driven out of the kingdom. He is replaced as king by Aethelred, the son of Aethelwald (King Aethelwald Moll of Northumbria, reigned 759-765).

791 – On 17 July Baldwulf is consecrated Bishop of Whithorn (Dumfriesshire or "Whithorn at Elvet") by Archbishop Eanbald of York and Bishop Aethelberht of Hexham, Northumberland.

792 – Archbishop Jaenberht of Canterbury dies and is succeeded by Aethelheard (of the

---

Manuscript "A" (Winchester or Parker): Trebuchet.
Manuscript "B" (Abingdon I) & Manuscript "C" (Abingdon II): 18thCentury.
Manuscript "D" (Worcester): Swiss 721 Hv BT.
Manuscript "E" (Peterborough or Laud): Courier New.
Manuscript "F" (Canterbury): Alexa.
Manuscript "H" (Winchester): Calligraphic.

monastery of Louth in Lincolnshire).

793 – "In this year terrible portents appeared over Northumbria, and miserably frightened the inhabitants: these were exceptional **high winds and** flashes of lightning, and fiery dragons were seen flying in the air. A great famine followed these signs; and a little after that in the same year on 8 January (probably a mistake for 8 June) the harrying of the heathen miserably destroyed God's church in Lindisfarne (Northumberland) by rapine and slaughter." On 22 February Sicga (see **788** above) dies.

794 – King Offa of Mercia orders King Aethelberht of East Anglia "head to be struck off". (Was this action due to a misunderstanding about the intention of Aethelbert's visit to Offa's court in Herefordshire? Did he want Offa's kingdom or had he come to seek agreement to his marriage to Offa's daughter Etheldreda who subsequently became a nun at Crowland Abbey, Lincolnshire and later venerated as a saint? Alternatively did Offa see this as an opportunity to further his ambitions on the East Anglian kingdom?) On 1 August Ealdorman Aethelheard (no further information readily available) dies. On 14 September on his return from exile, the former King Osred II of Northumbria, is seized and killed (he had attempted to stage a comeback); he is buried at Tynemouth, Northumberland. On 29 September King Aethelred of Northumbria marries Aelfled (daughter of King Offa of Mercia). Northumbria is attacked by the heathen and the monastery at Donemuth (Jarrow, County Durham) is looted. Some of their ships are shattered by storms and many of their men and one of their leaders (no further information readily available) are either killed or drowned at the mouth of the River Don in County Durham.

796 – Pope Adrian I dies (on 25 December 795). King Aethelred of Northumbria is killed by a retainer (on 28 March at Corbridge, Northumberland). On 28 March "between cock-crow and dawn" there is an eclipse of the moon.

On 14 May Eardwulf becomes King of Northumbria and on 26 May is consecrated and enthroned by Archbishop Eanbald of York, Bishop Aethelberht of Hexham, Northumberland, Bishop Hygebald of Lindisfarne, Northumberland and Bishop Baldwulf of Whithorn (Dumfrieshire or "Whithorn at Elvet").

King Offa of Mercia dies **on 29 July**/10 August **(29 July is the accepted day)** and is succeeded by his son Ecgfrith who dies later in the year. On 10 August Archbishop Eanbald of York dies and is buried at York. He is succeeded by another Eanbald (II, he was taught by Alcuin of York) who is consecrated on 14 August.

Manuscript "A" (Winchester or Parker): Trebuchet.
Manuscript "B" (Abingdon I) & Manuscript "C" (Abingdon II): 18thCentury.
Manuscript "D" (Worcester): Swiss 721 Hv BT.
Manuscript "E" (Peterborough or Laud): Courier New.
Manuscript "F" (Canterbury): Alexa.
Manuscript "H" (Winchester): Calligraphic.

Bishop Ceolwulf of Lindsey (Lincolnshire) and Bishop Eadbald of London leave the country (it is not known whether this was for the purposes of pilgrimage, exile or any other reason but Manuscript E indicates Bishop Ceolwulf dies). "Eadberht, whose nickname was Praen" (this has been interpreted as meaning priest), takes possession of the kingdom of Kent.

797 – On 8 September Archbishop Eanbald II of York receives the pallium (vestment of office, a cloak). Bishop Aethelberht of Hexham, Northumberland dies on **16 October, and is succeeded by Heardred (no further information readily available) on** 30 October.

798 – King Coenwulf of Mercia "harried the Kentishmen as far as Romney Marsh", Kent and captures King Eadberht Praen of Kent; he takes him bound back to Mercia *and has his eyes put out and his hands cut off. Archbishop Aethelheard of Canterbury holds a synod and confirms and ratifies the ordinances covering monasteries decreed during the reign of King Wihtgar of Wessex and other kings (no further information readily available). Bishop Alfhun of Dommoc (probably Dunwich in Suffolk, but a possible alternative is Walton Castle, Felixstowe in Suffolk) dies at Sudbury in Suffolk and is buried at Dunwich in Suffolk; Tidfrith (no further information readily available) is elected in his place. King Sigeric of Essex goes to Rome. The body of (Saint) Wihtburh (founder of the monastery) at Dereham in Norfolk is found to be uncorrupted fifty-five years after her death.* On 2 April a great battle at Whalley (Lancashire) in Northumbria. Alric, son of Heardberht, (no further information readily available) and many others are killed.

799 – The Romans cut off the tongue and put out the eyes of Pope Leo III who is then banished; with God's help his sight and speech are restored and he resumes his duties as Pope.

800 – On the second hour of the eve of 16 January there is an eclipse of the moon.

801 – Archbishop Aethelheard of Canterbury and Bishop Cyneberht of Wessex (Winchester, Hampshire) go to Rome.

802 – King Beorhtric of Wessex and Ealdorman Worr die. (Ealdorman Worr was a favourite of King Beorhtric and Beorthtric's queen, Eadburh, jealous of Worr's influence poisoned him; Beorthtric drank the same poison and so both died.) Beorhtric is succeeded as King of Wessex by Egbert. Ealdorman Aethelmund of the Hwicce (whose father Ingild had been given land in Wiltshire by King Uhtred of the Hwicce) rides with his men from the lands of the Hwicce (Gloucestershire, Worcestershire and the western half of Warwickshire) and crosses the River Thames at Kempsford, Gloucestershire where a battle takes place against Ealdorman Weohstan (presumably of Wiltshire) and the men of Wiltshire. Both ealdormen are killed; the men of Wiltshire are victorious. On 20 December at dawn there is an eclipse of the moon.

Manuscript "A" (Winchester or Parker): Trebuchet.

Manuscript "B" (Abingdon I) & Manuscript "C" (Abingdon II): 18thCentury.

Manuscript "D" (Worcester): Swiss 721 Hv BT.

Manuscript "E" (Peterborough or Laud): Courier New.

Manuscript "F" (Canterbury): Alexa.

Manuscript "H" (Winchester): Calligraphic.

803 – On 24 June Bishop Hygebald (his letters to Alcuin of York describe the Viking raid on Lindisfarne in 793) of Lindisfarne, Northumberland dies and is succeeded by Egbert who is consecrated on 11 June.

804 – Beornmod is consecrated Bishop of Rochester, Kent.

805 – Archbishop Aethelheard of Canterbury dies and is succeeded by Wulfred. Abbot Forthred dies (Abbot of three monasteries in Yorkshire: Stonegrave, Coxwold and Donaemuthe – this site has not been confidently identified).

806 – Archbishop Wulfred of Canterbury receives the pallium (vestment of office, a cloak). *On Wednesday 4 June at dawn "the sign of the holy cross appeared in the moon". On 30 August "a marvellous ring appeared around the sun"/*on 1 September there is an eclipse of the moon.

King Eardwulf of Northumbrian is expelled from his kingdom (no further information readily available). Bishop Eanberht of Hexham, Northumberland, dies.

807 – King Cuthred of Kent, Abbess Ceolburh of Berkley, Gloucestershire, and Ealdorman Heahberht/Heabryht/Heabriht/**Heardbryht** of Kent, die.

809 – *On Tuesday 16 July "at the beginning of the fifth hour of the day" there is an eclipse of the sun.*

814 – Charlemagne, Emperor of the Franks, dies. Archbishop Wulfred of Canterbury and Bishop Wigberht of Wessex (Sherborne, Dorset) go to Rome.

815 – Archbishop Wulfred of Canterbury returns home with the blessing of Pope Leo III. King Egbert of Wessex campaigns in Cornwall from east to west.

816 – Pope Leo III dies and is succeeded by Stephen IV.

817 – Pope Stephen IV dies and is succeeded by Paschal I. "The English Quarter"/ "the School of the English" (used by ecclesiastics, pilgrims and other visitors, on the Vatican Hill in Rome) is burnt down.

821 – King Coenwulf of Mercia dies and is succeeded by Ceolwulf. Ealdorman Eadberht (no further information readily available) dies.

823 – King Ceolwulf of Mercia is "deprived of his kingdom" (no further information readily available).

824 – Two Mercian ealdormen, Burhhelm and Muca are killed in battles with the West Saxons. Synod of Clofeshoh (possibly Brixworth, Northamptonshire. At this synod the archbishopric of Lichfield – see **787** above – is reduced to that of a bishopric).

Manuscript "A" (Winchester or Parker): Trebuchet.
Manuscript "B" (Abingdon I) & Manuscript "C" (Abingdon II): 18thCentury.
Manuscript "D" (Worcester): Swiss 721 Hv BT.
Manuscript "E" (Peterborough or Laud): Courier New.
Manuscript "F" (Canterbury): Alexa.
Manuscript "H" (Winchester): Calligraphic.

825 – Battle at Galford (near Lydford in Devon) between the Britons of Cornwall and the men of Devon. King Egbert of Wessex defeats King Beornwulf of Mercia in battle at Ellendun (this site is arguably either Lydiard Tregoze or Wroughton in the Swindon area of Wiltshire) where many are killed. King Egbert sends some of his levies, led by Aethelwulf (his son), Bishop Ealhstan (Alfstan) of Sherborne, Dorset, and Ealdorman Wulfheard (no further information readily available) into Kent. King Baldred of Kent flees north of the River Thames and as a result the men of Kent, Surrey, Sussex and Essex submit to King Egbert; they restore their earlier allegiance to the Kings of Wessex. King Athelstan I of East Anglia and his court look to King Egbert of Wessex as "their protector and guardian against the fear of Mercian aggression". The East Angles (in revolt against their Mercian overlord, and led by their King Athelstan I) kill King Beornwulf of Mercia (as he tries to suppress their revolt).

827 – King Ludeca of Mercia and five of his Ealdorman are killed. Wiglaf succeeds as King of Mercia.

829 – There is an eclipse of the moon on Christmas morning (at 2 a.m. on 25 December 828). King Egbert of Wessex conquers Mercia and "all that was south of the Humber (separating Yorkshire from Lincolnshire) and he was the eighth king to be "Ruler of Britain" (Bretwalda). (The other seven are then listed :) Aelle, King of Sussex; Ceawlin, King of Wessex; Aethelberht, King of Kent; Raedwald, King of East Anglia; Edwin, King of Northumbria; Oswald, King of Northumbria; Oswy, King of Northumbria. King Egbert leads his levies to Dore, South Yorkshire, where the Northumbrians offer him submission and peace.

830 – Wiglaf is restored as King of Mercia. Bishop Aethelwald of Lichfield, Staffordshire, dies. King Egbert of Wessex leads his levies into Wales and receives the submission of the Welsh (no further information given).

832 – Archbishop Wulfred of Canterbury dies. *Feologild is elected to succeed him on 25 April and is consecrated on the 9 June. Feologild dies on 30 August 832* (see **833** below).

833 – Abbot Feologild dies (see **832** above). Ceolnoth is elected and consecrated Archbishop of Canterbury.

834 – Archbishop Ceolnoth of Canterbury receives the pallium (vestment of office, a cloak).

835 – The heathen devastate Sheppey, Kent.

836 – King Egbert of Wessex fights thirty-five/`twenty-five` ships' companies at Carhampton, Somerset where many are killed – the Danes are victorious. Bishop Wigthegn (and his successor as Bishop of Winchester, Hampshire) Bishop Herefrith, and Ealdormen Dudda and Osmod (both possibly of Kent – no further information readily available) die.

838 – King Egbert of Wessex defeats a combined force of Danes and the Britons of Cornwall at Hingston Down near Plymouth, Devon.

Manuscript "A" (Winchester or Parker): Trebuchet.

Manuscript "B" (Abingdon I) & Manuscript "C" (Abingdon II): 18thCentury.

Manuscript "D" (Worcester): Swiss 721 Hv BT.

Manuscript "E" (Peterborough or Laud): Courier New.

Manuscript "F" (Canterbury): Alexa.

Manuscript "H" (Winchester): Calligraphic.

839 – King Egbert of Wessex dies. Thirteen years before he became King, Egbert had been expelled to the land of the Franks by King Offa of Mercia and King Beorhtric of Wessex; Beorhtric had married Offa's daughter Eadburh and this is why he supported Offa. Aethelwulf succeeds as King of Wessex and appoints his **second** son Athelstan as King of Kent, Essex, Surrey and Sussex.

840 – Ealdorman Wulfheard (no further information readily available) defeats thirty-three ships' companies in battle at Southampton, Hampshire. Ealdorman Wulfheard dies later in the year. Ealdorman Aethelhelm (no further information readily available) with the men of Dorset fight the Danes at Portland, Dorset – the Ealdorman is killed and the Danes were victorious.

841 – The heathen kill Ealdorman Hereberht (possibly of Kent – no further information readily available) and many people in Romney Marsh and in the county of Kent, in Lindsey (Lincolnshire) and in East Anglia.

842 – The Danes kill many people in London and Rochester, Kent and in Cwantawic/Cantwic (in the vicinity of Etaples in France – this site has not been confidently identified).

843 – King Aethelwulf of Wessex loses a battle at Carhampton, Somerset, to thirty-five ships' companies of Danes.

848 – Ealdorman Eanwulf (no further information readily available) with the men of Somerset, Ealdorman Osric (no further information readily available) with the men of Dorset, and Bishop Ealhstan of Sherborne, Dorset defeat the Danes in battle near the mouth of the River Parrett, Somerset; many are killed.

850 – Ealdorman Ceorl (no further information readily available) with the men of Devon defeat the heathen in battle at Wiceganbeorg (possibly Wigborough in Somerset or Weekaborough in Devon) and many are killed. King Athelstan (who ruled Sussex, Surrey and Kent and was the younger brother of King Aethelwulf of Wessex) and Ealdorman Ealhhere (no further information readily available) destroy a great host at Sandwich, Kent, capture nine ships, and drive off the rest of the ships in the fleet. (Manuscript E attributes the encounter at Sandwich to **851**.) For the first time the heathen remain in England over winter.

851 – Three hundred and fifty Danish ships come to the mouth of the River Thames and their crews destroy London and Canterbury and "put to flight" King Beorhtwulf of Mercia and his levies. The Danes then cross the River Thames and go into Surrey and are defeated in the battle of Acleah (probably at Ockley in Surrey) by King Aethelwulf of Wessex and his son Aethelbald and their levies – the greatest number of Danes to date are killed.

852 – Abbot Ceolred of Medeshamstede (Peterborough) leases the estate of Sempringham, Lincolnshire, to Wulfred (no further information readily

Manuscript "A" (Winchester or Parker): Trebuchet.

Manuscript "B" (Abingdon I) & Manuscript "C" (Abingdon II): 18thCentury.

Manuscript "D" (Worcester): Swiss 721 Hv BT.

Manuscript "E" (Peterborough or Laud): Courier New.

Manuscript "F" (Canterbury): Alexa.

Manuscript "H" (Winchester): Calligraphic.

available), on condition that on his decease the estate reverts to the monastery at Medeshamstede. In return Wulfred gives to the monastery at Medeshamstede the estate of Sleaford, Lincolnshire, and every year gives the monastery sixty wagon loads of wood, twelve wagon loads of brushwood, six wagon loads of faggots, two casks full of clear ale, two cattle for slaughter, six hundred loaves (of bread), ten measures of Welsh ale, a horse and thirty shillings and a day's supply of food. This grant is witnessed by King Burhred (Burgred) of Mercia, Archbishop Ceolnoth of Canterbury, Bishop Tunberht of Lichfield, Staffordshire, (Abbot) Bishop Ceolred of Medeshamstede, Bishop Ealhhun of Worcester, Bishop Beorhtred of Lindsey (Lincolnshire), Abbot Wihtred (no information readily available), Abbot Werheard (no information readily available), Ealdorman Aethelheard(no information readily available), Ealdorman Hunberht (no information readily available) and many others.

853 – King Burgred of Mercia and his councillors seek the help of King Aethelwulf of Wessex to subjugate Wales. King Aethelwulf agrees and their joint forces campaign successfully in Wales. King Aethelwulf sends his son Alfred (the future Alfred the Great) to Rome. Pope Leo IV consecrates Alfred king and stands sponsor to him at his confirmation. Ealdorman Ealhhere (no further information readily available) with the men of Kent and Ealdorman Huda (no further information readily available) fight "a heathen host" in Thanet, Kent with many men killed and drowned on both sides including the two ealdormen. After Easter, King Aethelwulf gives his daughter Aethelswith in marriage to King Burgred of Mercia.

855 – The Danes winter in Sheppey, Kent for the first time. King Aethelwulf of Wessex grants a tenth of his lands to the Church and journeys to Rome where he stays for twelve months. On King Aethelwulf's return journey he marries *Judith* the daughter of Charles, King of the Franks. Two years after returning King Aethelwulf dies and is buried at Winchester, Hampshire. His son Aethelbald succeeds as King of Wessex and another son Aethelberht succeeds as King of Kent, Essex, Surrey and Sussex.

860 – King Aethelbald of Wessex dies and is buried at Sherborne, Dorset. Aethelberht succeeds to the "entire kingdom" of Wessex and rules in "good peace and in great tranquillity". A great pirate host lands and storms Winchester, Hampshire but loses the battle in the vicinity involving Ealdorman Osric of Hampshire with the men of Hampshire and Ealdorman Aethelwulf of Berkshire with the men of Berkshire. King Aethelberht of Wessex is buried at Sherborne, Dorset (he dies in 865). *(Manuscript F attributes these events to* **861**.*)*

861 – *Saint Swithun, Bishop of Winchester, Hampshire dies.*

865 – The heathen host stay in Thanet, Kent and are promised money by the Kentishmen if they keep the peace. The heathen host travel inland secretly at night and devastate the eastern part of Kent. Aethelred succeeds as King of Wessex. The great host come to England and stay the winter in East Anglia where they were provided with horses and where "they

---

Manuscript "A" (Winchester or Parker): Trebuchet.
Manuscript "B" (Abingdon I) & Manuscript "C" (Abingdon II): 18thCentury.
Manuscript "D" (Worcester): Swiss 721 Hv BT.
Manuscript "E" (Peterborough or Laud): Courier New.
Manuscript "F" (Canterbury): Alexa.
Manuscript "H" (Winchester): Calligraphic.

(the East Angles) made peace with them".

866 – The host leave East Anglia, cross the River Humber separating Yorkshire from Lincolnshire and go to York. The Northumbrians make war on the host late in the year despite the dissent among the people caused by their repudiation (no further information readily available) of their king, Osberht and his replacement by Aella who was not of royal birth.

867 – On 21 March the Northumbrians attack the Danes in York. In the battle King Osberht of Northumbria who had been deposed as king by the Northumbrians themselves, and replaced by King Aella, are both killed. Many of the Northumbrians are killed both inside and outside the city and those that survive "made peace with the host". Bishop Ealhstan of Sherborne, Dorset dies and is buried in the churchyard of the Abbey at Sherborne. The host stay the winter in Nottingham in Mercia. King Burgred of Mercia and his councillors "begged" King Aethelred of Wessex and his brother Alfred to help them fight the host.

868 – King Burgred of Mercia and King Aethelred of Wessex and their armies march to the fortifications of the host at Nottingham but there is no major battle; the Mercians make peace with the host.

869 – The host go back to York from Nottingham and remain there a year. The host ride across Mercia into East Anglia and stay the winter at Thetford, Norfolk. At wintertime King Edmund of East Anglia is defeated in battle by the Danes *who are led by Ingware (no further information readily available) and Ubba (Hubba, one of the sons of Ragnar Lodbrok the legendary Viking leader at one time King of Denmark and part of Sweden).* King Edmund is killed and the Danes take over his kingdom. They destroy all the monasteries they come to, and burn and demolish Medeshamstede (Peterborough) where they kill the Abbot (Hedda) and his monks "reducing to nothing what had once been a very rich foundation".

870 – Archbishop Ceolnoth of Canterbury dies (Manuscript E attributes this to **869**) and is succeeded by Bishop Aethelred of Wiltshire. The host go to Reading, Berkshire. Three days afterwards two jarls, one of whom was Sidroc (no further information readily available on the other jarl) from the host ride up-country with their forces and are defeated in battle at Englefield, Berkshire by the forces of Ealdorman Aethelwulf of Berkshire. Sidroc is killed.

871 – Four days after the battle of Englefield, Berkshire (see **870** above) King Aethelred of Wessex and his brother Alfred (later King Alfred the Great of Wessex) leading "great levies" are defeated by the Danes at the battle of Reading, Berkshire; many are killed on both sides. Ealdorman Aethelwulf of Berkshire is killed in the battle (he is buried at Derby, despite being a Mercian he continued as Ealdorman after Berkshire became part of Wessex sometime around 853).

Four days later at the battle of Ashdown, Berkshire, King Aethelred and his brother Alfred

Manuscript "A" (Winchester or Parker): Trebuchet.

Manuscript "B" (Abingdon I) & Manuscript "C" (Abingdon II): 18thCentury.

Manuscript "D" (Worcester): Swiss 721 Hv BT.

Manuscript "E" (Peterborough or Laud): Courier New.

Manuscript "F" (Canterbury): Alexa.

Manuscript "H" (Winchester): Calligraphic.

defeat the Danish kings Bagsecg (probably one-time King of Denmark; local legend has him buried at Wayland Smithy, Berkshire) and Halfdan (Ragnasson, King of London 871-72 and founder of the Norse kingdom based in York – reigning 875-77). The Danes fight in two divisions, one including the two kings is defeated by King Aethelred – King Bagsecg is killed, and the other division including the jarls is defeated by Alfred. Jarl Sidroc the Old is killed. (According to Manuscripts B, C, **D** and E a Jarl Sidroc was killed at the battle at Englefield in 870 see **870** above). Also killed are jarls Sidroc the Young, Osbern, Fraena and Harold (no further information readily available about any of these jarls). Thousands are killed and the battle continues until nightfall.

A fortnight later King Aethelred and his brother Alfred are defeated by the Danes at the battle of Basing, Hampshire.

Two months later King Aethelred and his brother Alfred fight the Danes at the battle of Meretun/Maeredun (probably in Hampshire). King Aethelred and Alfred fight in two divisions and for most of the day they seem to be winning but the Danes eventually triumph; many are killed including Bishop Heahmund of Sherborne, Dorset. After this battle a "great summer host" (one based abroad) came to Reading, Berkshire.

King Aethelred of Wessex dies (of wounds received at the battle of Meretun) and is buried at Wimborne, Dorset. He is succeeded as King of Wessex by his brother Alfred. One month later Alfred with a small force fights the entire host at the battle of Wilton, Wiltshire; for most of the day Alfred seems to be winning but the Danes eventually triumph.

In this year there are nine general engagements and other innumerable forays south of the River Thames involving Alfred, single ealdormen (no further information readily available) and king's thanes and the Danes; nine jarls and a king are killed in these battles. The West Saxons "make peace" with the host. (The scribe tries to inject a greater degree of accuracy with the sequence of the battles in this year; some of his accounts seem similar.) The host move from Reading, Berkshire to London for their winter quarters. The Mercians "make peace" with the host.

872 – The host go to Northumbria and move to winter quarters in Torksey, in Lindsey (Lincolnshire). The Mercians "make peace" with the host (again).

873 – The host move from Torksey, in Lindsey (Lincolnshire) to winter quarters in Repton, Derbyshire.

874 – The host conquer all of Mercia and expel King Burgred of Mercia who goes to Rome to live. King Burgred dies in Rome and is buried at St Mary's Church in "the English quarter"/"the School of the English" (see **817** above). The host puts Ceolwulf a "foolish king's thane" in charge of the government of Mercia who swears oaths and provides hostages, and promises that the kingdom "should be at their disposal whenever they might require it". (This thane is King Ceolwulf II, last independent King of Mercia. The Danes partition the

---

Manuscript "A" (Winchester or Parker): Trebuchet.

Manuscript "B" (Abingdon I) & Manuscript "C" (Abingdon II): 18thCentury.

Manuscript "D" (Worcester): Swiss 721 Hv BT.

Manuscript "E" (Peterborough or Laud): Courier New.

Manuscript "F" (Canterbury): Alexa.

Manuscript "H" (Winchester): Calligraphic.

kingdom, Ceolwulf rules the western part and the Danes rule the eastern part themselves.) (Manuscript E attributes these events to **873**.)

Part of the host under Halfdan (joint leader with his brother Ivarr the Boneless of the "Great Army" which came to England in 865. Halfdan reigns as king of York 875-7) go from Repton, Derbyshire to Northumbria, and conquer the kingdom; they take winter quarters "on" the River Tyne and the lands thereabout. The host make frequent raids against the Picts and the Strathclyde Britons (no further details given). The three kings Guthrum (leader of the "great summer-army" which came to England in 871; he becomes King of East Anglia 879-90 (using his baptismal name Athelstan) after his defeat by Alfred the Great at the battle of Edington, Wiltshire in 878), Oscytel (no further information readily available) and Anund (no further information readily available) and a great host go from Repton, Derbyshire to Cambridge where they stay for a year.

875 – In the summer King Alfred of Wessex defeats a fleet of seven ships' companies of Danes capturing one of their ships and causing the others to flee. The host eludes the West Saxon levies and take Wareham, Dorset.

876 – King Alfred of Wessex makes peace with the host, they swear oaths on a sacred ring that they will leave Wessex speedily; never before had the host sworn such an oath. Under cover of this agreement the host elude the West Saxon levies at night and the "mounted host" take Exeter, Devon. Halfdan shares out the lands in Northumbria to the soldiers in his army and "they were engaged in ploughing and in making a living for themselves".

The host move from Wareham, Dorset to Exeter, Devon. The pirate host sail "west about" and lose one hundred and twenty ships off the coast near Swanage, Dorset in a great storm at sea. King Alfred and his mounted forces are unable to prevent the mounted host from reaching the unassailable fortress at Exeter, Devon. At Exeter the host provide "preliminary hostages" as many as are wanted, and swear solemn oaths to keep the peace (whilst King Alfred is clearly one of the parties involved, the leader of the host is not identified). *Rollo the Viking (a frequent campaigner in France) invades Normandy.* (Manuscript E attributes these events to **875**.)

877 – In the autumn the host go into Mercia and share out the land among them; they also give land to King Ceolwulf II of Mercia.

878 – Secretly in midwinter after Twelfth Night the host go to Chippenham, Wiltshire and then ride over to occupy Wessex; a "great part of the inhabitants" flee overseas, the rest submit. King Alfred of Wessex with a small company escape into the woods and inaccessible places in marshes (the location is not given). A brother (no name given) of the Danish kings Ivar and Halfdan goes to Devon, in Wessex, with twenty-three ships and is killed along with eight hundred men and forty men in his retinue – their banner "The Raven" is captured.

Manuscript "A" (Winchester or Parker): Trebuchet.

Manuscript "B" (Abingdon I) & Manuscript "C" (Abingdon II): 18thCentury.

Manuscript "D" (Worcester): Swiss 721 Hv BT.

Manuscript "E" (Peterborough or Laud): Courier New.

Manuscript "F" (Canterbury): Alexa.

Manuscript "H" (Winchester): Calligraphic.

At Easter, King Alfred and a small company of his men build a fortification at Athelney, Somerset and with the men of Somerset in the locality continues to fight the host. In the seventh week after Easter King Alfred rides to Ecgbryhtesstan to the east of Selwood Forest, to meet the men of Somerset and Wiltshire, and the men from Hampshire "on this side of the sea" (this could mean the men living to the west of Southampton Water); "they received him warmly" (Ecgbryht's/Egbert's Stone, possibly Willoughby Hedge, Wiltshire, commemorates this meeting). One day later King Alfred goes to Iley Oak, Wiltshire, and a day later he defeats the "entire host" at the battle of Edington, Wiltshire. He pursues the fugitives from the battle and besieges their fortification (presumed to be Chippenham in Wiltshire) for a "fortnight". The host provide preliminary hostages and swear oaths to leave his kingdom, and promise that their king (Guthrum) will receive baptism. Three weeks later, thirty of the "most honourable men in the host", including King Guthrum, come to King Alfred at Aller, near Athelney, Somerset. King Alfred stands sponsor to King Guthrum at his baptismal ceremony at Wedmore, Somerset. King Guthrum and his companions stay with King Alfred for twelve days who honours them "with riches" (no further information readily available).

The host go from Chippenham, Wiltshire to Cirencester, Gloucestershire and stay there one year. A "band of pirates" gather and occupy Fulham by the River Thames in London. The sun is eclipsed for one hour of the day (on 29 October 878).

879 – The host go from Cirencester, Gloucestershire to East Anglia where they occupy and share out the land. The host who have occupied Fulham, London go to Ghent in Belgium "in the land of the Franks" and stay there one year.

881 – "The host go "deeper" into the land of the Franks and after fighting the Franks they are supplied with horses. The host go up the River Meuse in Belgium "far into the land of the Franks" and stay there a year.

882 – King Alfred of Wessex leads naval forces in battle and defeats four ships' companies of Danes, capturing two ships, and all the crew are killed; he receives the surrender of the other two ships after their crews suffer heavy casualties – *two crew members escape.* The host go up the River Scheldt in Belgium to (the French province of) Condé and stay there a year.

Pope Marius I sends King Alfred a fragment of the True Cross (this fragment may be preserved in the "Brussels Cross" in the Cathedral of St Michel and Gudule in Brussels in Belgium).

Sigehelm (probably Swethelm, Bishop of Sherborne, Dorset) and Athelstan (no further information readily available) take to Rome and also to India to (the Indian Christians worshipping at the churches of) Saint Thomas and Saint Bartholomew· (the sites of these churches have not been confidently identified) the alms that King Alfred had promised to send for his success in besieging the host in London (the reference to London is probably a mistake, there is no record of King Alfred

---

Manuscript "A" (Winchester or Parker): Trebuchet.

Manuscript "B" (Abingdon I) & Manuscript "C" (Abingdon II): 18thCentury.

Manuscript "D" (Worcester): Swiss 721 Hv BT.

Manuscript "E" (Peterborough or Laud): Courier New.

Manuscript "F" (Canterbury): Alexa.

Manuscript "H" (Winchester): Calligraphic.

involved in operations around London until 886).

883 – In France the host travel along the River Somme to Amiens and stay there a year.

884 – The host in northern France divides into two groups, one goes "east" (no further information provided) and the other besiege Rochester, Kent where they build a fortification (no further details provided). The host in East Anglia break their peace with King Alfred (no further details provided).

Before midwinter Carloman, king of the Franks, dies after being mauled by a wild boar; one year earlier his brother Louis had died. Like their father Louis the Stammerer who died in 879 the year in which there was an eclipse of the sun (it was in 878 – see **878** above – the dating difference is due to the year being recorded as beginning 24 September); both had ruled the western kingdom of France. Louis the Stammerer was the son of Charles the Bald whose daughter (Judith) had married King Aethelwulf of Wessex (presumably the reason for the inclusion of this detailed information).

A "great pirate host" assembles among the "Old Saxons" (in north-western Germany, no further details provided) and is defeated in two battles (probably Norden in Fresia in 884 and in Saxony in 885) by the Old Saxons and their Frisian allies. Charles the Fat succeeds to the western kingdom of the Franks.

Pope Marius I dies. He had freed "the School of the English" (see **817** above) from payment of dues as requested by King Alfred of Wessex. Pope Marius had sent King Alfred "great gifts" including a fragment of the True Cross (see **882** above).

885 – Rochester, Kent is relieved by King Alfred of Wessex. The host abandon their encampment and horses and go overseas (it is not identified where) in the summer. King Alfred sends a fleet to East Anglia where it defeats at the mouth of the River Stour (on the border between Essex and Suffolk) a fleet of sixteen ships "of pirates" whose ships are captured and their crews killed. On their way home from this victory with their "booty" King Alfred's fleet are defeated by a "great fleet of pirates".

The host go west (from Louvain in Belgium) up the River Seine (Gaul-France) and takes up winter quarters in the city of Paris, Gaul (France).

886 – King Alfred of Wessex occupies London and all the English people submit to him except those within the Danelaw. King Alfred appoints Ealdorman Aethelred (ruler of Mercia, "Lord of the Mercians", married to King Alfred's daughter Ethelfleda) to govern London.

887 – In France the host go "up through the bridge" at Paris, up the River Seine and up the River Marne as far as Chézy-sur-Marne where they set up camp and at Yonne and stay two winters.

Manuscript "A" (Winchester or Parker): Trebuchet.
Manuscript "B" (Abingdon I) & Manuscript "C" (Abingdon II): 18thCentury.
Manuscript "D" (Worcester): Swiss 721 Hv BT.
Manuscript "E" (Peterborough or Laud): Courier New.
Manuscript "F" (Canterbury): Alexa.
Manuscript "H" (Winchester): Calligraphic.

Ealdorman Aethelhelm takes the alms of the West Saxons and King Alfred to Rome. (Aethelhelm was nephew of King Alfred of Wessex and the younger son of King Aethelred of Wessex. He was too young to succeed to the kingdom and so Alfred became king of Wessex in 871. He was possibly Ealdorman of Wiltshire.)

888 – (In 887) King Charles "the Fat" of the Franks is deprived of his kingdom by Arnulf, his brother's son, six weeks before he dies (on 13 January 888). The kingdom is divided into five with Arnulf overlord and king east of the River Rhine (Germany), Rudolf as king of the Middle Kingdom (Burgundy), Odo as king in the west (Neustria), and Berengar and Guido as kings of Lombardy and the territory "on that side of the Alps" – they often "lay waste" each other's lands and fight two major battles (no further information readily available).

Ealdorman Beocca (possibly of Somerset) takes the alms of the West Saxons and King Alfred to Rome. Queen Aethelswith (sister of King Alfred and daughter of King Aethelwulf of Wessex who had married King Burgred of Mercia) dies in Pavia (Italy – accompanying Ealdorman Beocca) *on the way to Rome.* Archbishop Aethelred of Canterbury and Ealdorman Aethelwald (no further information readily available) die in the one month.

889 – No West Saxon alms are taken to Rome; King Alfred sends two couriers with letters. The host (in France) go from the River Seine area to St Lo between the Bretons and the Franks.

890 – Abbot Beornhelm (no further information readily available) takes the alms of the West Saxons and King Alfred of Wessex to Rome. King Guthrum of East Anglia, who has the baptismal name Athelstan and who was godson of King Alfred, dies. In France in the vicinity of St Lo the host are defeated by the Bretons who drive them into a river drowning many (the river is not identified). Plegmund is chosen as Archbishop of Canterbury.

891 – The host go east (on the Continent) and King Arnulf of the Franks, with the East Franks, Saxons and Bavarians, defeat the "mounted host" before their ships are able to assist (no further details are provided). Dubhslaine, Macbeathadh and Maelinmhain (these spellings vary in manuscripts B, C, **D** and *F*) set out in a boat "without any oars" from Ireland on pilgrimage and land in Cornwall and go to King Alfred of Wessex. Suibhne, "the best teacher among the Scots" (no further information readily available), dies.

892 – After Easter a comet – "a long-haired star" – appears. In France the great host go from the east kingdom of the Franks to Boulogne where they are provided with ships to take them and all their horses. Two hundred and fifty ships bring the host to the mouth of the River Lympne in Kent, at the east end of the great forest of Andred (the Weald) which is at least one hundred and twenty miles long by thirty miles broad. They row their ships four miles up the river as far as the forest and occupy a half-built fort inhabited by a few peasants. Haesten (one of the most famous and notorious Vikings who fought in France, Spain, and England. He sailed into the Mediterranean and his raids included sites forming part of the Byzantine empire) brings eighty ships to the mouth of the River Thames and builds a fort at Milton Royal (Milton Regis, Kent) and a fort for the other host (those that crossed from Boulogne) at Appledore, Kent.

893 – Two "hosts" invade Wessex. They are drawn from those who had built the fort in the east kingdom of the Franks at Louvain in Belgium, and the Northumbrians and East Anglians who had earlier given oaths and hostages and made peace with King Alfred of Wessex. King Alfred gathers his forces, half are kept home and half on active service; those that man the fortresses are exempted from these arrangements (this is the first time such arrangements are mentioned). King Alfred positions those on active service between the "two hosts" in the forest (Appledore, Kent, the larger force comprising 250 ships whose king or leader is now unknown) and on the water (Milton Regis, Kent – the smaller force comprising 80 ships with Haesten the Dane as their leader) so that his forces can attack either host should they venture out from their strongholds into open country. Only twice does the full force of the host leave their strongholds; once when they first landed before the levies were mustered, and twice when they wished to evacuate their strongholds – see this entry below. Encounters involving "gangs and bands" from the host, moving through the woods, and King Alfred's levies and forces from his fortresses take place almost every day, wherever the host perceive the territory is unguarded.

The host (from Milton Regis led by Haesten) leave their fortresses with much plunder intent on moving into Essex to meet ships in the River Thames. The host (from Appledore, after raiding Hampshire and Berkshire, attempt to join Haesten in Essex), but King Alfred's forces (led by his son the future King Edward the Elder) intercept and defeat them at Farnham, Surrey, recovering their plunder. The host then cross River Thames without using a ford, go up the River Colne, Hertfordshire, to an island (Thorney) in the river (near Iver Heath, Buckinghamshire) where they remain; their king (no further information readily available) had been wounded in the battle at Farnham. King Alfred's forces surround them on the island and stay until they complete their tour of duty and when their supplies of food run out. They make their way home while King Alfred is on his way with the other half of his forces as their replacements.

The Danes living in Northumbria and East Anglia assemble about one hundred ships which sail to besiege Exeter, Devon, and a further forty ships which sail to besiege an un-named fort in Devonshire in the Bristol Channel. When he hears of this King Alfred leads most of his forces to relieve the siege of Exeter; when he arrives the Danes retire to their ships.

Meanwhile some of King Alfred's forces (led by his son Edward and his son-in-law Ealdorman Aethelred, ruler of Mercia, "Lord of the Mercians") move eastwards where they gather support from the citizens of London and then go on to the Danish fort at Benfleet, Essex where the Danes from Milton Regis and Appledore had combined their forces; their leader, Haesten the Dane, is away at the time (with the main part of his army) plundering (Mercia). The "English" forces storm the fort and seize everything within and take the plunder, with the women and children, to London whilst breaking-up or burning the Danish ships or taking them to London or Rochester, Kent. Haesten's wife (no further information readily available)

Manuscript "A" (Winchester or Parker): Trebuchet.
Manuscript "B" (Abingdon I) & Manuscript "C" (Abingdon II): 18thCentury.
Manuscript "D" (Worcester): Swiss 721 Hv BT.
Manuscript "E" (Peterborough or Laud): Courier New.
Manuscript "F" (Canterbury): Alexa.
Manuscript "H" (Winchester): Calligraphic.

and his two sons (no further information readily available) are brought to King Alfred who sends them back to Haesten because one son is the godson of King Alfred and the other is the godson of Ealdorman Aethelred. Haesten returns to Benfleet, rebuilds his fort and resumes his campaign in Mercia.

Whilst King Alfred of Wessex is preoccupied with events in Devonshire, "both the hosts" concentrate their forces at Shoebury, Essex where they build a fort. The combined force then marches westwards along the River Thames, on the way they receiving reinforcements from East Anglia and Northumbria. The combined force reaches and continues up along the River Severn. The English forces assemble including Ealdorman Aethelred of Mercia, Ealdorman Aethelhelm (no further information readily available), Ealdorman Aethelnoth (no further information readily available), and the king's thanes (no further information readily available) who were occupying the forts east of the River Parret in Somerset, the forts to both the west and east of Selwood Forest in eastern Somerset and northern Dorset borders, the forts to the north of the River Thames and the forts to the west of the River Severn; some Welsh also join them. The English forces surround the host on both sides of the river at "Buttington on Severn shore" (near Welshpool, Powys). After many weeks the host run out of food, some die of hunger and others eat their horses. Others sail to fight the English camped on the east side of the river and lose the battle; many are killed with the remnants escaping to their fort and ships at Shoebury, Essex. The English losses include Ordheh, a king's thane (no further information readily available), and many other thanes (no further information readily available).

The Danes, now back in Essex, gather their forces from East Anglia and Northumbria and place their women, ships and property in the safety of East Anglia. They then march their forces without a break by day and night until they reach the deserted Roman fort at Chester in The Wirral, Cheshire. The English forces are not able to catch the Danes before they reach the fort which they besiege for two days, but they do kill stragglers, seize all the cattle in the vicinity, burn all the corn in the vicinity and allow their horses to eat all the fodder they could so that the "neighbourhood was bare".

894 – The host move from the Wirral in Cheshire but are unable to remain there because the area has had its crops and livestock removed by the Mercians and consequently there is insufficient cattle and corn to sustain them. The host move into Wales (plundering the kingdoms of Brycheiniog, Gwent and Glywysing) and then march across Northumbria and East Anglia taking their plunder with them; the levies are unable to confront them until they reach the island of Mersea in Essex. The host who had besieged Exeter in Devon (see **893** above) sail home (no further information readily available) and on their way plunder inland near Chichester in Sussex where the garrison (presumably from Chichester) fight them, killing many hundreds and capturing some of their ships. Before wintertime the host at Mersea in Essex row their ships up the River Thames and then up the River Lea bordering Hertfordshire and Essex. The host have been away from home for two years.

895 – The host build a fort by the River Lea bordering Hertfordshire and Essex. The (English)

Manuscript "A" (Winchester or Parker): Trebuchet.
Manuscript "B" (Abingdon I) & Manuscript "C" (Abingdon II): 18thCentury.
Manuscript "D" (Worcester): Swiss 721 Hv BT.
Manuscript "E" (Peterborough or Laud): Courier New.
Manuscript "F" (Canterbury): Alexa.
Manuscript "H" (Winchester): Calligraphic.

garrison of London with support from others (no further information readily available) attack the fort and are repulsed, four king's thanes are killed (no further information readily available). In the autumn King Alfred of Wessex and his levies set up camp near the fort while the corn is being harvested to prevent the Danes interfering. King Alfred identifies where the River Lea might be blocked to prevent the Danes using their ships. He orders the construction of two forts, one on each side of the river. When the host see what is happening they abandon both their fort and their ships and go across country until they reach Bridgnorth in Shropshire by the River Severn where they build a fort. King Alfred's levies ride after the host. The men of London seize the ships of the host (at the fort in the River Lea), breaking-up the unserviceable and taking the serviceable back to London. Before the Danes leave their fort by the River Lea they place their women in safety in East Anglia (no further information readily available). The Danes remain at Bridgnorth for the winter. It has been three years since the Danes had first arrived in England from overseas at the mouth of the River Lympne in Kent.

896 – In the summer the host disperse (presumably from Bridgnorth in Shropshire), some go to East Anglia (no further information readily available), some go to Northumbria (no further details given) and those "without stock" acquire ships and sail to the River Seine in France. During the three years since the host arrived England has been afflicted by murrain (infectious disease in cattle) and with plague among the population. Many of "the best" of the king's servants have died; the most distinguished being Bishop Swithwulf of Rochester in Kent, Ealdorman Ceolmund of Kent, Ealdorman Beorhtwulf of Essex, Ealdorman Wulfred of Hampshire, Bishop Ealhheard of Dorchester-on-Thames in Oxfordshire, Eadwulf the king's thane in Sussex, Beornwulf reeve in Winchester Hampshire, and Ecgwulf the king's marshal.

The hosts from Northumbria and East Anglia raid the south coast using warships built "many years" before. King Alfred of Wessex "ordered warships to be built to meet the Danish ships: they were almost twice as long as the others, some had sixty oars, some had more; they were both swifter, steadier, and with more freeboard than the others; they were built neither after the Frisian design nor after the Danish, but as it seemed to himself that they could be most serviceable."

The crews from six Danish warships raid the Isle of Wight, Devon and along the coast. King Alfred sends nine of his new ships to blockade the entrance to the open sea (probably Poole Harbour in Dorset). The crews of three of the Danish ships sail their ships to fight the English, the three other ships are beached in the upper end of the harbour and their crews go off overland (no further information readily available). In the ensuing naval engagement the English seize two of the Danish ships but the third escapes with only five of her crew. At least three English ships run aground where three other Danish ships have been beached and a fight ensues when the tide ebbs far away. At this battle the following are killed: Lucumon the king's reeve, the Friesians Wulfheard, Aebbe and Aethelhere, and Aethelfrith of the king's household. Sixty-two English and Friesians are killed and one hundred and twenty Danes. The Danes refloat three of their beached ships and row out to sea; the tide has not ebbed sufficiently for the beached English ships to be refloated at the same time. However

Manuscript "A" (Winchester or Parker): Trebuchet.
Manuscript "B" (Abingdon I) & Manuscript "C" (Abingdon II): 18thCentury.
Manuscript "D" (Worcester): Swiss 721 Hv BT.
Manuscript "E" (Peterborough or Laud): Courier New.
Manuscript "F" (Canterbury): Alexa.
Manuscript "H" (Winchester): Calligraphic.

the crews of the Danish ships are wounded and exhausted and are unable to row past Sussex. Two of the Danes (ships – it is not clear whether the reference is to two ships or two men) are washed ashore where the men are seized and taken to King Alfred of Wessex at Winchester in Hampshire: the King has them hung. One single ship of the Danes with its wounded crew reaches East Anglia (no further information readily available). In the summer twenty ships (presumably Danish) and all their crews are lost off the south coast (no further information readily available). Wulfric, the king's marshal who had also been the Welsh reeve (an official responsible for collecting tribute from the Welsh), dies.

897 – Ealdorman Aethelhelm of Wiltshire dies nine nights before midsummer. Bishop Heahstan of London dies.

899 – King Alfred "the Great" of Wessex dies six nights before All Hallows Day (1 November). **(Manuscripts D and** E **give the day as 26 October.)** King Alfred is succeeded by his son Edward the Elder. Edward's cousin Aethelwold seizes the manors of Wimborne and Christchurch both in Dorset without the consent of the king and his councillors. King Edward leads his levies and camps at Badbury Rings near Wimborne in Dorset where Aethelwold and his men have barricaded themselves. Under cover of darkness Aethelwold escapes, and, despite being pursued by the king's forces, reaches the host in Northumbria **who receive him as king.** The king's forces "arrest" a nun (no further information readily available) whom Aethelwold had abducted without the king's consent. Ealdorman Aethelred of Devon dies four weeks before King Alfred.

902 – Ealdorman Aethelwulf brother of Ealhswith wife of King Alfred (in the ninth century Wessex did not designate the wife of their kings as queen) and Abbot Virgilius from Ireland die. Grimbald the priest dies on 8 July. (He was dean at the "New Minster", Winchester in Hampshire.) **(Manuscripts D and** F **attribute these events to 903.)** A battle of Holm (possibly Holme in Cambridgeshire, but why Kentishmen are involved) takes place between the Danes and the men of Kent.

903 – Aethelwold, cousin of King Edward the Elder of Wessex, comes with a fleet to Essex (no further information readily available). **(Manuscript D attributes these events to 904.)** *New Minster in Winchester, Hampshire is consecrated and the relics of Saint Judoc (a Breton nobleman who became a hermit) are translated to the New Minster.*

904 – Aethelwold, cousin of King Edward the Elder of Wessex, encourages the host in East Anglia to commence hostilities against the English. The host attack Mercia and cross the River Thames at Cricklade in Wiltshire and seize all they can in the countryside surrounding Braydon Forest in Wiltshire and then head **eastwards** home. King Edward marches his levies in pursuit and ravages their territory between the dikes (Cambridgeshire) and the River Wissey in Norfolk as far north as the Fens. The men of Kent disobey King Edward's order to retire despite being sent seven messengers conveying the order. The Kentishmen are trapped by the host and in the ensuing battle Ealdorman Sigewulf (no further information readily available) and his son Sigeberht (no further information readily available), Ealdorman

---

Manuscript "A" (Winchester or Parker): Trebuchet.
Manuscript "B" (Abingdon I) & Manuscript "C" (Abingdon II): 18thCentury.
Manuscript "D" (Worcester): Swiss 721 Hv BT.
Manuscript "E" (Peterborough or Laud): Courier New.
Manuscript "F" (Canterbury): Alexa.
Manuscript "H" (Winchester): Calligraphic.

Sigehelm of Kent, Eadwold the king's thane, Abbot Cenwulf (no further information readily available), Eadwold son of Acca (no further information readily available) and many others are killed on the English side. Eohric, King of the Danes in East Anglia, Prince (aetheling – a male of royal blood, the heir apparent,) Aethelwold (cousin of King Edward the Elder of Wessex) "who had incited him (Eohric) to this rebellion", **who the Danes had elected as their king,** Beorhtsige son of Prince (an aetheling) Beornnoth (no further information readily available) and the Scandinavian barons Ysopa (no further information readily available) and Oscytel (no further information readily available – but see **874** above) and many others are killed on the Danish side. Although the Danes win the battle they lose more men. **(Manuscript D attributes these events to 905.)**

Ealhswith wife of King Alfred the Great of Wessex dies. (Manuscript C attributes her death to **902** and **Manuscript D to 905.**) An eclipse of the moon takes place.

905 – Alfred the reeve of Bath in Somerset dies. A peace treaty between King Edward the Elder of Wessex and the host from East Anglia and with the Northumbrians is ratified at Tiddingford in Buckinghamshire. **(Manuscript D attributes these events to 906.** Manuscript E also attributes the peace treaty to **906** and adds that Edward was "compelled" to make peace.) A comet appears **on 20 October.**

907 – The city of Chester rebuilt.

908 – Bishop Denewulf of Winchester, Hampshire dies. **(Manuscript D attributes this event to 909.)**

909 – Frithustan becomes Bishop of Winchester in Hampshire. Bishop Asser of Sherborne in Dorset dies. King Edward the Elder of Wessex sends his levies drawn from Wessex and Mercia north who campaign for five weeks "destroying both people and every kind of cattle" and killing many Danes. **(Manuscript D attributes these events to 910.)**

The body of Saint Oswald, King of Northumbria 634-42, is translated from Bardney in Lincolnshire to Mercia (Saint Oswald's Priory, Gloucester — his head was preserved in the coffin of Saint Cuthbert on Lindisfarne, Northumberland.) **(Manuscript D attributes this event to 906.)**

910 – The Northumbrian host break the peace and campaign in Mercia "rejecting with scorn" any offers of peace made to them by King Edward the Elder of Wessex. King Edward is in Kent mustering one hundred ships which sail east along the south coast to meet him. The host think King Edward's fleet is his main strength and can plunder where they please. King Edward sends his (land) levies drawn from both Mercia and Wessex to intercept them which they do when the host are on their way home. In the ensuing battle **on 6 (5 is often quoted) August** at Tettenhall (Wednesfield, Wolverhampton in Staffordshire/West Midlands) the English defeat the Danes; many thousands are killed including King Eowils (joint King of Northumbria with Halfdan), **King Halfdan (joint King of Northumbria with Eowils), and (with no further information readily available on any of the following), Jarl Ohtor, Jarl Scurfa**

Manuscript "A" (Winchester or Parker): Trebuchet.
Manuscript "B" (Abingdon I) & Manuscript "C" (Abingdon II): 18thCentury.
Manuscript "D" (Worcester): Swiss 721 Hv BT.
Manuscript "E" (Peterborough or Laud): Courier New.
Manuscript "F" (Canterbury): Alexa.
Manuscript "H" (Winchester): Calligraphic.

and Anlaf the Black, **the Scandinavian barons Athulf,** Agmund, Benesing, Guthferth (there are two people named Guthferth), Osferth Hlytte, and Thurferth.

Aethelflaed, "Lady of the Mercians" builds a fortress at Bremesburh (this site has not been confidently identified.) **(Manuscript D attributes the battle of Tettenhall and the building of the fortress at Bremesburh to 909, it mentions the battle again in the entry for 910 and provides the details – similar to those in** Manuscript A **– in the entry for 911 but does not name the battle.) A great pirate host comes from Brittany in France and harries along the River Severn (bordering Somerset and Gloucestershire) causing much destruction but almost all of them died there (no further information readily available).**

911 – Ealdorman Aethelred of Mercia dies and King Edward the Elder of Wessex takes over all the lands belonging to him including London and Oxford. **(Manuscripts D and** E **attributes these events to 910. In addition Manuscript D includes these details in the entry for 912.)**

912 – Around Martinmas (11 November) King Edward the Elder of Wessex has built the more northerly fortress at Hertford (north of the River Lea) and between the Rivers Maran, Beane and Lea – all in Hertfordshire. Between April and Midsummer Day King Edward takes some of his levies to Maldon in Essex where they camp whilst the fort at Witham in Essex is being built. Whilst at Maldon numbers of people who had previously been subjects of the Danes submit to him. At the same time another part of his forces build a fortress at Hertford on the south bank of the River Lea in Hertfordshire. **(Manuscript D attributes these events to 913.)** Aethelflaed, Lady of the Mercians, builds fortresses at Scergeat (this site has not been confidently identified) on 2 May and later in the year at Bridgnorth in Shropshire.

913 – Aethelflaed, Lady of the Mercians, builds fortresses at Tamworth in the early summer and before 1 August at Stafford (both in Staffordshire).

914 – Early in the summer Eddisbury in Cheshire and late in the autumn Warwick are fortified. **(Manuscript D attributes the fortification of Warwick to 915.)**

915 – After Christmas the fortresses at Chirbury in Shropshire, Weardburh (this site has not been confidently identified), and before Christmas Runcorn in Cheshire are built.

916 – After Easter separate raiding parties from the host ride out from Leicester and Northampton. One party kills many inhabitants of Hook Norton in Oxfordshire and as they return home they combine with a second party heading towards Luton in Bedfordshire. Local people fight and defeat them (the site has not been confidently identified) recovering the plunder taken, and most of the raiding parties' horses and weapons. **(Manuscript D attributes these events to 914.)**

On 16 June Abbot Ecgberht is killed together with his companions; he "had done nothing to deserve it" (no

Manuscript "A" (Winchester or Parker): Trebuchet.
Manuscript "B" (Abingdon I) & Manuscript "C" (Abingdon II): 18thCentury.
Manuscript "D" (Worcester): Swiss 721 Hv BT.
Manuscript "E" (Peterborough or Laud): Courier New.
Manuscript "F" (Canterbury): Alexa.
Manuscript "H" (Winchester): Calligraphic.

further information is provided about who was involved and where it took place). Three days later, Aethelflaed, Lady of the Mercians, sends an army into Wales and takes Brecenanmere (an artificial island housing a royal residence, a crannog at Llangorse Lake, near Brecon) capturing the wife of the King (Tewdwr ab Elise of Brycheiniog) and thirty-three others.

917 – Before the 1 August, Aethelflaed, Lady of the Mercians, takes Derby and the surrounding region it controlled; four of her thanes (no further information readily available) are killed within the city gates.

A "great pirate host" from Brittany in France led by Jarls Ohtor (no further information readily available) and Hroald (no further information readily available) sail up the River Severn and campaign along the Welsh coast. They seize Bishop Cyfeiliog of Archenfield (on the borders of Herefordshire and Gloucestershire) and take him to their ships. King Edward the Elder of Wessex pays forty pounds ransom for him. The host move inland intent on renewing their raids towards Archenfield where they are defeated in battle by the men from Herefordshire and Gloucestershire and from the nearest fortresses (these are not identified). Jarl Hroald and the brother of Jarl Ohtor (no further information readily available) and a great many of the host are killed. The survivors are driven into an enclosure (no further information readily available) and are forced to give hostages and promise that they will leave King Edward's domain. King Edward makes arrangements to ensure the south shoreline of the River Severn is guarded from Cornwall in the west to the mouth of the River Avon in Gloucestershire in the east so that the host are prevented from landing. However, on two separate occasions at night, the host land at Watchet in Somerset and at Porlock in Somerset but are driven off by the English with only a few escaping by swimming to their ships. The survivors from these raids camp on the island of Flatholm/**Steepholme** in the Bristol Channel until they reduce their food supplies to such an extent that some die of hunger. The survivors go to Dyfed in South Wales and eventually to Ireland. Before 11 November King Edward goes to Buckingham staying there four weeks to oversee the building of fortresses, one each side of the river (the Great Ouse). Jarl Thurcytel (no further information readily available), all the Scandinavian barons (no further information readily available), and almost all who owed allegiance to the host at Bedford and many who owe allegiance to Northampton submit to King Edward. **(Manuscript D attributes these events to 915**.)

918 – Before Martinmas (11 November) King Edward the Elder of Wessex leads his army to Bedford and occupies the fortress where most of the garrison submit to him. He stays for four weeks and orders the building of a new fortress on the south side of the River Great Ouse. In the early part of the year, Aethelflaed, Lady of the Mercians, takes Leicester by "peaceful means" and the majority of the Danes become her subjects; likewise the people of York swear allegiance to her.

919 – Before midsummer King Edward Elder of Wessex occupies Maldon in Essex and builds and garrisons a fortress. Jarl Thurcytel (no further information readily available) and those of his men who wish, go to France "under the protection" of King Edward and with his assistance. Aelfwynn, the daughter of Aethelred, lord of the Mercians, is deprived of her authority in Mercia and taken to Wessex three weeks before Christmas (see **921** below).

Manuscript "A" (Winchester or Parker): Trebuchet.
Manuscript "B" (Abingdon I) & Manuscript "C" (Abingdon II): 18thCentury.
Manuscript "D" (Worcester): Swiss 721 Hv BT.
Manuscript "E" (Peterborough or Laud): Courier New.
Manuscript "F" (Canterbury): Alexa.
Manuscript "H" (Winchester): Calligraphic.

920 – Before Easter King Edward the Elder of Wessex builds and garrisons the fortress at Towcester in Northamptonshire and then after Rogationtide (end of April) he builds and garrisons a fortress at Wigingamere (this site has not been confidently identified) in Essex. Between Midsummer (21 June) and Lammas (1 August) the host from Northampton, Leicester, and the lands to the north (no further information readily available) break the peace. They spend a day trying to take the fortress at Towcester but give up when the garrison receive reinforcements. Small bands of the host go out at night taking captives and cattle in the area between Bernwood and Aylesbury in Buckinghamshire. The host from Huntingdon in Cambridgeshire and from East Anglia build a fortress at Tempsford in Bedfordshire abandoning their fortress at Huntingdon. They sally out and suffer substantial losses when the garrison at Bedford repulses their attack.

The host from Mercia and East Anglia assemble and fail to capture the fortress of Wigingamere (this site has not been confidently identified) in Essex and after capturing cattle leave the area. King Edward assembles a "great force" including men from the fortresses in the area surrounding Tempsford in Bedfordshire; he captures this fortress from the host killing their King (Guthrum II of East Anglia), Jarl Toglos (no further information readily available) and his son (no further information readily available), Jarl Manna (no further information readily available) and his brother (no further information readily available) and all in the garrison who resisted, the others they make captive; they seize everything inside the fortress. King Edward with men from Kent, Surrey, Essex and from the nearest fortresses (no further information readily available) capture the Danish fortress at Colchester in Essex killing everyone inside apart from the men who escape over the wall; they also seize "everything" inside.

In the autumn, in retaliation, the East Anglian Danes, and those "they had enticed to their aid", unsuccessfully besiege Maldon in Essex. When English reinforcements arrive the garrison sally out and with this additional help many hundreds of "pirates and others" (no further information readily available) are killed. King Edward goes with his levies from Wessex to Passenham in Northamptonshire whilst the fortress of Towcester is being reinforced with a stone wall. Jarl Thurferth, leader of the host at Northampton, the Scandinavian barons (no further information readily available) and those in the host owing allegiance to Northampton as far north as the River Welland (Northamptonshire/Lincolnshire), submit to King Edward.

When one part of King Edward's levies (divided into two groups; one group on campaign, the other group farming and maintaining the economic life of the country) go home, the other part take their place and occupy and repair the fortress which had been destroyed at Huntingdon in Cambridgeshire. The inhabitants of the district submit to King Edward. Before Martinmas (11 November) King Edward takes his West Saxon levies to Colchester in Essex where they occupy and repair the fortress which had been destroyed. Many of the people from East Anglia and Essex who had previously been under Danish control submit to King Edward. The entire Danish Host in East Anglia submit to King Edward as do those who hold allegiance to the host in Cambridge: "the treaty was ratified with oaths exactly as he drew it up".

Manuscript "A" (Winchester or Parker): Trebuchet.

Manuscript "B" (Abingdon I) & Manuscript "C" (Abingdon II): 18thCentury.

Manuscript "D" (Worcester): Swiss 721 Hv BT.

Manuscript "E" (Peterborough or Laud): Courier New.

Manuscript "F" (Canterbury): Alexa.

Manuscript "H" (Winchester): Calligraphic.

921 – Between Rogationtide (end of April) and Midsummer (21 June) King Edward the Elder of Wessex marches his levies to Stamford in Lincolnshire where he builds a fortress on the south bank of the River Welland (Northamptonshire/Lincolnshire) and receives the submission of the inhabitants of the district. During his time at Stamford his sister Aethelflaed, Lady of the Mercians, dies at Tamworth in Staffordshire on 12 June. She is buried in the east chapel of St Peter's Church (Gloucester Cathedral) in Gloucester. (Manuscripts C and E attribute her death to **918**). King Edward takes over the fortress at Tamworth in Staffordshire and receives the submission of all those in Mercia who had owed allegiance to Aethelflaed and the Kings of Wales: Hywel, Clydog and Idwal and all the people in Wales. King Edward builds a fort at Cledemutha at the mouth of the River Clwyd in Wales. King Edward goes to Nottingham which he occupies and repairs the fortress, which he garrisons with both Englishmen and Danes; all the people in Mercia, both English and Danish submit to him.

```
(In the entry for 921 Manuscript E records events relating to earlier
years.) King Sihtric (Sigtrygg or Sihtric Cáech, Norse King of Dublin
917-921, Norse King of York 921-927) kills King Niall Glúndub of
Ireland (the accepted date is 919). He also kills his brother Sigefrith
(the accepted date is 888).
```

922 – King Edward the Elder of Wessex leads his levies to Thelwall in Warwickshire where he builds and garrisons a fortress. Whilst there he sends Mercian levies to occupy, repair and garrison the fortress in Manchester in Northumbria. Archbishop Plegmund of Canterbury dies.

923 – King Raegnald I (leader of the Norse from Dublin) storms York. Before midsummer (21 June) King Edward the Elder of Wessex leads his levies to Nottingham where he builds a fortress on the south side of the River Trent opposite the existing fortress on the north side of the river; he also builds a bridge to link the two fortresses together. King Edward then goes to Bakewell in Derbyshire and builds and garrisons a fortress in the vicinity. King Constantine II and all the people of Scotland accept King Edward as their "father and lord". Similar submissions to King Edward are made by King Raegnald I of York (he dies in 921 and his recorded submission to King Edward the Elder of Wessex is 920) and the sons (Ealdred and Uhtred) of King Eadwulf II of Northumbria (who each ruled part of Northumbria) and all the inhabitants of Northumbria, English and Danish, Norwegian and others; together with the King Dyfnwal of the Strathclyde Welsh and all his subjects. *(Manuscript F attributes the submission of the kings and peoples to King Edward to **924**.)*

924 – King Edward the Elder of Wessex dies at Farndon-on-Dee in Cheshire in Mercia; his son Aelfweard dies **16 days** afterwards at Oxford and both are buried at Winchester in Hampshire. His son Athelstan succeeds to the throne is accepted as king by the Mercians and is consecrated at Kingston in Surrey (he later becomes the first King of All England). King Athelstan gives his sister (Aedgyth) **in marriage to (the future Holy Roman Emperor) Otto, son of the King (Henry I) of the Old Saxons.** Dunstan is born (later Archbishop of Canterbury and venerated as a saint. However, it is thought more likely that he was born in 909.) Bishop Wulfhelm of Wells,

---

Manuscript "A" (Winchester or Parker): Trebuchet.

Manuscript "B" (Abingdon I) & Manuscript "C" (Abingdon II): 18thCentury.

Manuscript "D" (Worcester): Swiss 721 Hv BT.

Manuscript "E" (Peterborough or Laud): Courier New.

Manuscript "F" (Canterbury): Alexa.

Manuscript "H" (Winchester): Calligraphic.

Somerset is consecrated Archbishop of Canterbury.

925 – King Athelstan of England and King Sihtric of Northumbria (of York) meet at Tamworth, Staffordshire on 30 January and King Athelstan gives his sister (her identity is a matter of conjecture) in marriage to King Sihtric.

926 – Fiery rays of light appear in the northern sky. King Sihtric of Northumbria (of York) dies and his kingdom is annexed by King Athelstan of England. King Athelstan receives the submission of all the kings on the island of Britain, Hywel, King of the West Welsh, Constantine, King of Scots, Owain, King of Gwent, and Ealdred Ealdulfing from Bamburgh, Northumberland. On 12 July at Eamont Bridge in Cumbria these rulers establish a "covenant of peace" with pledges and oaths and forbid "all idolatrous practices."

927 – King Athelstan of England drives out King Guthfrith of York. Archbishop Wulfhelm of Canterbury goes to Rome.

928 – *William Longsword becomes Duke of Normandy.*

931 – On 29 May Beornstan is consecrated Bishop of Winchester in Hampshire.

932 – Bishop Frithustan of Winchester in Hampshire dies. *(Manuscript F attributes his death to* **931** *followed by the consecration of Beornstan his replacement.)*

933 – King Athelstan of England invades Scotland with both and land and naval forces and "harried much of the country". **(Manuscripts D, E and F attribute this event to 934.)** Bishop Beornstan of Winchester in Hampshire dies on 1 November. Prince Edwin (aetheling – a male of royal blood, the heir apparent – the younger son of King Edward the Elder and Aelfflaed, his second wife) drowns at sea (his body is washed ashore in France and he is buried at the monastery of Saint Bertin at Saint Omer).

934 – Aelfheah becomes Bishop of Winchester, Hampshire. *(Manuscript F attributes this to* **935***.)*

937 – In Manuscript A the entry for this year consists of the poem "The Battle of Brunanburh". This explains that Athelstan with his brother Edmund (aetheling, a male of royal blood, the heir apparent), lead a combined Mercian and West Saxon army to Brunanburh (South Yorkshire – although other sites including the Wirral in Cheshire are favoured by some) and fights in battle a combined force of Vikings and Scots led by King Anlaf (Olaf III) Sihtricsson of York (called "Cuaran", who was to become King of Dublin in Ireland, the Isle of Man and the Western Isles), and by King Constantine II of Scotland (they were also joined by King Owen I of Strathclyde/Cumbria.) Athelstan (and his brother) are victorious and five young kings and (eight) jarls are killed as are a countless number of Norseman and Scots, including the young son (Cellach) of the King of Scots. The Norsemen who escape make for Dublin in

Manuscript "A" (Winchester or Parker): Trebuchet.
Manuscript "B" (Abingdon I) & Manuscript "C" (Abingdon II): 18thCentury.
Manuscript "D" (Worcester): Swiss 721 Hv BT.
Manuscript "E" (Peterborough or Laud): Courier New.
Manuscript "F" (Canterbury): Alexa.
Manuscript "H" (Winchester): Calligraphic.

Ireland. "Never before in this island, as the books of ancient historians tell us, was an army put to greater slaughter by the sword."

941 – King Athelstan of England dies on 27 October at Gloucester, "forty years all but a day after King Alfred" the Great. His brother Edmund succeeds him at the age of eighteen. At this time Wulfhelm was Archbishop of Canterbury. **(Manuscripts D and** E **attribute Athelstan's death to 940 – the accepted year is 939.) The Northumbrians are "false to their pledges" and choose as their King Anlaf (Olaf III) Sihtricsson (called "Cuaran", who was to become King of Dublin in Ireland, the Isle of Man and the Western Isles) from Ireland.**

942 – King Edmund of England conquers Mercia as far as Dore in South Yorkshire and the Whitwell Gap in Derbyshire and the River Humber (separating Yorkshire from Lincolnshire). He also conquers the "Five Boroughs" of Leicester, Nottingham, Derby, Lincoln and Stamford in Lincolnshire. (The scribe provides a eulogy when describing these events.)

King Edmund stands sponsor for the baptism of King Anlaf (Olaf III) Sihtricsson of York (called "Cuaran", who was to become King of Dublin in Ireland, the Isle of Man and the Western Isles). Much later in the year he stands sponsor for the baptism of King Raegnald II (Guthfrithson) of York (successor to Anlaf/Olaf III Sihtricsson). (Manuscript E records King Edmund standing sponsor for King Raegnald's baptism in **943**.) Archbishop Wulfhelm of Canterbury dies. (Manuscript E records King Anlaf's death in **942** – is this a mistake? In **944** it refers to Anlaf (surely the same person) and Raegnald both "of royal blood" being driven out.)

943 – King Edmund of England gives the Abbey of Glastonbury in Somerset "into the charge of St Dunstan who later became its first abbot". **King Anlaf (Olaf III) Sihtricsson of York (called "Cuaran", who was to become King of Dublin in Ireland, the Isle of Man and the Western Isles) storms Tamworth in Staffordshire, and takes much booty away; many are killed on both sides. During this raid Wulfrun is taken prisoner (a Mercian noblewoman after whom the town of Wolverhampton in Staffordshire/West Midlands is named). King Edmund besieges King Anlaf and Archbishop Wulfstan of York in Leicester and might have captured them had not they escaped at night. Afterwards King Anlaf "obtained" King Edmund's friendship.**

944 – King Edmund of England brings all Northumbria under his control expelling King Anlaf (Olaf III) Sihtricsson (called "Cuaran", who was to become King of Dublin in Ireland, the Isle of Man and the Western Isles) and King Raegnald Guthfrithson (both were at one time kings in York).

945 – King Edmund of England "ravaged all Strathclyde, and ceded it to Malcolm, King of Scots, on condition that he would be his fellow worker both by sea and land".

946 – King Edmund of England dies on St Augustine's day, *(26 May);* **"it is widely known"**

Manuscript "A" (Winchester or Parker): Trebuchet.
Manuscript "B" (Abingdon I) & Manuscript "C" (Abingdon II): 18thCentury.
Manuscript "D" (Worcester): Swiss 721 Hv BT.
Manuscript "E" (Peterborough or Laud): Courier New.
Manuscript "F" (Canterbury): Alexa.
Manuscript "H" (Winchester): Calligraphic.

how he met his death – he was stabbed by Liofa at Pucklechurch in Gloucestershire. His queen (a second marriage) was Aethelflaed of Damerham, Hampshire, daughter of Ealdorman Aelfgar (probably) of Essex. Edmund is succeeded by his brother Eadred who subjugates the Northumbrians and receives oaths from the Scots "to do his will in all things". (Manuscript E attributes King Edmund's death and Eadred's actions to **948**.)

947 – King Eadred of England goes to Tanshelf (Pontefract, West Yorkshire) to meet Archbishop Wulfstan of York and all the councillors of Northumbria who pledge their allegiance, "but within a short while they were false both to their pledges and oaths".

948 – King Eadred of England campaigns against the Northumbrians who had made Erik Bloodaxe (former King of Norway) their king. During this campaign the minster built at Ripon in North Yorkshire by Saint Wilfrid is destroyed by fire. On his way home the host of Erik destroy the rearguard of King Eadred's forces at Castleford, West Yorkshire, killing many. King Eadred is so enraged he wants to renew his campaign and "completely devastate" Yorkshire but on hearing this, the "council of the Northumbrians" abandon Erik and make reparations to King Eadred.

949 – King Anlaf (Olaf III) Sihtricsson (called "Cuaran", formerly of York who was to become King of Dublin in Ireland, the Isle of Man and the Western Isles) comes to Northumbria (to York to become king again).

951 – Bishop Aelfheah of Winchester, Hampshire dies on 12 March.

952 – King Eadred of England imprisons Archbishop Wulfstan of York at Iudanburh (this site has not been confidently identified) because of his opposition. King Eadred puts to death many in the borough of Thetford in Norfolk because they killed Abbot Eadhelm (probably abbot of St Peter's and St Paul's – now St Augustine's – Abbey, Canterbury). The Northumbrians expel from York their King, Anlaf (Olaf III) Sihtricsson (called "Cuaran", who was to become King of Dublin in Ireland, the Isle of Man and the Western Isles) and accept Erik Bloodaxe (former King of Norway and their King in York 947-948, see **948** above) as their king.

954 – The Northumbrians "drive out" Erik Bloodaxe (former King of Norway) as their king. King Eadred of England succeeds to the Northumbrian kingdom. Archbishop Wulfstan of York is released from prison and "restored" to the bishopric of Dorchester-on-Thames, Oxfordshire.

955 – King Edred of England dies on 23 November at Frome in Somerset. **He is buried at the Old Minster, Winchester, Hampshire.** He is succeeded in Wessex by Eadwig **and by**

Manuscript "A" (Winchester or Parker): Trebuchet.

Manuscript "B" (Abingdon I) & Manuscript "C" (Abingdon II): 18thCentury.

Manuscript "D" (Worcester): Swiss 721 Hv BT.

Manuscript "E" (Peterborough or Laud): Courier New.

Manuscript "F" (Canterbury): Alexa.

Manuscript "H" (Winchester): Calligraphic.

Edgar in Mercia. (Manuscripts B and C attribute these events to **956**.)

956 – King Eadwig of England exiles Saint/Abbot Dunstan of Glastonbury (he goes to Flanders). **(Manuscript D attributes these events to 957.)**

957 – Prince Edgar (King Eadwig's brother) becomes King in Mercia (and Northumbria. Two alternative reasons: both kingdoms had rejected King Eadwig, or, given that they were age 15 and 14, the division of the country had been agreed earlier). **Archbishop Wulfstan of York dies on 16 December and is buried at Oundle in Northamptonshire.** (Manuscript E attributes his death to **956**.)

958 – **Archbishop Oda of Canterbury dissolves the marriage of King Eadwig of Wessex/England and Aelgifu (daughter of King Edward the Elder) on grounds of consanguinity.**

King Eadwig of (Wessex) England dies on 1 October and is succeeded by Edgar who ruled Wessex, Mercia and Northumbria at the age of sixteen. (Manuscripts B, C and E attribute these events to **959**).

959 – King Edgar of England sends for Saint Dunstan and appoints him Bishop of Worcester, and afterwards adds the bishopric of London. (Manuscript E contains a eulogy to King Edgar although it does refer to "one grave fault", he was "too fond of foreign, vicious customs, and introduced heathen practices too eagerly".)

961 – Archbishop Oda of Canterbury dies and Saint Dunstan, Bishop of Worcester and London succeeds him. (Aelfsige had been appointed archbishop after Oda set out for Rome to receive his pallium (vestment of office, a cloak) but died in the winter cold whilst crossing the Alps.)

962 – Ealdorman Aelfgar of Devon, King Edgar of England's kinsman dies and is buried at Wilton in Wiltshire. King Sigferth kills himself and is buried at Wimborne, Dorset. (Sigferth was a Danish Viking who made the daughter of the Count of Flanders pregnant and he killed himself because of the consequences.) There was a great pestilence (no further information provided) and a fire in London which destroyed St Paul's Church – it was rebuilt in the same year. Aethelnod the priest (no further information readily available) went to Rome and died there on 15 August.

963 – Wulfstan the Deacon (no further information readily available) dies on 28 December and later Gyric the priest (no further information readily available) dies. Abbot Aethelwold of Abingdon, Oxfordshire becomes Bishop of Winchester, Hampshire and is consecrated by Archbishop Dunstan of Canterbury (venerated as a saint) on Sunday 29 November.

(The remaining text for this entry from Manuscript E is thought to have been added sometime onwards from the early twelfth century.)

Manuscript "A" (Winchester or Parker): Trebuchet.
Manuscript "B" (Abingdon I) & Manuscript "C" (Abingdon II): 18thCentury.
Manuscript "D" (Worcester): Swiss 721 Hv BT.
Manuscript "E" (Peterborough or Laud): Courier New.
Manuscript "F" (Canterbury): Alexa.
Manuscript "H" (Winchester): Calligraphic.

Bishop Aethelwold establishes many new monasteries, driving out from Winchester Cathedral, Hampshire the secular clergy because they will not observe any monastic rule; he replaces them with monks. Bishop Aethelwold establishes two monasteries, one of monks, one of nuns, at Winchester. In response to his request King Edgar of England gives Bishop Aethelwold all the monasteries destroyed by the heathen so that they can be restored.

First of all Bishop Aethelwold has the monastery at Ely in Cambridgeshire rebuilt; this is where Saint Aethelthryth is buried. He consecrates one of his monks Byrhtnoth as Abbot; he provides monks where formerly there had been nuns. Bishop Aethelwold richly endows the monastery with the lands and income from the many villages he buys from King Edgar.

Bishop Aethelwold next goes to the monastery at Medeshamstede (Peterborough) where only "old walls and wild woods" survive (see **869** above). Hidden in the old walls he finds written by Abbot Hedde documents explaining that the monastery had been built at the request of King Wulfhere of Mercia and his brother Aethelred. He also finds documents relating to the charter of King Wulfhere of Mercia in 656 under which the monastery was freed from all obligations to king, bishop and secular authorities and also that this charter had been agreed by Pope Agatho (see **675** above) and Archbishop Deusdedit of Canterbury(see **656** above). Bishop Aethelwold appoints Ealdwulf as abbot and provides monks. (It is thought Ealdwulf was a layman and chancellor to King Edgar who had accidentally killed his own son. Rather than go to Rome to seek absolution as he intended he participated in the refounding of the monastery, first as a monk and then as abbot.) Bishop Aethelwold takes the documents to King Edgar who with a new charter reaffirms the exclusion of the monastery from the jurisdiction of others as set out in the original charter and confirms and adds to the land-holdings of the monastery. In the new charter King Edgar declares the monastery and all its lands "free, that is with sake and with soke, with toll and with team, and with infangenetheof". (These terms are commonly found in the Domesday Book and their precise definition is a subject of ongoing debate. They involve the judicial rights of a lord to hold a court for criminal and civil matters if he has a sufficient number of tenants to make it necessary. The process in the ensuing proceedings requires a "sake" – a cause, a lawsuit – or a "soke" – seeking a cause, services – and "infangenetheof", empowers a lord to judge thieves within the limits of his jurisdiction and to retain fines imposed for the crime). King Edgar's charter is witnessed by Archbishop Dunstan of Canterbury, Archbishop Oswald of York, Bishop

Manuscript "A" (Winchester or Parker): Trebuchet.
Manuscript "B" (Abingdon I) & Manuscript "C" (Abingdon II): 18thCentury.
Manuscript "D" (Worcester): Swiss 721 Hv BT.
Manuscript "E" (Peterborough or Laud): Courier New.
Manuscript "F" (Canterbury): Alexa.
Manuscript "H" (Winchester): Calligraphic.

Aethelwold of Winchester, Bishop Aelfstan of London, Bishop Aethelwulf (no further information readily available), Abbot Aescwig(no further information readily available), Abbot Osgar of Abingdon, Oxfordshire, Abbot Aethelgar of the New Minster in Winchester, Ealdorman Aelfhere of Mercia, Ealdorman Aethelwine of East Anglia, Ealdorman Byrhtnoth of Essex, Ealdorman Oslac of southern Northumbria and many other prominent men.

Abbot Ealdwulf buys many estates and richly endows the monastery. Abbot Ealdwulf remains at Medeshamstede until the death of Archbishop Oswald of York (see **992** below) whom he is elected to succeed. Cenwulf is elected by the monks at Medeshamstede and appointed Abbot in succession to Ealdwulf. Cenwulf is the first to build a wall around the monastery and then gave it the name "Burh" (see **656** above). Abbot Cenwulf remains at Medeshamstede now Peterborough (its modern name) until he is appointed Bishop of Winchester. Aelfsige is elected by the monks at Medeshamstede and appointed Abbot in succession to Cenwulf. Abbot Aelfsige exhumes the bodies of Saint Cyneburh and Saint Cyneswith who were buried at Castor (Peterborough), and exhumes the body of Saint Tibba who was buried at Ryhall, Rutland; he brings all three to the monastery at Peterborough. (Cyneburh and Cyneswith were sisters and daughters of King Penda of Mercia – who reigned 632-654/655 – and sisters of King Peada of Mercia – who reigned 655-656/657 – and founded the monastery at Medeshamstede. Both sisters acted as witnesses to the Medeshamstede charter of their brother King Wulfhere of Mercia – who reigned 657-675) – see **656** above. Cyneburh probably founded the abbey at Castor and all three were abbesses in turn; Cyneburh was succeeded as abbess by Cyneswith and then by Tibba, a relative.)

964 – King Edgar of England replaces priests with monks at both the Old and New Minsters at Winchester in Hampshire (see **963** above for the detail provided by Manuscript E), Chertsey in Surrey and Milton Abbas in Dorset. He appoints Abbot Aethelgar to the New Minster in Winchester, Ordberht to Chertsey and Cyneweard to Milton Abbas.

965 – King Edgar of England marries Aelfthryth, daughter of Ealdorman Ordgar of Devon.

966 – Thored (he may be the Thored who was Ealdorman of Northumberland 979-92) ravages Westmorland. Oslac becomes Ealdorman of Northumbria.

969 – King Edgar of England orders the whole of the Isle of Thanet in Kent to be harried (no further information readily available).

971 – Prince Edmund aetheling (a male of royal blood, the heir apparent, brother of

Manuscript "A" (Winchester or Parker): Trebuchet.

Manuscript "B" (Abingdon I) & Manuscript "C" (Abingdon II): 18thCentury.

Manuscript "D" (Worcester): Swiss 721 Hv BT.

Manuscript "E" (Peterborough or Laud): Courier New.

Manuscript "F" (Canterbury): Alexa.

Manuscript "H" (Winchester): Calligraphic.

King Aethelred II of England and half-brother of King Edward the Martyr of England) dies (Manuscript E attributes his death to **970**) and is buried at Romsey Abbey, Hampshire.   Archbishop Oscytel of York, formerly Bishop of Dorchester-on-Thames in Oxfordshire, dies on 1 November at Thame in Oxfordshire. Abbot Thurytel of Bedford his kinsman "carries" the bishops body to Bedford where he had at one time been abbot.

973 – Coronation of King Edgar of England at Bath in Somerset on Sunday 11 May at the age of twenty-nine - the entry includes a eulogy. Soon after his coronation King Edgar leads all his fleet to Chester where six kings make submission to him and "pledged themselves to be his fellow workers by sea and land". (Manuscript E attributes these events to **972**.)

975 – King Edgar of England dies and the entry for the year includes a eulogy to him including references to the succession of his young son Edward II, to the death of Bishop Cyneweard of Wells, Somerset and to the expulsion of many wise servants of God in Mercia, the banishment of Earl Oslac of Northumbria (appointed by King Edgar), the arrival of a comet in the autumn and widespread hunger followed by a restoration of the food supply. (Manuscripts B and C have the same eulogies to King Edgar, **Manuscripts D and** E **have a shortened version**, *and Manuscript F simply records his death.*)

The next year a great famine and very many disturbances occur (no other information provided). "God's adversaries broke God's laws". Ealdorman Aelfhere of Mercia (accused as being a leader of the anti-monastic, anti-reformers and hostile to Saint Oswald, Bishop of Worcester) and "many others" are accused of hindering monastic reform, destroying monasteries which King Edgar had ordered Bishop Aethelwold to found, dispersing monks, robbing widows. All this leads to "many injustices and evil crimes" flourishing. The situation goes "from bad to worse". (Manuscript C attributes the famine to **976**.)

977 – After Easter a "great assembly" takes place at Kirtlington in Oxfordshire where suddenly Bishop Sideman of Devonshire, dies on 30 April. Despite his wish to be buried at Crediton in Devon King Edward of England and Archbishop Dunstan of Canterbury order his body be taken to Saint Mary's Abbey, Abingdon in Oxfordshire where it is buried on the north side of Saint Paul's Chapel.

Manuscript B of the Chronicle ends in 977.

978 – At a meeting of the leading councillors of England the upper storey of a building at Calne in Wiltshire collapses resulting in the injury and death of several people. The entry records that Archbishop Dunstan "alone remained standing on a beam" (this is quoted as an example of secular buildings as well as churches having more than one storey).

Manuscript "A" (Winchester or Parker): Trebuchet.
Manuscript "B" (Abingdon I) & Manuscript "C" (Abingdon II): 18thCentury.
Manuscript "D" (Worcester): Swiss 721 Hv BT.
Manuscript "E" (Peterborough or Laud): Courier New.
Manuscript "F" (Canterbury): Alexa.
Manuscript "H" (Winchester): Calligraphic.

At Corfe "passage", Dorset, in the evening of the 18 March, **King Edward of England, "The Martyr" is murdered** and is buried at Wareham in Dorset with no royal honours. There is then a lament "no worse deed for the English was ever done than this" referring to his sainthood and his fame. **Aethelred, his brother, succeeds as King of England.** Aelfwold, Bishop of Dorset, dies and is buried in Sherborne Cathedral in Dorset.

979 – On the Sunday a fortnight after Easter, Aethelred (II) is consecrated King of England at Kingston in Surrey in the presence of two archbishops (Dunstan of Canterbury and Oswald of York) and ten bishops (no other information provided). Frequently in the year, around midnight, a cloud as red as blood with the appearance of fire is seen, resulting in rays of light of various colours; at the first streak of dawn they vanish.

980 – On 2 May Abbot Aethelgar is consecrated Bishop of Selsey in Sussex. The pirate host in seven ships either kill or take prisoner most of the people of Southampton in Hampshire. (Manuscript E attributes the raid on Southampton to **981**.) The Isle of Thanet in Kent is also raided and a separate pirate host from the north raids Cheshire. Ealdorman Aelfhere of Mercia conveyed, with great ceremony the body of King Edward of England, "The Martyr" from Wareham in Dorset to Shaftesbury Abbey in Dorset.

981 – The Danes harry the coasts of Devon and Cornwall; Padstow in Cornwall is wasted. Aelfstan, Bishop of Wiltshire dies and is buried in the abbey at Abingdon in Oxfordshire; he is succeeded by Wulfgar. Abbot Womaer of Ghent in Belgium dies.

982 – Danes from three ships companies land and ravage the Isle of Portland in Dorset. A great fire occurs in London. Ealdorman Aethelmar of Hampshire dies and is buried in the New Minster in Winchester, Hampshire. Ealdorman Eadwine of Sussex dies and is buried at Abingdon Abbey in Oxfordshire. Abbess Herelufu of Shaftesbury in Dorset and Abbess Wulfwynn of Wareham in Dorset die. Otto II, Emperor of the Romans, wins a hardfought victory in Italy against a great host of the Saracens who had landed from ships; there is great slaughter on both sides. On his way home, Otto his brothers son, (Otto I, Duke of Swabia and Bavaria in Germany, 955-982) dies. He was the son of Prince Liudolf who was himself the son of Otto I (reigned as Holy Roman Emperor 962-973) and his wife Eadgyth, a daughter of King Edward the Elder of Wessex.

983 – **Ealdorman Aelfhere of Mercia dies** and is succeeded by Aelfric. Pope Benedict VII dies.

984 – **Bishop Aethelwold of Winchester, Hampshire dies** on 1 August. **Aelfheah, who is also known as Godwine, is consecrated Bishop of Winchester on 19 October.**

985 – Ealdorman Aelfric of Mercia is banished (accused of treason against the king). Eadwine is consecrated abbot of the abbey at Abingdon in Oxfordshire. (Manuscript E attributes Eadwine's consecration to **984**.)

986 – King Aethelred II of England lays waste Rochester in Kent (no further information readily available). The "great pestilence" among cattle first comes to England.

Manuscript "A" (Winchester or Parker): Trebuchet.
Manuscript "C" (Abingdon II): 18thCentury.
Manuscript "D" (Worcester): Swiss 721 Hv BT.
Manuscript "E" (Peterborough or Laud): Courier New.
Manuscript "F" (Canterbury): Alexa.
Manuscript "H" (Winchester): Calligraphic.

988 – Watchet in Somerset is raided by the Danes and Goda the Devonshire thane is killed along with many others. (Manuscript E attributes the raid on Watchet to **987**.) Archbishop Dunstan of Canterbury dies and is succeeded by Bishop Aethelgar of Selsey, Sussex who lives for no more than one year three months.

990 – Bishop Sigeric of Ramsbury, Wiltshire is appointed Archbishop of Canterbury *and goes to Rome for his pallium (vestment of office, a cloak)*. Abbot Eadwine of Abingdon, Oxfordshire dies and is succeeded by Wulfgar. (Manuscript E attributes these events to **989** but does not mention Rome.)

991 – Anlaf (Olaf Tryggvason, later King of Norway) arrives at Folkestone in Kent with ninety-three ships and ravages the surrounding countryside. He moves on to Sandwich in Kent and then on to Ipswich in Suffolk taking similar action. On 10 August Anlaf and his host defeat Ealdorman Byrhtnoth of Essex and his levies at the battle of Maldon in Essex. On the advice of Archbishop Sigeric of Canterbury and Bishop Aelfheah of Winchester, Hampshire, King Aethelred II of England makes peace and stands as sponsor for Anlaf at his confirmation. On the advice of Archbishop Sigeric "In this year it was decided for the first time to pay tribute to the Danes because of the great terror they inspired along the sea coast. On this first occasion it amounted to ten thousand pounds".

992 – Archbishop Oswald of York dies and is succeeded by Abbot Ealdwulf of Peterborough. He is appointed to the see of both York and Worcester. Cenwulf is appointed Abbot of Peterborough monastery. Ealdorman Aethelwine of East Anglia dies.

King Aethelred II of England and his councillors decide that all ships of value should collect in London and that the levies be commanded by Ealdorman Aelfric of Hampshire, Earl Theored of Northumbria, Bishop Aelfstan of London, and Bishop Aescwig of Dorchester-on-Thames, Oxfordshire. King Aethelred gives them instructions to try and entrap the host somewhere out to sea. Ealdorman Aelfric warns the host (commanded by Anlaf/Olaf Tryggvason, future King of Norway who reigned 995-1000). The night before the day of the intended battle Ealdorman Aelfric deserts the levies to "his own great disgrace" and the host escape except one ship whose crew is killed. The host engage the ships from East Anglia and London killing many and capturing Ealdorman Aelfric's ship.

993 – Bamburgh in Northumberland is destroyed by the host and much plunder is taken. The host go to the mouth of the River Humber, which separates Yorkshire from Lindsey (Lincolnshire), and do much damage to the surrounding countryside. Great levies were gathered but when they should have joined battle with the host their leaders, Fraena

---

Manuscript "A" (Winchester or Parker): Trebuchet.

Manuscript "C" (Abingdon II): 18thCentury.

Manuscript "D" (Worcester): Swiss 721 Hv BT.

Manuscript "E" (Peterborough or Laud): Courier New.

Manuscript "F" (Canterbury): Alexa.

Manuscript "H" (Winchester): Calligraphic.

(of Rockingham, Northamptonshire – a landowner and benefactor of Peterborough Abbey), Ealdorman Godwine of Lindsey (Lincolnshire) and Frithugist, a Lincolnshire thane, fled. King Aethelred II of England orders Aelfgar, the son on Ealdorman Aelfric of Hampshire, to be blinded.

994 – Archbishop Sigeric of Canterbury dies (Manuscripts E and *F* attribute this to **995**) **and is succeeded by Bishop Aelfric of Wiltshire** *(in 995 according to Manuscript F, see* **995** *below). Bishop Aelfric is chosen by King Aethelred II of England and all his councillors on 21 April at Amesbury, Wiltshire.* Bishop Aelfric is consecrated at Christ Church (Canterbury Cathedral. Manuscript E attributes this to **996**.)

Anlaf (Olaf Tryggvason later King of Norway) and King Swein Forkbeard of Denmark come to London on 8 September with ninety-four ships. They unsuccessfully attack the city and intend to set it on fire but they suffer heavy losses and leave. Instead they burn, harry and slaughter along the coast and inland in Essex, Kent, Sussex and Hampshire. They obtain horses and go "wherever they pleased" and "continued to do unspeakable damage". King Aethelred and his councillors agree to offer the host tribute and supplies if they would stop their harrying. The host accept the offer and take up winter quarters in Southampton, Hampshire where they receive sixteen thousand pounds and provisions from the whole of Wessex. King Aethelred sends Bishop Aelfheah of Winchester, Hampshire and Ealdorman Aethelweard of the Western Shires (Cornwall, Devon, Dorset, Somerset and Wiltshire) to meet Anlaf and bring him to the king at Andover in Hampshire; hostages being sent to Anlaf's ships beforehand. King Aethelred stands sponsor for Anlaf at confirmation and provides him with gifts. Anlaf promises never to come to England with warlike intent and keeps his promise.

995 – A star comet appears.

(As indicated in **994** *above Manuscript F attributes the succession of Aelfric as Archbishop of Canterbury to the year* **995** *and includes a detailed account of his actions to remove secular clergy from the Christ Church, Canterbury – the cathedral. This addition describes him as "a very wise man, and there was no wiser man in all England".)*

The secular clergy (i.e., those who "lived in the world" and do not follow a "Rule") are described as those who "were most distasteful to him". He consults "the most learned men he knew" and refers to the law as had been established when St Augustine had first come to England (see **595** *above) and to Bede's "Ecclesiastical History of the English People". Aelfric and those he consults agree that the secular clergy should be expelled from Christ Church Canterbury subject to the agreement of King Aethelred II of England. Archbishop Aelfric goes to King Aethelred who advises him to go to Rome and obtain his pallium (vestment of office, a cloak) at the same time seeking the advice of Pope John XV about the secular clergy.*

Manuscript "A" (Winchester or Parker): Trebuchet.
Manuscript "C" (Abingdon II): 18thCentury.
Manuscript "D" (Worcester): Swiss 721 Hv BT.
Manuscript "E" (Peterborough or Laud): Courier New.
Manuscript "F" (Canterbury): Alexa.
Manuscript "H" (Winchester): Calligraphic.

When the secular clergy hear of Aelfric's intention to go to Rome they decide to send two of their number (no further information readily available) to Rome where they arrive before Aelfric; they offer the Pope "treasures and silver" if he gives them the pallium. The Pope refuses on the grounds they brought no letter from King Aethelred or the English people and orders them to leave.

Archbishop Aelfric arrives and the Pope gives him his pallium and orders him to "fill your cathedral" with "regular" clergy (i.e., those who are a member of a religious order and observe a "Rule") not "secular" clergy. Archbishop Aelfric returns to England and reports to King Aethelred, he then goes to Canterbury Cathedral where he replaces the secular clergy with regular clergy.

*(Manuscript F includes these events in the entry for **995** but in its entry for **997** it only says "Archbishop Aelfric went to Rome for his pallium".)*

996 – *Wulfstan (II, later Archbishop of York) is consecrated Bishop of London.*

997 – The host campaign in Devonshire, in the lands around the River Severn, in Cornwall, Wales and Devon. They land at Watchet in Somerset where they cause great havoc burning and killing people. Afterwards they sail around Land's End and enter the River Tamar between Devon and Cornwall and up to Lydford, Devon killing "everything they meet". They burn to the ground the thegn Ordwulf's abbey church at Tavistock, Devon and take an "indescribable amount" of plunder to their ships.

998 – The host go into the mouth of the River Frome and into Dorset: "Many a time levies were gathered to oppose them; but, as soon as battle was about to begin, the word was given to withdraw, and always in the end the host had the victory." The host base themselves in the Isle of Wight and take supplies from Hampshire and Sussex.

999 – The host sail up the River Thames and up the River Medway to Rochester in Kent. The men of Kent oppose them but without the support they should have had they are defeated. The host get horses and ride where they wish destroying and laying waste most of West Kent. King Aethelred II of England and his councillors decide to oppose them with both land and naval forces but when the ships are ready delays occur from day to day which saps the morale of the "unhappy sailors" manning the vessels. "Time after time the more urgent a thing was the greater delay from one hour to the next, and all the while they were allowing the strength of their enemies to increase; and as they kept retreating from the sea, so the enemy followed close on their heels. So in the end these naval and land preparations were a complete failure, and succeeded only in adding to the distress of the people, wasting money, and encouraging their enemy."

Manuscript "A" (Winchester or Parker): Trebuchet.
Manuscript "C" (Abingdon II): 18thCentury.
Manuscript "D" (Worcester): Swiss 721 Hv BT.
Manuscript "E" (Peterborough or Laud): Courier New.
Manuscript "F" (Canterbury): Alexa.
Manuscript "H" (Winchester): Calligraphic.

1000 – King Aethelred II of England (with an army) marches into Cumberland and lays waste most of the county. His fleet sail to Chester but are unable to contact him as planned and so they harry the Isle of Man. The enemy fleet has in the meantime sailed in the summer to Normandy in France, the realm of Duke Richard II.

1001 – There are constant hostilities with the pirate host who "harried and burnt almost everywhere". In a single movement they penetrate inland as far as Aethelingadene (possibly Alton in Hampshire). They are opposed by the men of Hampshire and in the ensuing battle (this site has not been confidently identified) the Danes are victorious despite their greater losses. The English losses amount to eighty-one men in total and include Aethelweard the king's high-reeve, Leofric who lived at Whitchurch in Hampshire, Leofwine the king's high-reeve, Wulfhere the bishop's officer, Godwine who lived at Worthy (King's Worthy in Hampshire), and the son of Bishop Aelfsige of Winchester (no further information readily available regarding any of these individuals).

The host go to Devon where they are joined by Pallig (a Dane, husband of Gunnhildr, sister of King Swein Forkbeard of Denmark) who deserts from his service to King Aethelred II of England. (Gunnhildr and Pallig are both killed in the massacre of St Brice's Day – see **1002** below.) The host burn Kingsteignton in Devon and many other places the scribe does not know the names of (as he records in the text). Peace is made with them. The host move from the mouth of the River Exe in Devon and up to a fortress (at Exeter?) which withstands their attacks. They then follow their "usual tactics" of slaying and burning the surrounding countryside. In one continuous drive they move towards Pinhoe in Devon where they defeat in battle the local forces "vast levies of the men of Devon and Somerset" commanded by Kola the king's high-reeve and Eadsige the king's reeve; there are many casualties. The next morning they burn down the manors of Pinhoe and Broad Clyst (both in Devon) and many other places the scribe did not know the names of (as he records in the text). They move to the Isle of Wight and the following morning they burn down the manor at Bishop Waltham in Hampshire and many other villages. Soon afterwards peace is made with them. (Manuscript E provides details of the peace; see the entry for **1002** below.) "No fleet by sea nor levies on land dared approach them, however far inland they went".

1002 – King Aethelred II of England and his councillors decide to make peace with the Danes. King Aethelred sends Ealdorman Leofsige of Essex, Middlesex, Hertfordshire and Buckinghamshire to their fleet to arrange a truce on the basis that they will receive maintenance and tribute from the King. A truce is agreed and twenty-four thousand pounds is paid to the Danes. During the arrangements for the peace Ealdorman Leofsige kills Aefic, the king's "high reeve" and as a result King Aethelred banishes Ealdorman Leofsige from the kingdom.

In the spring Emma, the daughter of Duke Richard II of Normandy, comes

---

Manuscript "A" (Winchester or Parker): Trebuchet.

Manuscript "C" (Abingdon II): 18thCentury.

Manuscript "D" (Worcester): Swiss 721 Hv BT.

Manuscript "E" (Peterborough or Laud): Courier New.

Manuscript "F" (Canterbury): Alexa.

Manuscript "H" (Winchester): Calligraphic.

to England (she becomes the second wife of King Aethelred). Archbishop Ealdwulf of York dies.

King Aethelred gives orders for all the Danish people in England to be killed on St Brice's Day (13 November) because he had been told that the Danes planned to murder him and his councillors and take over his kingdom.

1003 – Exeter is destroyed and much plunder is taken by the Danes through/*because of* Hugh, "a French fellow" (no further information readily available) appointed by Queen Emma of England as her reeve. The great levies of Wiltshire and Hampshire gather to fight the host under the command of Ealdorman Aelfric of Hampshire. (The scribe records that) Ealdorman Aelfric "was up to his old tricks", as soon as the opposing sides were in sight of each other he pretends illness – self-induced vomiting – leaving his men "in the lurch"; the English levies disperse. When King Swein Forkbeard of Denmark, leader of the host, sees this he takes his forces to Wilton, Wiltshire, where he sacks the town and burns it down; they then go to Salisbury, Wiltshire and back to their ships (no further information readily available as to where their ships were located).

1004 – King Swein Forkbeard of Denmark and his fleet sack and burn Norwich in Norfolk. Ulfcytel (Ulfkell, a thane who exercised power similar to an ealdorman in East Anglia) and the chief men of East Anglia decide they should "buy peace" with King Swein before they do too much damage since they had come unexpectedly to Norwich before there was time to gather the levies to oppose them. Under cover of a truce, and within three weeks of sacking Norwich, King Swein and his forces go secretly to Thetford, Norfolk *(Manuscript F records Hertford)* where they spend a night pillaging and burning the borough. When Ulfcytel discovers this he sends men to destroy the Danish ships – they "fail in their duty" (no further information readily available). Ulfcytel gathers as strong a force of levies as he can and on the day after the sacking of Thetford engages the Danes in battle where many are killed on both sides including the chief men (no further information readily available) of East Anglia. Had Ulcytel's forces been up to full strength the Danes would not have got back to their ships at Norwich "as they themselves admitted".

1005 – Archbishop Aelfric of Canterbury dies and is succeeded by Bishop Aelfheah of Winchester, Hampshire. (Manuscript E attributes these events to **1006**.) In this year there is a great famine throughout England, the worst in living memory. King Swein Forkbeard of Denmark's fleet briefly returns to Denmark but sails back to England.

Manuscript "A" (Winchester or Parker): Trebuchet.

Manuscript "C" (Abingdon II): 18thCentury.

Manuscript "D" (Worcester): Swiss 721 Hv BT.

Manuscript "E" (Peterborough or Laud): Courier New.

Manuscript "F" (Canterbury): Alexa.

Manuscript "H" (Winchester): Calligraphic.

1006 – Aelfheah is consecrated Archbishop of Canterbury. Bishop Beorhtwold is appointed to the Bishopric of Wiltshire (Bishop of Ramsbury, Wiltshire). Wulfgeat (no further information readily available) is deprived of all his property. Ealdorman Aelfhelm of York is killed (murdered by Eadric Streona at Shrewsbury, Shropshire) and his sons Wulfheah and Ufegeat are blinded. Bishop Cenwulf of Winchester, Hampshire dies.

After midsummer the Danish fleet sack Sandwich, Kent. King Aethelred II of England calls out all the levies from Wessex and Mercia who embark on a campaign against the Danes all the autumn, "but with no more success than very often in the past"; the Danes go wherever they want. The campaign causes "all manner of distress to the inhabitants, so that neither the home levies nor the invading host did them any good!" After 11 November the Danes return to their safe base on the Isle of Wight. At Christmas the Danes proceed through Hampshire into Berkshire to "their well-stocked food depot at Reading" and as usual lit their beacons (war signals) as they went. The Danes burn Wallingford, Oxfordshire, to the ground and spend one night at Cholsey, Oxfordshire. They then proceed along the Berkshire Downs to Cuckhamsley Knob – it was said that if they ever reached Cuckhamsley Knob they would never reach the sea again. Levies assemble at East Kennet in Wiltshire and are soon defeated by the Danes who return to their ships from a distance of more than fifty miles inland with their plunder; on the way the people of Winchester, Hampshire watch an "arrogant and confident host" passing their gates.

While this was happening King Aethelred crosses the River Thames on his way to Shropshire where he spends the Christmas period. The terror inspired by the host results in no one providing a plan to get them out of the country or defeat them; they have "left their mark on every shire of Wessex". King Aethelred discusses with his ministers how the country can be saved before it is destroyed, they decide that circumstances dictate that the host be given tribute "however distasteful it might be to them all". King Aethelred offers, and the host accept a truce subject to payment and supply of provisions; these are supplied from all parts of England.

1007 – Tribute money amounting to thirty/thirty-six thousand pounds is paid to the hostile host. Eadric Streona is appointed Ealdorman of Mercia. **Archbishop Aelfheah of Canterbury goes to Rome to receive his pallium (vestment of office, a cloak).**

1008 – King Aethelred II of England orders ships to be speedily built throughout England; one large warship to be provided by every three

Manuscript "A" (Winchester or Parker): Trebuchet.
Manuscript "C" (Abingdon II): 18thCentury.
Manuscript "D" (Worcester): Swiss 721 Hv BT.
Manuscript "E" (Peterborough or Laud): Courier New.
Manuscript "F" (Canterbury): Alexa.
Manuscript "H" (Winchester): Calligraphic.

hundred hides (a hide, the amount of land which could be tilled with one plough in a year to support one family and its dependants), a cutter from every ten hides, and a helmet and corselet from every eight hides.

1009 – The new English fleet, larger than any before in any reign, assemble off Sandwich, Kent "but no more than on previous occasions were we to enjoy the good fortune or the honour of naval operations which would be advantageous to this land". A Sussex nobleman Wulfnoth, *father of Earl Godwine*, manages to win over twenty ships (from the fleet) and harries the south coast after accusations against him are made to King Aethelred II of England by Beorhtric, brother of Ealdorman Eadric Streona of Mercia. Beorhtric takes eighty ships from the fleet to apprehend Wulfnoth. Beorhtric's ships are either wrecked in a storm or burnt by Wulfnoth. On hearing this news King Aethelred, the ealdormen (no further information readily available) and the chief councillors (no further information readily available) abandon the fleet and go home. The remaining ships return to London "thus inconsiderately allowing the effort of the whole nation to come to naught". After 1 August the Danes/Thurkil's (the future Earl Thurkil (Thorkell) the Tall of East Anglia) host go to Sandwich and on to Canterbury whose citizens and the whole of East Kent agree a truce with them and pay them three thousand pounds.

The Danes harry Sussex, the Isle of Wight, Hampshire and Berkshire. King Aethelred orders out all the nation's levies. On one occasion, when the Danes are heading for their ships, the English levies surround them and prepare for battle but no battle ensues because Ealdorman Eadric Streona prevents it "as was always the case". After 11 November the Danes return to Kent and take up winter quarters along the River Thames receiving supplies from both Kent and Essex. The Danes make frequent, and unsuccessful, attacks on London suffering heavy losses. After Christmas the Danes pass through the Chiltern Hills (Berkshire, Buckinghamshire, Oxfordshire) and go to Oxford and burn the town. They return to Kent along both sides of the River Thames crossing the river at Staines, Middlesex, having been forewarned that the levies will oppose them in London.

1010 – After Easter the host go to East Anglia and land at Ipswich, Suffolk, where they believe Ulfcytel (a thane who exercised power similar to an ealdorman in East Anglia) and his levies are. (The battle of Ringmere on 5 May, in the vicinity of Thetford in Norfolk – the precise site is a matter of debate – ensues. The scribe refers to the aftermath rather than the battle itself.) The East Anglians soon take flight but the men of Cambridgeshire/*Cambridge* resist. Athelstan, son-in-

---

Manuscript "A" (Winchester or Parker): Trebuchet.

Manuscript "C" (Abingdon II): 18thCentury.

Manuscript "D" (Worcester): Swiss 721 Hv BT.

Manuscript "E" (Peterborough or Laud): Courier New.

Manuscript "F" (Canterbury): Alexa.

Manuscript "H" (Winchester): Calligraphic.

law to King Aethelred II of England, with Oswy (son-in-law to Ealdorman Byrhtnoth of Essex who was killed at the Battle of Maldon in **991** – see above) and his son(no further information readily available), Wulfric, the son of Leofwine of the Hwicce, and Eadwig, Aefic's brother(possibly, Aefic, Dean of Evesham Abbey in Worcestershire), and many other good thanes and countless number of people are killed. Thurcytel "Mare's Head" (could he be Thurcytel the hostage put to death in 1016?– see **1016** below) instigates the flight from the battle and the Danes have the victory. The Danes obtain horses and control East Anglia; for three months they harry the countryside, even uninhabited parts, killing men and cattle and burning the fens. They burn Thetford and Cambridge and then turn south towards the River Thames and go west into Oxfordshire, Buckinghamshire and along the River Ouse into Bedford and to Tempsford in Bedfordshire burning as they go. They return to their ships taking their plunder with them.

"and when they were dispersing to the ships, then levies should have been out, ready in case they should intend to go inland. Then, however, the levies were on their way home. And when the enemy was in the east, then our levies were mustered in the west; and when they were in the south, then our levies were in the north. Then all the councillors were summoned to the king, for a plan for defence of the realm had to be devised then and there, but whatever course of action was decided upon it was not followed even for a single month. In the end there was no leader who was willing to raise levies, but each fled as quickly as he could; nor even in the end would one shire help another."

Before 30 November the Danes destroy Northampton. They cross the River Thames into Wessex and to the marshland at All Cannings and Bishop's Cannings both in the Vale of Pewsey, Wiltshire destroying everything with fire. At Christmas they return to their ships.

1011 – King Aethelred II of England sues for peace. By this time the host have overrun East Anglia, Essex, Middlesex, Oxfordshire, Cambridgeshire, Hertfordshire, Buckinghamshire, Bedfordshire, half of Huntingdonshire, a great part of Northamptonshire, and south of the River Thames all Kent, Sussex, the district around Hastings (not included in Sussex as it is today), Surrey, Berkshire, Hampshire and most of Wiltshire. "All these misfortunes befell us by reason of bad policy in that tribute was not offered them in time or resistance made; but when they had done their worst." Notwithstanding the peace and tribute the host roam the countryside in bands robbing and killing people.

Between 8 September and 29 September the host successfully besiege

---

Manuscript "A" (Winchester or Parker): Trebuchet.

Manuscript "C" (Abingdon II): 18thCentury.

Manuscript "D" (Worcester): Swiss 721 Hv BT.

Manuscript "E" (Peterborough or Laud): Courier New.

Manuscript "F" (Canterbury): Alexa.

Manuscript "H" (Winchester): Calligraphic.

Canterbury through the treachery of Archdeacon Aelfmaer(no further information readily available) whose life had been saved (no further information readily available) by Archbishop Aelfheah of Canterbury. Archbishop Aelfheah (known later as Saint Alphege), Aelfweard the king's reeve, Abbot Leofwine (more correctly Abbess Leofrun) of Minster in Thanet in Kent, Bishop Godwine of Rochester, Kent, are captured by the host. Many men and women in holy orders are killed or captured; they release Abbot Aelfmaer of Saint Augustine's Abbey, Canterbury (the church of Saint Peter and Saint Paul was rededicated in 978 by Archbishop Dunstan of Canterbury to Saint Augustine). They take Archbishop Aelfheah with them to their ships and keep him prisoner until they martyr him – see **1012** below.

1012 – Before 13 April (Easter) Ealdorman Eadric Streona of Mercia and all the chief councillors both spiritual and temporal remain in London until after Easter when the host is paid forty-eight (Manuscripts C and **D**)/eight thousand pounds in tribute. On the evening of Saturday 19 April, the host(under the command of the future Earl Thurkil (Thorkell) the Tall of East Anglia), drunk with wine brought to them from the south, lose patience with Archbishop Aelfheah of Canterbury as he refuses to pay them any money or allow a ransom to be paid. They pelt him with bones and the heads of cattle – he is finally killed by a hit on the head with an axe. In the morning (presumably 20 April) the Archbishop's body is recovered by Bishop Eadnoth (? of Rochester, Kent) and Bishop Aelfhun of London. They take the body to London for burial at St Paul's Church (the predecessor to St Pauls' Cathedral). When tribute is paid the host disperse. Forty-five Danish ship's crews ally themselves with King Aethelred II of England on condition he feed and clothe them.

1013 – Bishop Lyfing of Wells, Somerset is appointed Archbishop of Canterbury. Before August King Swein of Denmark, Norway and England brings his fleet to Sandwich in Kent. He then sails around East Anglia, into the River Humber which separates Yorkshire from Lincolnshire and up the River Trent bordering Nottinghamshire and Lincolnshire until reaching Gainsborough, Lincolnshire. Earl Uhtred of Northumbria and all the Northumbrians submit to King Swein as do all the people of Lindsey (Lincolnshire), the Five Boroughs (Leicester, Nottingham, Derby, Lincoln and Stamford in Lincolnshire), all the Danes north of Watling Street. Hostages are provided by each shire.

King Swein orders provisions and supplies of horses. He delegates to his son Cnut (the future King of England) command of his ships and the hostages. King Swein then moves south with his whole force crossing Watling Street (i.e., out of the Danelaw) King Swein devastates

---

Manuscript "A" (Winchester or Parker): Trebuchet.
Manuscript "C" (Abingdon II): 18thCentury.
Manuscript "D" (Worcester): Swiss 721 Hv BT.
Manuscript "E" (Peterborough or Laud): Courier New.
Manuscript "F" (Canterbury): Alexa.
Manuscript "H" (Winchester): Calligraphic.

the countryside - doing "the greatest mischief that any host was capable of" - and receives the submission of the people of Oxford and Winchester, Hampshire; he is provided with further hostages. Moving towards London a great part of King Swein's host are drowned in the River Thames "because they did not bother to look for any bridge". London, with King Aethelred II of England and Thurkil (the future Earl Thurkil (Thorkell) the Tall of East Anglia who had defected to join King Aethelred) within its walls, does not submit. King Swein goes to Wallingford, Oxfordshire and Bath, Somerset where he receives the submission of Ealdorman Aethelmaer (probably of the Western Shires, Wessex) and the thanes from the west; they provide him with hostages.

King Swein turns northwards towards his ships - "the whole nation accepted him as their undisputed king". The citizens of London submit to King Swein who demands tribute in full and supplies; as does Thurkil (the future Earl Thurkil (Thorkell) the Tall of East Anglia), leader of the host at Greenwich (Kent/London). Despite this the host "went harrying as often as they pleased. At this time nothing went right for the nation, neither in the south nor in the north". For a time King Aethelred stays with his fleet in the River Thames whilst his Queen Emma, accompanied by Abbot Aelfsige of Peterborough, go to her brother Duke Richard II in Normandy. King Aethelred sends "across the sea" his sons Edward and Alfred in the charge of Bishop Aelfhun of London. At Christmas King Aethelred leaves the fleet and spends the festival on the Isle of Wight after which he goes to Duke Richard. King Aethelred stays there "until the opportunity presented by Swein's death".

Abbot Aelfsige goes to Bonneval monastery in France and buys the body of Saint Florentine - minus the head - for five hundred pounds. The monastery had been pillaged and the abbot and monks were destitute. On his return to England he gave it as an offering to "Christ and Saint Peter" (presumably at Peterborough Abbey).

1014 – King Swein of Denmark, Norway and England dies on 2 February and the men in his fleet all choose his son Cnut as his successor. King Cnut (not yet recognised as King of England but King as far as the host is concerned) stays in Gainsborough in Lincolnshire until Easter; he reaches an agreement with the people and is provided with horses.

All the spiritual and temporal councillors in England send for King Aethelred II of England "if only he would govern his kingdom more justly than he had done in the past". King Aethelred sends his son Edward to negotiate; he agrees on his father's behalf to address their concerns and "a complete and friendly agreement was reached and

---

Manuscript "A" (Winchester or Parker): Trebuchet.

Manuscript "C" (Abingdon II): 18thCentury.

Manuscript "D" (Worcester): Swiss 721 Hv BT.

Manuscript "E" (Peterborough or Laud): Courier New.

Manuscript "F" (Canterbury): Alexa.

Manuscript "H" (Winchester): Calligraphic.

ratified with word and pledge on either side" – every Danish king is outlawed from England forever.

During Lent King Aethelred returns to England and takes his levies at full strength to Lindsey (Lincolnshire) burning and killing before the host "is prepared". King Cnut sails to Sandwich, Kent where he puts ashore the hostages given to his father as surety minus their hands, ears and noses. King Aethelred gives orders to pay the host at Greenwich (Kent/London) twenty-one thousand pounds.

On 28 September a swollen incoming tide floods many areas, reaching inland further than ever before, submerging many homesteads and drowning many people.

1015 – Ealdorman Eadric Streona of Mercia murders Siferth and Morcar, "the chief thanes of the Seven Boroughs" (this is the only time the phrase the "Seven Boroughs" is used and probably refers to Torksey in Lincolnshire and York as well as the "Five Boroughs" of Leicester, Nottingham, Derby, and Lincoln and Stamford in Lincolnshire) in his chambers at the great council at Oxford. King Aethelred II of England seizes the thane's property and orders Siferth's widow Eadgyth to be brought to Malmesbury, Wiltshire. Against King Aethelred's will, Prince Edmund marries Eadgyth and goes to the Five Boroughs where he seizes all the property of Siferth and Morcar and receives the submission of the people.

King Cnut (not yet recognised as King of England but King as far as the host is concerned) sails to Sandwich, Kent, and then sails around Kent to Wessex, into the mouth of the River Frome, Somerset and harries Somerset, Dorset and Wiltshire. At this time King Aethelred is sick in Cosham, Hampshire. Ealdorman Eadric gathers the levies and Prince Edmund (later Edmund II, "Ironside") gathers levies in the north and they join forces, but before giving battle with the host, Ealdorman Eadric leaves Edmund thus leaving the "field clear for their foes". Ealdorman Eadric takes forty of King Aethelred's ships and their crews and submits to King Cnut. The West Saxons submit to the host and supply them with hostages and horses; the host spend the winter in Wessex.

1016 – King Cnut leader of the Scandinavian forces in England returns to England with one hundred and sixty ships **and with Ealdorman Eadric Streona of Mercia. He crosses the River Thames at Cricklade in Wiltshire into Mercia spending Christmas in Warwickshire, harrying, burning and killing all around. Prince Edmund (son of King Aethelred II of England) gathers levies but they "would not be satisfied" unless King Aethelred were with them and they had the support of London. The**

Manuscript "A" (Winchester or Parker): Trebuchet.

Manuscript "C" (Abingdon II): 18thCentury.

Manuscript "D" (Worcester): Swiss 721 Hv BT.

Manuscript "E" (Peterborough or Laud): Courier New.

Manuscript "F" (Canterbury): Alexa.

Manuscript "H" (Winchester): Calligraphic.

expedition is abandoned.

After Christmas an order is issued to the levies calling up every man fit for military services on penalty of the "full fine" (no further information readily available) for failure to report for duty. Word is sent to King Aethelred in London to join them with a request he bring with him as many reinforcements as possible. "Then when they all met, it came to nothing, as so often before". This second expedition is abandoned when King Aethelred leaves the assembly and returns to London after he had been informed that there were plans to betray him.

Prince Edmund goes to Northumbria and joins Earl Uhtred of Bamburgh and Northumbria. Everyone expects them to collect levies to oppose King Cnut but instead they harry Staffordshire, Shrewsbury in Shropshire and Chester. King Cnut harries Buckinghamshire, Bedfordshire, Huntingdonshire, Northamptonshire, along the fen to Stamford (in Lincolnshire) and Lincolnshire, to Nottinghamshire and to Northumbria towards York. When Earl Uhtred hears that King Cnut is in Northumbria he leaves Prince Edmund and submits to King Cnut together with the Northumbrians. Despite giving hostages Earl Uhtred and Thurcytel (could he be Thurcytel "Mare's Head" who instigated the flight from the battle of Ringmere in Norfolk with the Danes in 1010? – see above) are put to death on the advice of Ealdorman Eadric Streona. **(Uhtred is murdered by his enemy Thurbrand the Hold (a rank below a jarl and probably a hereditary landowner), prominent among the Anglo-Danes in York). King Cnut appoints (his brother-in-law) Eric as Earl of Northumbria.**

Both Prince Edmund and King Cnut make their separate ways to London. Before King Cnut arrives by ship King Aethelred dies on 23 April "after a life of much hardship and many difficulties". The councillors, who were all in London, and its citizens, chose Prince Edmund as king who "defended his kingdom valiantly during his lifetime".

During 7 to 9 May Danish ships sail to Greenwich in Kent/London and then on to London. There the crews dig a great channel on the south bank of the River Thames and drag their ships to the west side of London Bridge; they build earthworks so that no one can get in or out of London. They repeatedly attack London, but are unsuccessful. King Edmund II "Ironside" goes to Wessex and receives the submission of the inhabitants. King Edmund fights the Danes at Penselwood in Somerset and after midsummer, Sherston in Wiltshire – both battles are inconclusive with many casualties on both sides. Ealdorman Eadric Streona and Ealdorman Aelfmaer Darling (no further information readily available) assist King Cnut.

King Edmund assembles his levies for a third time and relieves the siege of London, he keeps to the north of the River Thames coming through the wooded slopes by Clayhill (Farm, Tottenham, North London). **Two days later he then crosses the River Thames at Brentford, Middlesex and defeats the host; however, many English are "drowned through their**

Manuscript "A" (Winchester or Parker): Trebuchet.

Manuscript "C" (Abingdon II): 18thCentury.

Manuscript "D" (Worcester): Swiss 721 Hv BT.

Manuscript "E" (Peterborough or Laud): Courier New.

Manuscript "F" (Canterbury): Alexa.

Manuscript "H" (Winchester): Calligraphic.

own negligence" when they go in search of booty. King Edmund goes to Wessex and calls up the levies. The host march on London and unsuccessfully besiege it; they then go by ship into the River Orwell, Suffolk, land and proceed into Mercia destroying and burning everything on their way "as their custom is". They obtain supplies and send their ships and livestock into the River Medway in Kent.

King Edmund calls up the levies of all England for the fourth time and crosses the River Thames at Brentford in Middlesex and goes into Kent. The host flee before him with their horses into the Isle of Sheppey, Kent, many of them are killed. Ealdorman Eadric Streona transfers his allegiance to King Edmund at Aylesford in Kent –"no greater error of judgement was ever made than this" (of taking him back into favour).

The host go back into Essex and make their way to Mercia destroying everything before them. When he discovers this, King Edmund called up the levies of all England for the fifth time. He catches the host at a hill called "Ashingdon" in Essex and a battle ensues. During the battle the Magesaete (Magonsaete – men from Herefordshire and South Shropshire) and Ealdorman Eadric Streona did as he had "so often done before" being the first to leave the battle and betray "his royal lord and the whole nation." King Cnut is victorious and in so doing wins all England. Bishop Eadnoth of Dorchester-on-Thames, Oxfordshire, Abbot Wulfsige of Ramsey, Cambridgeshire, Ealdorman Aelfric of Hampshire, Ealdorman Godwine of Lindsey (Lincolnshire), Ulfcytel from East Anglia (a thane who exercised power similar to an ealdorman), Aethelweard, son of Ealdorman Aethelwine/**Aelfwine**/Aethelsige (no further information readily available), and the "flower of the English nation" are killed.

King Cnut goes to Gloucestershire on the basis of the information he receives about the location of King Edmund. Ealdorman Eadric Streona and the councillors advise the two kings to come to terms and exchange hostages. The two kings meet at Alney, near Deerhurst in Gloucestershire and make a treaty whereby after payment to the host, King Edmund is to rule in Wessex and King Cnut in the country to the north (for Cnut only Mercia is mentioned in Manuscripts E and F). The host go to their ships with all their plunder. The citizens of London come to terms with the host and buy peace from them. The host bring their ships and make their winter quarters in London. On 30 November King Edmund II, Ironside, dies (probably from wounds received at the battle of Ashingdon – see this entry above) and is buried with his grandfather King Edgar of England at Glastonbury, Somerset. Abbot Wulfgar of Abingdon, Oxfordshire dies and is succeed by Aethelsige.

1017 – Cnut is chosen as King of all England. **He divides the nation into four parts; he retains Wessex, gives East Anglia to Thurkil (Thorkell) the Tall, Mercia to Eadric Streona and Northumbria to Eric (confirming his appointment – see the entry for**

Manuscript "A" (Winchester or Parker): Trebuchet.

Manuscript "C" (Abingdon II): 18thCentury.

Manuscript "D" (Worcester): Swiss 721 Hv BT.

Manuscript "E" (Peterborough or Laud): Courier New.

Manuscript "F" (Canterbury): Alexa.

Manuscript "H" (Winchester): Calligraphic.

1016 above). Ealdorman Eadric Streona is killed (his head was cut off by Eric the new Earl of Northumbria on the explicit order of the King) *in London very justly.* **Northman, son of Ealdorman Leofwine of Mercia (he succeeded Eadric Streona), Aethelweard, son of Aethelmaer the Stout (no further information readily available), Beorhtric, son of Aelfheah of Devon (no further information readily available) are killed. King Cnut banishes Prince Eadwig aetheling (son of King Aethelred II of England, and as aetheling, a male of royal blood, the heir apparent)** and has him killed. **Eadwig "king of the peasants" (no further information readily available) is banished** (Manuscript C attributes this to **1020**).

Before 1 August King Cnut takes as his wife, *Aelfgifu in English and Emma in French,* **the widow of King Aethelred II of England and the youngest daughter of Richard I Duke of Normandy. (Emma of Normandy, King Cnut's second wife who was also known as Aelfgifu because she was considered a replacement for Cnut's first English Queen Aelfgifu. Queen Emma/Aelfgifu was the widow and second wife of King Aethelred II of England.)**

1018 – All England pays King Cnut of England a "tribute" of seventy-two thousand pounds plus ten thousand five hundred pounds paid by London. Part of the host return to Denmark, forty ships and their crews remain with King Cnut. The Danes and English agree at Oxford to observe King Edgar's (King of England 959-975) laws. Abbot Aethelsige of Abingdon, Oxfordshire dies and is succeeded by Aethelwine.

1020 – King Cnut of England takes nine ships with him and spends the whole winter in Denmark. (Manuscript E attributes this to **1019**. Cnut becomes King of Denmark in 1019). **King Cnut of England and Denmark returns to England and at Easter holds a great council at Cirencester in Gloucestershire. Ealdorman Aethelweard (referred to as Ealdorman of the Western Provinces – part of Wessex but not as extensive as the earldom was to become under the Godwine family) is banished. King Cnut, Earl Thurkil (Thorkell) the Tall of East Anglia, Archbishop Wulfstan of York with bishops, abbots and many monks (no further information readily available), go to Ashingdon in Essex and attend the consecration of the battlefield church**/*have a stone church built for the souls of those killed in the battle (of Ashingdon – see* **1016** *above.) and appoint as priest Stigand, the king's priest.* **Aelfstan, who was named Lyfing, Archbishop of Canterbury, dies; he was a "very prudent man" both in secular and ecclesiastical matters. On 13 November Aethelnoth the monk, dean at Christ Church Canterbury is consecrated Archbishop of Canterbury** *by Archbishop Wulfstan of York.*

1021 – On 11 November King Cnut of England and Denmark outlaws Earl Thurkil (Thorkell) the Tall of East Anglia (probably as a result of a trial of Thurkil's wife who was found guilty of poisoning his son by his first marriage with the help of a witch. Thurkil had sworn her innocence and lost face as a result.) The "charitable" Bishop Aelfgar of Elmham, Norfolk dies on Christmas Day.

Manuscript "A" (Winchester or Parker): Trebuchet.

Manuscript "C" (Abingdon II): 18thCentury.

Manuscript "D" (Worcester): Swiss 721 Hv BT.

Manuscript "E" (Peterborough or Laud): Courier New.

Manuscript "F" (Canterbury): Alexa.

Manuscript "H" (Winchester): Calligraphic.

1022 – King Cnut of England and Denmark sails with his fleet to the Isle of Wight. Archbishop Aethelnoth of Canterbury goes to Rome accompanied by Abbot Leofwine who had been "unjustly" driven from Ely in Cambridgeshire. **The Archbishop is received with great ceremony by Pope Benedict VIII who gives Aethelnoth his pallium (vestment of office, a cloak) and consecrates him archbishop on 7 October. Archbishop Aethelnoth sings the mass on the same day and feasts with Pope Benedict, takes his pallium from the altar of St Peter's and then returns home "joyously" to his native land.** The Pope clears Abbot Leofwine of all the charges made against him on the testimony of the Archbishop.

1023 – King Cnut of England and Denmark returns to England and is reconciled with Earl Thurkil the Tall of East Anglia. King Cnut makes Thurkil his regent in Denmark and provides him with his son Harthacnut to foster; Earl Thurkil gives King Cnut his son Haraldr to foster. King Cnut has/ **gives permission in Saint Paul's Church to Archbishop Aethelnoth of Canterbury and Bishop Beorhtwine of Sherborne, Dorset for** the relics of Saint Aelfeah (Alphege former Archbishop of Canterbury martyred by the host see **1012** above) to be transferred from London to Canterbury. **On 8 June Saint Aelfeah's body is conveyed by ship across the River Thames to Southwark (on the south side of the river opposite Saint Paul's) in the presence of King Cnut, the Archbishop, diocesan bishops (no further information readily available), earls (no further information readily available) and very many others including both laity and clergy. The Archbishop and "his companions" then take the body to Rochester, Kent. On the third day Queen Emma (Aelfgifu, Cnut's queen) and her son (and future king) Harthacnut convey Saint Aelfeah's body on the 11 June to Christ Church Canterbury with much pomp and circumstance. On 15 June Archbishop Aethelnoth, Bishop Aelfsige II of Winchester, Hampshire and Bishop Beorhtwine oversee the burial of Saint Aelfeah's body on the north side of the altar.** Archbishop Wulfstan of York dies and is succeeded by Aelfric (at one time at the New Minster, Winchester, Hampshire) *who is consecrated by Archbishop Aethelnoth in Canterbury.*

1025 – King Cnut of England and Denmark goes to Denmark and loses a battle at the Holy River (in Sweden) with a Swedish fleet and army including Ulf (Cnut's brother-in-law. Ulf's sister Gytha married Earl Godwine of Wessex in 1020) and Earl Eilaf (his brother, at one time Earl of Gloucestershire. After this battle he is reconciled with King Cnut); many Danes and Englishmen on Cnut's side are killed. (This battle takes place in 1026 with the Norwegian forces led by King Olaf II of Norway and the Swedish forces led by King Anund Jakob of Sweden opposing the forces of King Cnut.)

1026 – Archbishop Aelfric of York goes to Rome and receives his pallium (vestment of office, a cloak) from Pope John XIX on 12 November.

1027 – King Cnut of England and Denmark travels to Rome and on his return "home" he goes to Scotland where Malcolm, **King of Scots,** and two other kings,

Manuscript "A" (Winchester or Parker): Trebuchet.
Manuscript "C" (Abingdon II): 18thCentury.
Manuscript "D" (Worcester): Swiss 721 Hv BT.
Manuscript "E" (Peterborough or Laud): Courier New.
Manuscript "F" (Canterbury): Alexa.
Manuscript "H" (Winchester): Calligraphic.

Maelbeth and Iehmarc, **become his vassal; King Malcolm maintains his allegiance for a "short time".**

Robert 1 (becomes) Duke of Normandy (in 1027. In 1035) he goes to Jerusalem where he dies. He is succeeded by William, later King William I of England, who is still a child of about eight at the time.

1028 – King Cnut of England and Denmark sails from England with fifty ships *of English thanes* to Norway and secures the country for himself driving out King Olaf II of Norway.

1029 – King Cnut of England, Denmark and Norway returns to England.

1030 – King Olaf II of Norway is killed (at the battle of Stiklestad, near Thrandheim Fjord, Norway) fighting his own people and is later canonized. Earl Hakon of Worcestershire (who was made regent of Norway by King Cnut in 1028) dies at sea (in the Pentland Firth south of Orkney).

1031 – King Cnut of England, Denmark and Norway returns to England and immediately gives to Christ Church Canterbury the port of Sandwich in Kent with all the "dues that accrue from both sides of the harbour" as far inland as a small axe can be thrown by a man standing on a ship afloat in closest proximity to the shore whenever the tide is at its highest and full. Part of the charter is included but some has been erased from the manuscript.

1032 – Wildfire causes much damage throughout the country. Bishop Aelfsige II of Winchester dies and is succeeded by Aelfwine the king's chaplain.

1033 – Bishop Leofsige of Worcester dies and is buried at Worcester. He is succeeded by Beorhtheah. Bishop Merehwit of Somerset dies and is buried at Glastonbury Abbey, Somerset (where he had been abbot before becoming a bishop).

1034 – Bishop Aethelric of Dorchester-on-Thames, Oxfordshire dies and is buried at Ramsey, Cambridgeshire. **King Malcolm II of Scotland of Scotland dies.**

1035 – King Cnut of England, Denmark and Norway dies on 12 November at Shaftesbury in Dorset and is buried at the Old Minster in Winchester, Hampshire.

Soon after King Cnut dies a meeting of all the councillors is held in Oxford. Earl Leofric of Mercia and almost all the thanes north of the River Thames and King Cnut's household troops in London elect Harold I Harefoot (son of King Cnut and Aelfgifu) as regent of all England on behalf of himself and his brother Harthacnut (son of Cnut and Emma/ Aelfgifu of Normandy, widow of King Aethelred II of England) who was in Denmark. Earl Godwine of Wessex and almost all the prominent men in Wessex oppose the election of Harold but cannot prevent it. It is

---

Manuscript "A" (Winchester or Parker): Trebuchet.
Manuscript "C" (Abingdon II): 18thCentury.
Manuscript "D" (Worcester): Swiss 721 Hv BT.
Manuscript "E" (Peterborough or Laud): Courier New.
Manuscript "F" (Canterbury): Alexa.
Manuscript "H" (Winchester): Calligraphic.

decided that Queen Emma (Aelfgifu) Harthacnut's mother should reside in Winchester in Hampshire together with his housecarles and hold all Wessex in trust for her son. Earl Godwine is "her most devoted supporter". (Manuscript E includes this entry in **1036**.)

Queen Emma (Aelfgifu – see **1017** above) whilst in Winchester has all King Cnut's "best valuables" taken from her by King Harold I who mischievously claimed to be King Cnut's son by the other Aelfgifu (i.e., Queen Emma, the replacement Aelfgifu. Harold was in fact the younger, second, son of Cnut and his English wife Aelfgifu of Northampton).

1036 – Prince Alfred, aetheling (a male of royal blood, the heir apparent), son of King Aethelred II of England and Emma (Aelfgifu) of Normandy, comes from Normandy to visit his mother in Winchester, Hampshire "but Earl Godwine of Wessex would not permit him to, neither moreover would other men who wielded great power, because the popular cry was greatly in favour of King Harold I (Harold Harefoot of England), although it was unjust". Prince Alfred is captured on the way (near Guildford in Surrey) by Earl Godwine. some of Alfred's followers are murdered, some are sold for money, and some are mutilated. Prince Alfred is taken to Ely in Cambridgeshire and when he arrives his eyes are put out on board a ship. He is then taken to the monks at Ely Abbey where he remains for the rest of his life; he is buried at the west end of the church in the south aisle near the tower. (Included in the Chronicle is a ballad on Alfred's death.)

1037 – King Harold I (Harold Harefoot) is chosen everywhere as king. Harthacnut (son of King Cnut and Emma/Aelfgifu of Normandy see **1017** above) is repudiated because he remains too long in Denmark. Queen Emma (Aelfgifu) is exiled; she is given refuge in Bruges in Belgium by Count Baldwin V of Flanders . Earlier in the year, Aefic, Dean of Evesham Abbey in Worcestershire dies.

1038 – On 1 November Aethelnoth **The Good** , Archbishop of Canterbury, dies and is succeeded by Eadsige *the king's priest.* Aethelric, Bishop of Sussex **who did not want to outlive** Aethelnoth dies **within a week of him** and is succeeded by Grimcytel. On 20 December Beorhtheah, Bishop of Worcestershire, dies and is succeeded as Bishop of Worcestershire and Gloucestershire by Lyfing. Aelfric, Bishop of East Anglia dies soon after Bishop Beorhteah.

1039 – The year of the great gale (no other information provided). Bishop Beorhtmaer of Lichfield, Staffordshire dies. The Welsh forces (of King Gruffudd ap Llywelyn of Gwynedd) defeat the Mercian forces of Eadwine, brother of Earl Leofric of Mercia, and kill Eadwine, Thurkil (no further information readily available), Aelfgeat (no further information readily available) and many other good men. (The site of the battle is possibly Rhyd Y Gros, near Welshpool, Powys.) King Harthacnut of Denmark travels to Bruges in Belgium to visit his mother Queen Emma (Aelfgifu see **1017** above) of Normandy.

1040 – Archbishop Eadsige goes to Rome. King Harold 1 (Harold Harefoot) of England dies on 17 March at Oxford and is buried at Westminster. During his reign the crews of "sixteen ships of his navy were paid at the rate of eight marks a rowlock, just as had been done in Cnut's time". King Harthacnut of Denmark who is in Bruges in Belgium is sent for to become King of England. He comes to Sandwich,

Manuscript "A" (Winchester or Parker): Trebuchet.

Manuscript "C" (Abingdon II): 18thCentury.

Manuscript "D" (Worcester): Swiss 721 Hv BT.

Manuscript "E" (Peterborough or Laud) : Courier New.

Manuscript "F" (Canterbury): Alexa.

Manuscript "H" (Winchester): Calligraphic.

Kent with sixty/sixty-two ships to England before midsummer (on 17 June). He is received by both English and Danes (no further information readily available). King Harthacnut/his councillors impose a severe tax which "was borne with difficulty" the crews of his ships were to be paid at the fixed rate of eight marks a rowlock. The effect of this tax leads his loyal supporters to become disloyal. The scribe includes the comment "He never did anything worthy of a king while he reigned. He had the body of the dead King Harold I (Harold Harefoot) of England disinterred and cast into a marsh". (The body was thrown into the marshes along the River Thames; it was retrieved and buried in the cemetery belonging to the Danish troops – no further information readily available.) The price of a sester (a Roman unit of measurement, about two pints of liquid or sixteen bushels of dry) of wheat rises to fifty-five pence and more.

1041 - The tax amounting to twenty-one thousand and ninety-nine pounds is paid to the fleet. Subsequently a further sum of eleven thousand and forty-eight pounds is paid to thirty-two ships. In retribution for the killing of two housecarles (Feader and Thorstein) inside the minster church of St Mary's in Worcester, who were collecting the "heavy tax" (new unpopular ship tax). King Harthacnut of England and Denmark has all Worcestershire harried. Edward, son of King Aethelred II and Emma (Aelfgifu, see **1017** above) who "had long been in exile from this country" comes to England from Normandy and is sworn in as future king; he remains at King Harthacnut's court. Despite guaranteeing his safety King Harthacnut has Earl Eadwulf III of Bamburgh, Northumberland killed and thereby Harthacnut breaks his pledge.

1042 – On 11 January Aethelric is consecrated Archbishop of York (his election is quashed later in the year). On 8 June King Harthacnut of Denmark and England dies at Lambeth in London whilst drinking "he suddenly fell to the ground with a horrible convulsion – he never spoke again before he dies". He is buried in the Old Minster, Winchester, Hampshire. Edward, son of King Aethelred II of England and Queen Emma (Aelfgifu) of Normandy (see the entry for **1017** above), is chosen as king by right of birth (he is known to history as "Edward the Confessor").

"this was a most disastrous year", the weather was severe, the crops suffered and more cattle died because of diseases or the weather than anyone remembered before. Abbot Aelfsige of Peterborough dies and is replaced by Earnwig the monk who is elected abbot because "he was a very good man and very sincere".

1043 - On 3 April at Winchester, Hampshire, Edward the Confessor of England is consecrated king by Archbishop Eadsige of Canterbury. Stigand the priest is consecrated Bishop of East Anglia (cathedral at North Elmham, Norfolk). **Two weeks before the 30 November King Edward of England is advised (by whom is not explicitly stated) to ride from Gloucester with Earl Leofric of Mercia, Earl Godwine of Wessex and Earl Siward of Northumbria and "their band" to Winchester, Hampshire. There they take Queen Emma (Aelfgifu – see 1017 above) "unaware" and** King Edward "had all the lands which his mother owned confiscated for his own use, and took from her all she possessed, an indescribable number of things of gold and silver because she had been too tightfisted with him" **and had done "less for him than he wished" both before and**

Manuscript "A" (Winchester or Parker): Trebuchet.

Manuscript "C" (Abingdon II): 18thCentury.

Manuscript "D" (Worcester): Swiss 721 Hv BT.

Manuscript "E" (Peterborough or Laud): Courier New.

Manuscript "F" (Canterbury): Alexa.

Manuscript "H" (Winchester): Calligraphic.

after his accession to the throne. They allow Queen Emma to remain in residence. soon afterwards Bishop Stigand is dismissed from his post and all he possessed is confiscated by King Edward because he is considered Queen Emma's close confidant.

1044 – Archbishop Eadsige of Canterbury resigns from his post for reasons of ill-health, and with the agreement of the counsel of King Edward the Confessor of England and Earl Godwine of Wessex, he consecrates Siward, Abbot of Abingdon, Oxfordshire, as his suffragan. (Siward became an auxiliary bishop known as the "Bishops of Saint Martin's", the first church established in Canterbury. This involved his acting on behalf of Archbishop Eadsige with the expectation that Siward would eventually become Archbishop.) The intention of Archbishop Eadsige was known to few beforehand because he feared that someone else in whom he had less confidence or would not want, might be appointed if they asked or purchased it.

In this year there is a very great famine in the whole of England, with corn dearer than anyone remembered; a "sester" (a Roman unit of measurement, about two pints of liquid or sixteen bushels of dry) of wheat rose in price to sixty pence and higher.

King Edward sails to Sandwich in Kent with thirty-five ships. Athelstan the sacristan becomes Abbot of Abingdon, Oxfordshire. **On 25 July Bishop Aelfweard of London dies at Ramsey, Cambridgeshire where he had "retired"; he had formerly been Abbot of Evesham, Worcestershire and had done much to promote the good of the abbey. Manni (Mannig or Wulfmaer) is elected Abbot of Evesham and consecrated on 10 August. The noblewoman Gunhild (niece of King Cnut of England, Denmark and Norway) is expelled by King Edward (reasons are not given); she stays in Bruges in Belgium before going to Denmark.** Stigand is reinstated as Bishop of East Anglia (cathedral at North Elmham, Norfolk).

1045 – On 23 January King Edward the Confessor of England marries Edith, daughter of Earl Godwine of Wessex. On 22 April Bishop Beorthwold of Sherborne, Dorset dies and is succeeded by Hereman, King Edward's chaplain. In the summer King Edward sails with his ships to Sandwich in Kent where the largest fleet of English ships ever seen assembles **because of the threatened invasion of King Magnus of Norway (son of Saint Olaf King of Norway). The invasion does not take place because of the conflict between King Magnus and King Swein Estrithson of Denmark (nephew of King Cnut of England, Denmark and Norway).** On 26 December Wulfric is consecrated Abbot of St Augustine's Abbey in Canterbury because of Abbot Aelfstan's "great infirmity".

1046 – On 20/**23** March Bishop Lyfing of Crediton, Devon dies; **he had held three sees, one in Devonshire, one in Cornwall and one in Worcester.** Leofric, King Edward the Confessor's chaplain succeeds **to the sees of Devonshire and Cornwall and Bishop Ealdred (Abbot of Tavistock, Devon) to Worcester.** On 5 July Abbot Aelfstan of St Augustine's Abbey in Canterbury dies.

Earl Swein (eldest son of Earl Godwine and Earl of Herefordshire, Gloucestershire, Oxfordshire, Berkshire and Somerset) with King Gruffudd ap Llywelyn of Gwynedd campaign in Wales. On his way home Earl Swein

Manuscript "A" (Winchester or Parker): Trebuchet.

Manuscript "C" (Abingdon II): 18thCentury.

Manuscript "D" (Worcester): Swiss 721 Hv BT.

Manuscript "E" (Peterborough or Laud): Courier New.

Manuscript "F" (Canterbury): Alexa.

Manuscript "H" (Winchester): Calligraphic.

abducts, but eventually releases, Abbess Edgiva of Leominster in Herefordshire (the abbey was dissolved shortly afterwards as a direct result of this incident). Before Christmas Osgod Clappa (a Dane, probably at one time in the service of King Cnut of England, Denmark and Norway) **the staller (someone with duties in the royal court)** is outlawed. **King Magnus of Norway conquers Denmark.**

1047 – In February the winter is more severe than any living man could remember because of the death of men and cattle. There was frost and snow and widespread storms and birds and fish die because of the hard frost and from hunger. Earl Swein (eldest son of Earl Godwine and Earl of Herefordshire, Gloucestershire, Oxfordshire, Berkshire and Somerset) goes to Bruges where Count Baldwin of Flanders rules and stays the winter; Swein then goes on to Scandinavia in the summer. Bishop Grimcytel of Sussex dies and is buried in Christ Church, Canterbury. He is succeeded by Heca, King Edward of England's chaplain. On 29 August Bishop Aelfwine of Winchester, Hampshire dies and is succeeded by Bishop Stigand (formerly Bishop of East Anglia – see **1043** and **1044** above). **The former King of Denmark, Swein Estrithson, asks (King Edward the Confessor of England) for fifty ships to help him against King Magnus of Norway who had conquered Denmark. This is considered a "foolish plan" and his request is refused because King Magnus had a powerful fleet. King Magnus then drives out Swein Estrithson and conquers Denmark (again – see 1046 above) with great slaughter. The Danes pay King Magnus money and accept him as their king; King Magnus dies later in the year.**

1048 - On 29 March, Athelstan, Abbot of Abingdon, Oxfordshire, dies and is succeeded by Spearhafoc a monk from Bury St Edmunds, Suffolk. There is a "very great mortality" **of men and cattle** over all England (no further information readily available) **with wildfire spreading over Derbyshire and some other places, doing much damage**. **On the 1 May** there is a severe earthquake throughout England/**in many places, at Worcester, Droitwich, (both in Worcestershire), Derby and elsewhere.** Lothen (no further information readily available) and Yrling (no further information readily available) with twenty-five ships raid Sandwich in Kent and the Isle of Wight where the "best men" (no further information readily available) are killed seizing "indescribable booty both in captives and in gold and silver so that no one knew what it amounted to in all". They sail around Thanet, in Kent, but are resisted by the inhabitants who prevent them from raiding. They move on to Essex where they raid and take captives. They sail to Flanders to sell their plunder and then sail east from whence they had come. King Edward the Confessor of England and the earls (they are not identified) sail out to pursue them in their ships.

Siward (one of the auxiliary Bishops of Saint Martin's, Canterbury see **1044** above) resigns his post on account of ill-health, returns to Abingdon Abbey in Oxfordshire where he dies on 23 October **(Manuscript D attributes his death to 1049).** Archbishop Eadsige of Canterbury resumes his duties.

Swein Estrithson returns to Denmark. Harold Hardrada, an uncle of King Magnus of Norway, goes to Norway after the death of King Magnus of Norway (see 1047 above) and is accepted as king and makes his peace with England. Swein Estrithson

---

Manuscript "A" (Winchester or Parker): Trebuchet.

Manuscript "C" (Abingdon II): 18thCentury.

Manuscript "D" (Worcester): Swiss 721 Hv BT.

Manuscript "E" (Peterborough or Laud): Courier New.

Manuscript "F" (Canterbury): Alexa.

Manuscript "H" (Winchester): Calligraphic.

asks King Edward for at least fifty ships to help him (in his battles against the Norwegians) – the "whole nation" opposes this request (this is a similar request and response to the events also recorded in Manuscript D for 1047 above).

1049 – The Holy Roman Emperor, Henry III, assembles a "countless host" with Pope Leo **and the patriarch (was this the Patriarch of Constantinople – unlikely given the later exchanges about papal primacy and the Great Schism between the church in the East and the West in 1054 – or one of the patriarchs from Aquileia or Grado in Italy)** and many other "famous men of many nations" (no further information readily available), to make war on Count Baldwin V of Flanders. Count Baldwin had seized his palace at Nijmegen in The Netherlands and taken other actions (no further information readily available) against the Emperor. The Emperor also requests naval support from King Edward the Confessor of England to prevent Count Baldwin escaping. King Edward agrees and assembles a large naval force in Sandwich in Kent which stays there until Henry III the Holy Roman Emperor obtains "satisfaction" from Count Baldwin **and as a result many (English) ships go home but King Edward remains in Sandwich, Kent with a few ships.**

Earl Swein (Earl of Herefordshire, Gloucestershire, Oxfordshire, Berkshire and Somerset) comes **from exile in Denmark where he had "cooked his goose with the Danes"** with seven ships to Bosham in Sussex to ask King Edward for a grant of land to maintain himself, claiming he wished to be the vassal of King Edward and begged Earl Beorn of Northamptonshire (his cousin) to be his friend at court/ **promised to help him.** Earl Swein makes his peace with King Edward and is promised that all his legal right to all his former possessions would be recognised. Earl Harold of East Anglia (his brother) and Earl Beorn object and refuse to restore anything to Swein that King Edward had granted to them. King Edward refuses every request made by Earl Swein. Earl Swein is given four days safe passage to return to his ships/ *ordered to leave the country.* Earl Swein goes to Bosham to his ships *where he speaks to his father Earl Godwine of Wessex and Earl Beorn (it is presumed they had all agreed to go to Bosham first and then on to Sandwich).*

The King hears that hostile ships are harrying off to the west (no further information readily available). Earl Godwine with Earl Beorn sail from Sandwich with forty-two ships to Pevensey in Sussex/with two ships of the royal navy (this is the first time this description is used), one ship is commanded by Earl Harold and the other by Tostig (later Earl of Northumbria) and is joined by forty-two ships manned by men on national service (this is the first time this expression is used). At Pevensey the ships are "weather-bound".

King Edward allows the Mercian contingent in his fleet to go home. King Edward is informed that Osgod Clappa the Staller (see **1046** above) had twenty-nine/**thirty-nine** ships lying at Wulpe in Belgium. King Edward sends a summons to his ships at the northern mouth of the River Stour in Kent. Osgod Clappa takes his wife (no further information readily available) to Bruges in Belgium and returns to Wulpe in Belgium with six ships sending other ships from his fleet to plunder the Naze in Essex/**Sussex; a violent gale occurs and all the ships are destroyed except four which are later destroyed across the sea (no further information readily available).**

Manuscript "A" (Winchester or Parker): Trebuchet.

Manuscript "C" (Abingdon II): 18thCentury.

Manuscript "D" (Worcester): Swiss 721 Hv BT.

Manuscript "E" (Peterborough or Laud): Courier New.

Manuscript "F" (Canterbury): Alexa.

Manuscript "H" (Winchester): Calligraphic.

While Earl Godwine and Earl Beorn are with their ships at Pevensey, Earl Swein speaks to his father (Earl Godwine) /persuades Earl Beorn to accompany him to King Edward at Sandwich where he intends to swear an oath of loyalty to/**improve his relations with**/the king/help him win the king's friendship. Earl Beorn is accompanied by only three of his followers "never thinking he would betray them". He/is persuaded on the way to ride to Bosham as if they were on their way to Sandwich to prevent the crews deserting Earl Swein's ships. As soon as they arrive at Bosham, Earl Beorn refuses to go on board the ships, but Swein's sailors throw him into a boat, bind him, and row out to their ships/ Earl Beorn is bound and led on board ship. Earl Swein's ships sail to Dartmouth/Axmouth in Devon where Earl Beorn is killed and deeply buried/buried him in a church. **The men of Hastings seize two of Earl Swein's ship, kill all their crews and take their ships to King Edward at Sandwich.** Earl Harold/his (Beorn's) friends and household troops come from London exhumes Earl Beorn's body and takes it to the Old Minster, Winchester, Hampshire. Earl Beorn is buried beside his uncle, King Cnut of England, Denmark and Norway. King Edward and the whole army declare Earl Swein to be a "nithing" (a man without honour). Earl Swein sails with only two out of his original eight ships (the crews of six ships had deserted) to Bruges and spends the winter with Count Baldwin.

Thirty-six Scandinavian ships come from Ireland, sail up the Welsh River Usk and raid the countryside with the aid of Gruffydd, King of Gwynedd and Powys. On the 29 July these forces defeat Bishop Ealdred's of Worcester levies, who are too few in number, and are taken by surprise early in the morning; many are killed but some escape including the Bishop.

Bishop Eadnoth of Dorchester-on-Thames, Oxfordshire dies and is replaced by Ulf, King Edwards chaplain, a "bad appointment". **He was later expelled because "he did nothing worthy of a bishop", and it "brings shame to us to speak further about it" (see 1050 below).** Abbot Oswy of Thorney, Cambridgeshire dies **in Oxfordshire**. Abbot Wulfnoth of Westminster Abbey in London dies. Bishop Siward (see **1044** above) dies and is buried at Abingdon, Oxfordshire.

The cathedral at Rheims in France is consecrated in the presence of Pope Leo IX and the Holy Roman Emperor, Henry III. A "great synod" is held in Rheims presided over by Pope Leo IX; attended by the Archbishops of Burgundy, Besançon, Rhiems and Trèves (all four in France, no further information readily available) and **many bishops and abbots** and laymen. **Two were sent from England** King Edward sends Bishop Duduc of Wells, Somerset, Abbot Wulfric of **(from) St Augustine's Abbey, Canterbury** and Abbot Aelfwine of **(and) Ramsey Abbey in Cambridgeshire to the synod** so that they can report back to the King. **(This synod is part of Pope Leo IX's reformation of the Church. It focuses on celibacy and simony – the purchase of preferment in the church.)**

1050 – King Edward the Confessor of England pays off nine ships of the royal fleet (the fleet founded by King Cnut of England, Denmark and Norway), five ships remain and he promises their crews twelve months pay. King Edward sends Bishop Hereman of Sherborne, Dorset and Bishop Ealdred of Worcester on a mission (it is unclear what precisely the purpose of this mission was – moving the seat of the Devonshire bishopric of Crediton

Manuscript "A" (Winchester or Parker): Trebuchet.

Manuscript "C" (Abingdon II): 18thCentury.

Manuscript "D" (Worcester): Swiss 721 Hv BT.

Manuscript "E" (Peterborough or Laud): Courier New.

Manuscript "F" (Canterbury): Alexa.

Manuscript "H" (Winchester): Calligraphic.

to Exeter, or to secure the release of the king from a vow to go on a pilgrimage) to see Pope Leo IX in Rome; they return the same year. (Manuscript E has the two bishops attending a synod in Rome; they arrive on the eve of Easter.) Pope Leo holds a synod at Vercelli in Italy attended by Bishop Ulf of Dorchester-on-Thames, Oxfordshire, who provides "exceptionally costly gifts" without which he would have been deprived of his bishopric because "he did not know how to perform his offices as well as he ought to have done". Earl Swein (Earl of Herefordshire, Gloucestershire, Oxfordshire, Berkshire and Somerset) returns to England; his sentence of outlawry is revoked. On 29 October Archbishop Eadsige of Canterbury dies.

1051 – On 22 January Archbishop Aelfric Puttoc of York dies and is buried at Peterborough. At mid Lent King Edward the Confessor of England holds a council in London and appoints as Archbishop of Canterbury Robert, **the "Frenchman" who had been Bishop of London**. He also appoints Abbot Spearhafoc of Abingdon, Oxfordshire as Bishop of London, who is replaced as abbot by "bishop" Rudolf a kinsman of King Edward. **Abbot Spearhafoc is deprived of his see before he is consecrated. (Manuscript D attributes these appointments to 1050).** In the spring Archbishop Robert goes to Rome for his pallium (vestment of office, a cloak). Archbishop Robert returns from Rome with his pallium on 26 June and is installed as Archbishop at Christ Church (Canterbury Cathedral) Canterbury on 29 June. He goes to King Edward but on the way Abbot Spearhafoc meets him with the king's letter to the effect that Archbishop Robert should consecrate him Bishop of London; the Archbishop refuses on two separate occasions on the grounds that Pope Leo XI has forbidden it. Despite this Spearhafoc takes up the duties of Bishop of London with the king's consent.

King Edward pays off all his household troops **and abolishes the tax which King Aethelred had instituted to buy off the Danes in the thirty-ninth year after it had been introduced; this tax took priority over all others and was the most oppressive.**

Eustace of Boulogne, formerly married to King Edward's sister (Goda, who died in 1047), lands at Dover, Kent. After visiting King Edward he proceeds home via Canterbury where he and his men have a meal. They then proceed towards Dover. Outside Dover he and his men put on their armour and then go into the town. There they **behave "foolishly" when looking for quarters killing a townsman, one of the Frenchmen is killed. A further seven men are killed and "much evil was done on either side with horse and with weapons".**/One of the Frenchman approaches a householder who refuses him lodging. The Frenchman wounds the householder who then kills the Frenchman. Eustace with his other companions, mount their horses, kill the householder in his house. The Frenchmen kill in the town more than twenty others while the townsmen kill nineteen of the Frenchmen and wound many others. **Eustace and his men escape to seek King Edward's protection who is residing at Gloucester** and there they give "a one-sided account of how they fared" / *"told the king it was worse than it was"*. King Edward is

Manuscript "A" (Winchester or Parker): Trebuchet.

Manuscript "C" (Abingdon II): 18thCentury.

Manuscript "D" (Worcester): Swiss 721 Hv BT.

Manuscript "E" (Peterborough or Laud): Courier New.

Manuscript "F" (Canterbury): Alexa.

Manuscript "H" (Winchester): Calligraphic.

incensed with the people of Dover and summons Earl Godwine of Wessex. He orders Earl Godwine to "carry war" into Dover on the basis that Eustace had told him that the fault was with the townsmen, "but it was not so". Earl Godwine refuses the order because it was "abhorrent to him to injure the people of his own province". King Edward orders his council to attend him at Gloucester on the 8 September. Based in their castle in Herefordshire in Earl Swein's (Earl of Herefordshire, Gloucestershire, Oxfordshire, Berkshire and Somerset) territory the Frenchmen inflict "all the injuries and insults they possibly could upon the king's men".

Earl Godwine is concerned that these events should happen in his earldom and so he gathers his forces from all over his earldom, as do his sons Earl Swein (Earl of Herefordshire, Gloucestershire, Oxfordshire, Berkshire and Somerset), and Earl Harold (Earl of East Anglia). Their combined forces assemble around 1 September at Beverstone (in the)**, Longtree (Hundred) in Gloucestershire. They prepare for war against King Edward unless Eustace and his men are handed over to them; they also want handed over to them the Frenchmen in the castle (there are three castles in the vicinity at this time, Ewyas Harold and Hereford in Herefordshire and Richard's Castle on the Herefordshire/Shropshire border).** The Earls wish for an audience with King Edward but this is refused because the Normans tell the king that the Earls wish to use the occasion to betray him.

King Edward at Gloucester sends for Earl Siward of Northumbria and Earl Leofric of Mercia who bring with them a "moderate" number of troops, but when they realise the seriousness of the situation they send for reinforcements from all over their earldoms. Earl Ralph (nephew of King Edward, and subsequently appointed Earl of Herefordshire, Gloucestershire and Oxfordshire) also assembles troops to support King Edward. The forces in support of King Edward assemble in Gloucestershire and are resolved to attack Godwine's forces if King Edward wishes. Then some (they are not identified) consider it great folly if battle ensues between the forces of King Edward and those of Godwine as the inevitable casualties would leave the country open to invasion and bring "utter ruin". The two parties agree to exchange hostages and meet again at a council in Southwark in London on the 24 September **so that Earl Godwine and his sons can make their case.**

The two parties arrive at the agreed place and time in London. King Edward and his supporters include Earl Siward and Earl Leofric of Mercia who have called out all the levies in their earldoms; these are augmented by additional levies from "to the south and to the north of the River Thames". **As time progresses the supporters from Wessex of Earl Godwine decrease in number.**

All the thanes of Earl Harold are required to find sureties that they would become the king's men, **Earl Swein is outlawed. Earl Godwine decides not to meet King**

Manuscript "A" (Winchester or Parker): Trebuchet.
Manuscript "C" (Abingdon II): 18thCentury.
Manuscript "D" (Worcester): Swiss 721 Hv BT.
Manuscript "E" (Peterborough or Laud): Courier New.
Manuscript "F" (Canterbury): Alexa.
Manuscript "H" (Winchester): Calligraphic.

Edward. Earl Godwine and Earl Harold are summoned to King Edward and his council but they request protection and hostages so that they can go to and from the king without any fear of treachery. King Edward orders all the earls' thanes to acknowledge him as their overlord. King Edward orders Earl Godwine and Earl Harold to come with twelve men to the king's council. Earl Godwine requests protection and hostages so that he might clear himself of the charges against him. King Edward refuses the provision of hostages and gives Earl Godwine five days safe conduct to leave the country. **Earl Godwine leaves at night. The following morning King Edward holds a council which proclaims Earl Godwine, his sons and their supporters, outlaws**/Earl Godwine of Wessex and all his sons are banished from England.

Godwine, with his wife Gytha and his sons Swein (Earl of Herefordshire, Gloucestershire, Oxfordshire, Berkshire and Somerset), Tostig (later Earl of Northumbria) **and his wife Judith (the daughter of Count Baldwin IV and half sister to Baldwin V, the current Count of Flanders)** and Gurth (later Earl of East Anglia, Cambridgeshire and Oxfordshire when Harold becomes Earl of Wessex) go **to Thorney Island**/Bosham**, Sussex and then in one ship laden with as much treasure as possible** on to Bruges in Belgium where they stay all winter. Earl Harold (Earl of East Anglia) and Leofwine (later Earl of Kent, Essex, Middlesex, Hertford, Surrey and probably Buckinghamshire) go to **Bristol, Gloucestershire in the ship Earl Swein had previously provisioned for himself. King Edward sends Bishop Ealdred of London with a force to intercept Harold and Leofwine before they reach the ship but "they could not or would not". Harold with Leofwine sails out from the mouth of the River Avon, Somerset but encounter such severe weather that he barely survives; many of his men die. Harold with Leofwine sail to** Ireland (no other readily available information provided) and stay the winter. **(The scribe in Manuscript D includes the comment) that if any Englishman had been told that these events had happened he would have been very surprised for Godwine has risen to great eminence as if "he ruled the king and all England", his sons were earls and favourites of the king and his daughter was the king's wife.**

King Edward commits his wife Edith (one of earl Godwine's daughters) to the nunnery at Wherwell in Hampshire and deprives his queen (Edith) of all she owned, lands, gold and silver "and of everything". Odda is appointed earl over Devon, Dorset, Somerset and Cornwall, and Earl Leofric's son, Aelfgar is given the Earldom of East Anglia formerly held by Harold.

Duke William of Normandy with a great retinue of Frenchmen is received by King Edward. William the priest/the king's chaplain **(a Norman) is appointed Bishop of London in place of Abbot Spearhafoc.**

1052 – On **6**/14 March Emma/Aelfgifu (see **1017** above) dies; she is the mother of King Edward the Confessor of England (son of King Aethelred II of England) and the mother of King Harthacnut of Denmark and England (son of King Cnut of England, Denmark and Norway). She is buried alongside King Cnut in the Old

Manuscript "A" (Winchester or Parker): Trebuchet.

Manuscript "C" (Abingdon II): 18thCentury.

Manuscript "D" (Worcester): Swiss 721 Hv BT.

Manuscript "E" (Peterborough or Laud): Courier New.

Manuscript "F" (Canterbury): Alexa.

Manuscript "H" (Winchester): Calligraphic.

Minster at Winchester, Hampshire.

King Gruffydd ap Llywelyn of Gwynedd campaigns in Herefordshire. On the anniversary of the day in 1039 when Eadwine, brother of Earl Leofric of Mercia, was killed by the forces of King Gruffudd, a battle takes place near Leominster in Herefordshire. The Welsh are opposed by the local English and the Frenchmen from the castle (no further information provided, presumably Richard's Castle on the Herefordshire/Shropshire border); many English and French are killed.

Earl Harold of East Anglia sails from Ireland with nine ships and enters the mouth of the River Severn and lands at Porlock, Somerset, plundering the borderlands between Somerset and Devon. He defeats the local forces opposing him, killing thirty thanes (no further details given) and other men seizing cattle, captives and property; he sails around Lands End in Cornwall.

King Edward has forty small ships fitted out under the command of Earl Ralph of Herefordshire, Gloucestershire and Oxfordshire and Earl Odda of Devon, Dorset, Somerset and Cornwall. These ships are stationed at Sandwich, in Kent, for many weeks, to prevent the return of Earl Godwine of Wessex who had spent the winter in Bruges in Belgium. On 23 June Earl Godwine sails *from Bruges and the River Yser in Belgium and* puts to sea and reaches Dungeness, Kent. Unbeknown to King Edward's forces Earl Godwine secures the support of all the men of Kent, Sussex/**Essex** and Surrey and the shipmen from the Hastings district and everywhere along the sea coast (all the southeast of England) and many other places; *hostages and those ships found to be serviceable are seized.* King Edward's household troops at Sandwich, Kent, learn of Earl Godwine's landing and set out in pursuit; the levies are called out to oppose Earl Godwine who is warned of the approaching opposing forces and sails to Pevensey, Sussex. Earl Godwine evades them and so they give up/the weather becomes so stormy that the ships of Earl Ralph and Earl Odda are unable to find Earl Godwine who sails to Bruges. Earl Ralph and Earl Odda's troops/ships return to Sandwich and then home to London/it was decided that the ships of Earl Ralph and Earl Odda should sail to London where other earls (no further information readily available) and other "rowers" (new crews) would take over; however the ships are delayed so long in Sandwich that the crews decide they should all go home.

When Earl Godwine learns that the troops at Sandwich have gone home he sails towards the Isle of Wight where he harries the inhabitants until they pay him as much as he wants. He sails on to Portland in Dorset where he causes more damage. He awaits the arrival of Earl Harold with his forces. Other than seize provisions, the Godwine forces cause "no great harm" winning over the support of all those along the sea coast and up country (no further information readily available). The Godwine forces collect support from all shipmen they meet and take with them as many ships as are serviceable as they sail to Pevensey, Sussex, to Dungerness, Kent capturing all the ships in Romney, Hythe and Folkestone (all in Kent). At Dover, Kent, they land and seize as many ships and hostages as they please, repeating this practice when they reach Sandwich; by which time they have

---

Manuscript "A" (Winchester or Parker): Trebuchet.

Manuscript "C" (Abingdon II): 18thCentury.

Manuscript "D" (Worcester): Swiss 721 Hv BT.

Manuscript "E" (Peterborough or Laud): Courier New.

Manuscript "F" (Canterbury): Alexa.

Manuscript "H" (Winchester): Calligraphic.

an overwhelming force at their disposal. Everywhere they go they are provided with as many hostages and as much provisions as they require. The Godwine forces sail from the mouth of the River Stour in Kent on to London. Some of these ships sail to the Isle of Sheppey, Kent, where the crews damage the countryside and burn Milton Royal in Kent before joining the Godwine forces in London.

When King Edward learns of this he sends for reinforcements; but these are slow in coming. In the meantime Godwine's forces arrive at Southwark (on the south bank of the River Thames in London) on Monday 14 September, where they await the incoming high tide (on the east side of the bridge. Shipping from up river waited on the west side of the bridge for the outgoing tide. Note: bridges were important defensive measures to stop shipping from moving upstream, their arches restricted the height of mast clearance and their width restricted the use of oars). Whilst waiting Earl Godwine receives the support of the local citizenry. On the incoming high tide he sails "through" (there may have been sections of the bridge capable of being raised like a drawbridge rather than the bridge permanently horizontal supported by a series of connected arches) the bridge (London Bridge) near the south bank. The Godwine's forces line the south bank while King Edward's levies and shipmen, his earls (presumably Earl Ralph and Earl Odda) and fifty ships, line the north bank of the River Thames. Godwine's ships then sail towards the north bank of the River Thames as if to surround the kings ship's (presumably the ones previously at Sandwich). No one on either side wants to fight and leave the country wide open to foreign invasion — "there were few men else of any consequence except Englishmen on either side".

Earl Godwine and his sons request that they "might legally possess all of the things of which they had been wrongfully deprived". For quite a while King Edward rejects this request and consequently Godwine's supporters become so incensed against the King that Earl Godwine has difficulty in restraining them. Through the intervention of Bishop Stigand of Winchester in Hampshire, *the king's adviser and chaplain*, the two sides agree to exchange hostages. Intermediaries are appointed and a truce arranged between them. Earl Godwine and Earl Harold with as many of their troops they considered necessary land (presumably on the north bank) so that a meeting of the council could take place. Earl Godwine sets out his case. He establishes his innocence and those of all members of his family, with regard to all charges made against them. The council restore to the Godwines — the earl, his wife, his sons and daughter — their earldoms and everything they possess. The Council confirm the friendship between King Edward and the Godwines, promise to make good/**effective** laws for the whole nation, and outlaw   unconditionally Archbishop Robert of Canterbury and all Frenchmen who had promoted injustice, made unjust judgements and counselled evil in the country *"for they were the cause of all the ill feeling which had arisen between him (Earl Godwine) and the king"*, with the exception of those the council decided were loyal to both King Edward and all his people.

Archbishop Robert of Canterbury, Bishop William of London and Bishop Ulf of Dorchester-on-Thames, Oxfordshire and their French supporters escape with difficulty; some go west to Osbern Pentecost's castle at Ewias (Ewyas) Harold, Herefordshire and some go north to Robert's castle (probably Richard's Castle, Herefordshire).

Manuscript "A" (Winchester or Parker): Trebuchet.

Manuscript "C" (Abingdon II): 18thCentury.

Manuscript "D" (Worcester): Swiss 721 Hv BT.

Manuscript "E" (Peterborough or Laud): Courier New.

Manuscript "F" (Canterbury): Alexa.

Manuscript "H" (Winchester): Calligraphic.

Archbishop Robert and Bishop Ulf and their supporters leave London through the East Gate, killing many young men as they go; they ride to the Naze in Essex where they take an unseaworthy ship and fled overseas.

Bishop Stigand is appointed Archbishop of Canterbury. With King Edward's permission, and the agreement of the monks, Abbot Earnwig of Peterborough, although in good health gives his abbacy to Leofric the monk (Leofric was the nephew of Earl Leofric of Coventry and Lady Godiva was his aunt) who as abbot endows the monastery with land, gold and silver so that it becomes known as "The Golden Borough".

Earl Swein (formerly Earl of Herefordshire, Gloucestershire, Oxfordshire, Berkshire and Somerset) who had gone from Bruges in Belgium to Jerusalem on a pilgrimage dies on his way home at Constantinople on 29 September. (There are some unsubstantiated claims that Earl Swein was accompanied by Bishop Ealdred of Worcester.)

(A later entry in the same year records.) Godwine is taken ill soon after he lands at Southwark but he recovers. (The scribe in Manuscript C adds the comment) that he had made far too few amends for the church property he had taken from many holy places.

On 20 December there is a high wind which **lasts over Christmas and** does much damage throughout the country. Rhys, the brother of the Welsh King Gruffydd ap Llywelyn of Gwynedd, is put to death **for the crimes he had committed, and his head is brought to Gloucester on 5 January 1053.**

(Manuscript F attributes Queen Emma's death, the events it mentions relating to the return of the Godwines, and the appointment of Bishop Stigand of Winchester, Hampshire, as Archbishop of Canterbury to **1051***.)*

1053 – Earl Godwine of Wessex dies at Easter on 15 April after suffering a stroke; he and his sons Earl Harold of East Anglia and Tostig (later Earl of Northumbria), are with King Edward the Confessor of England at Winchester, Hampshire. Earl Godwine is buried in the Old Minster, Winchester. Harold succeeds as Earl of Wessex and Aelfgar (son of Earl Leofric of Mercia) succeeds Harold as Earl of East Anglia. **Before 1 November and within a month,** Bishop Wulfsige of Lichfield, Staffordshire, dies and is succeeded by Abbot Leofwine of Coventry, Warwickshire; Abbot Aethelweard of Glastonbury, Somerset dies **and is succeeded by Aethelnoth (no further information readily available);** Abbot Godwine of Winchcombe, Gloucestershire, dies **and is succeeded by Bishop Ealdred of Worcester**. **Aelfric, brother of Earl Odda (for a few months in 1051/1052 during the Godwine's exile he was Earl of Somerset, Dorset, Devon and Cornwall, but he loses these following the return of the Godwines; he receives some lands in Worcestershire and Gloucestershire by way of compensation) dies at Deerhurst, Gloucestershire, and is buried at Pershore, Worcestershire.** The Welsh kill a large number of "English frontier guards" (a new description) near Westbury in Gloucestershire. In this year there is no lawfully constituted archbishop in England, Archbishop Stigand holds (in plurality the Bishopric of Winchester and) the Archbishopric of Canterbury (he is excommunicated by five Popes because of this). Archbishop Cynesige of York, Bishop Leofwine of Lichfield, Staffordshire and Bishop Wulfwig of Dorchester-on-Thames, Oxfordshire go overseas to

---

Manuscript "A" (Winchester or Parker): Trebuchet.

Manuscript "C" (Abingdon II): 18thCentury.

Manuscript "D" (Worcester): Swiss 721 Hv BT.

Manuscript "E" (Peterborough or Laud): Courier New.

Manuscript "F" (Canterbury): Alexa.

Manuscript "H" (Winchester): Calligraphic.

be consecrated (because of Archbishop Stigand's position). Wulfric succeeds to the Bishopric of Dorchester-on -Thames during Bishop Ulf's lifetime and exile (in **1052**, see above and also **1049** and **1050**).

1054 – Earl Siward of Northumbria invades Scotland **by sea and land** defeating King Macbeth of Scotland (Shakespeare's Macbeth in which Earl Siward features) in battle (Dunsinane Hill, near Perth, Tayside) **on 27 July**. Siward suffers many Danish and English losses among his forces, including his son **Osbern, his sister's son Siward, among his and King Edward the Confessor of England's housecarles**. Bishop Ealdred of Worcester goes on a mission to **Cologne in** Germany (to seek assistance with the return from Hungary of Edward the Exile, son of King Edmund II, Ironside, of England) where he is received with great honour **and ceremony, and entertained by both Archbishop Hermann II of Cologne and Henry III, the Holy Roman Emperor; he stays nearly a year**. **(During Bishop's Ealdred's absence in Germany,) he gives permission for Bishop Leofwine of Lichfield, Staffordshire to consecrate the monastic** church at Evesham, Worcestershire; it is consecrated on 10 October. Osgod Clappa (a Dane, at one time with duties in the royal court of King Cnut of England, Denmark and Norway) dies suddenly in his bed (probably in Flanders, he had been outlawed, see **1046** above). **Pope Leo IX dies and is succeeded by Pope Victor II.** A great pestilence of cattle occurs, greater than anyone has known for many years before.

1055 – Earl Siward of Northumbria dies at York and is buried in the church he had built, Galmanhowe in York. (The records of Saint Olaf (Olave's) Church in York record that it is where Earl Siward is buried.) **Tostig Godwine becomes Earl of Northumbria. Archbishop Cynesige of York "fetched" his pallium (vestment of office, a cloak) from Pope Victor II**. At a council in London on 19 March Earl Aelfgar of East Anglia, son of Earl Leofric of Mercia, is unjustly outlawed and goes to Ireland where he acquires an additional eighteen ships to supplement his forces. He sails to Wales with his forces where he allies himself with King Gruffydd ap Llywelyn of Gwynedd. Earl Aelfgar and King Gruffydd raise great levies of Irish and Welsh **and march on Hereford.** Ralph the Frenchman, Earl of Hereford, gathers his levies to oppose them at Hereford but before the battle is joined the English flee "because they had been made to fight on horseback". About four or five hundred English are killed. On 24 October the forces of Earl Aelfgar and King Gruffydd burn Hereford to the ground, kill many of its inhabitants and take others hostage, and loot and burn St Aethelberht's (an East Anglian king killed on the orders of King Offa of Mercia – see **794** above) cathedral built by Bishop Athelstan of Hereford **killing many of the priests inside.** In response the English levies from all the surrounding area are called out, they proceed to Gloucester and then a little way into Wales. Meanwhile Earl Harold of Wessex has an earthwork built around Hereford and negotiates a peace treaty at Billingsley, Shropshire. Earl Aelfgar has his sentence of outlawry revoked and his **earldom and** possessions restored; his household troops on his ships go to Chester, Cheshire to await their promised pay. The Welsh Bishop Tremrig dies; he had been appointed, Bishop Athelstan of Hereford's deputy when the Bishop became an invalid (he had become blind).

1056 – **Bishop Aethelric of Durham gives up his bishopric (he was forced to retire because of financial irregularities) and retires to St Peter's (the present-day cathedral) Peterborough; he is replaced by his brother Aethelwine.** Bishop Athelstan of Hereford dies on 10 February and is buried at Hereford. He is succeeded by Leofgar who was Earl Harold of Wessex's Chaplain. (The scribe adds the comment) that Leofgar wore his moustaches during his priesthood until he became a bishop. After his consecration Bishop Leofgar joined the levies opposing King Gruffydd ap

---

Manuscript "A" (Winchester or Parker): Trebuchet.

Manuscript "C" (Abingdon II): 18thCentury.

Manuscript "D" (Worcester): Swiss 721 Hv BT.

Manuscript "E" (Peterborough or Laud): Courier New.

Manuscript "F" (Canterbury): Alexa.

Manuscript "H" (Winchester): Calligraphic.

Llywelyn of Gwynedd. In the fighting (the location is not identified) eight days before midsummer Bishop Leofgar is killed along with his priests (no further information readily available) who were with him and Aelfnoth the Sheriff of Hereford. Many other good men were killed and the rest escaped. (The scribe adds the comment) it is heartbreaking to tell of all the hardship, all the marching and campaigning, all the toil and the loss of men and horses endured by the English. When Earl Leofric of Mercia, Earl Harold, Bishop Ealdred of Worcester arrive they arrange a peace treaty with King Gruffydd. King Gruffydd agrees to be a loyal and faithful underking to King Edward the Confessor of England. Bishop Ealdred succeeds Bishop Leofgar, who had held the bishopric for eleven weeks and four days, as Bishop of Hereford. The Holy Roman Emperor "Cona"(Henry III) dies. On 31 August Earl Odda, who retired as a monk, dies and is buried at Pershore in Worcestershire (for a few months in 1051-1052 during the Godwines exile Odda was Earl of Somerset, Dorset, Devon and Cornwall, but he was deprived of his earldom following the return of the Godwine's, Odda received some lands in Worcestershire and Gloucestershire by way of compensation).

1057 – Prince Edward (the aetheling – a male of royal blood, the heir apparent,) arrives in England and dies a few days later; he is buried in St Paul's Cathedral in London. **He is the son of King Edmund II "Ironside" of England, the half-brother of King Edward the Confessor of England. King Cnut of England, Denmark and Norway banished Prince Edward and his brother Prince Edmund into Hungary (in 1017. The scribe is mistaken: Prince Edward and his brother Prince Edmund were banished to Sweden, taken to Russia before reaching Hungary.) He married Agatha (daughter rather than kinswoman) of The Holy Roman Emperor Henry III. (The scribe records that) "it was arranged that he could not see his kinsman, King Edward".**

On 30 October Earl Leofric of Mercia dies and is buried at Coventry, Warwickshire. He is succeeded by his son Earl Aelfgar of East Anglia. On 21 December Earl Ralph (nephew of King Edward, and subsequently appointed Earl of Herefordshire, Gloucestershire and Oxfordshire) dies and is buried at Peterborough. Pope Victor II dies and is succeeded by Pope Stephen IX who had been Abbot of Monte Cassino Abbey in Italy. **Bishop Heca of Sussex dies** (Manuscripts E and *F* attribute this event to **1058**) **and is succeeded by Aethelric (no further information readily available).**

1058 – Earl Aelfgar of Mercia is "driven out of the country" (no reasons indicated). He soon returns "with violence" with the help of King Gruffydd ap Llywelyn of Gwynedd (no further information provided). A pirate host comes from Norway: (with a commentary by the scribe) "it is tedious to tell how it all happened". Bishop Ealdred of Worcester consecrates the church of St Peter he had restored in Gloucester (the present Gloucester Cathedral). Bishop Ealdred goes to Jerusalem "with greater ceremony than any before him" and makes a gift of a golden chalice of "most admirable workmanship", worth five marks, to the Church of the Holy Sepulchre in Jerusalem.

Pope Stephen IX dies and is succeeded by Pope Benedict X (he is referred to

---

Manuscript "A" (Winchester or Parker): Trebuchet.
Manuscript "C" (Abingdon II): 18thCentury.
Manuscript "D" (Worcester): Swiss 721 Hv BT.
Manuscript "E" (Peterborough or Laud): Courier New.
Manuscript "F" (Canterbury): Alexa.
Manuscript "H" (Winchester): Calligraphic.

as the "Anti Pope", his election was considered irregular as his votes had been bought) who sends the pallium (vestment of office, a cloak) to Archbishop Stigand of Canterbury. Archbishop Stigand consecrates/ **Aethelric (a monk from Christ Church Priory, Canterbury) Bishop of Sussex and Abbot Siward (formerly Abbot of Chertsey Abbey, Surrey) is consecrated Bishop of Rochester, Kent.**

Manuscript F of the Chronicle ends in 1058.

1059 – Pope Benedict X (see 1058 above) is expelled from office and replaced by Nicholas II, the former Bishop of Florence in Italy. On 17 October the tower at Peterborough (on the site of the present Cathedral) is consecrated.

1060 – On the 4 July there is a great earthquake (no details provided as to where or how extensive). King Henry I of France dies. Archbishop Cynesige of York dies on 22 December and is buried at Peterborough; he is succeeded by Bishop Ealdred of Worcester. Walter (chaplain to Queen Edith, wife of King Edward the Confessor of England) becomes Bishop of Hereford. Bishop Duduc of Wells, Somerset dies and is succeeded by Giso the priest (chaplain to King Edward, notorious for acquiring land in his diocese.) (Manuscript E attributes this event to **1061**).

1061 – Archbishop Ealdred of York goes to Rome, Italy and receives his pallium (vestment of office, a cloak) from Pope Nicholas II. He travels with Earl Tostig of Northumbria and his wife Judith (daughter of Count Baldwin IV of Flanders and aunt of Matilda wife of Duke William of Normandy). On their return journey both the Archbishop and the earl suffer hardship (no further information readily available). Bishop Godwine of Saint Martin's, Canterbury, dies on 9 March **and Abbot Wulfric of Saint Augustine's Abbey, Canterbury, dies** on 18 April. **On 19 March Pope Nicholas II dies and is succeeded by Alexander II, Bishop of Lucca in Italy.** On hearing of the death of Abbot Wulfric of St Augustine's Abbey, Canterbury, King Edward the Confessor of England appoints Aethelsige, a monk from the Old Minster in Winchester, Hampshire in his place as Archbishop Stigand of Canterbury wanted. On 26 May Aethelsige is consecrated Abbot at Windsor, Berkshire.

1063 – After Christmas (1062) Earl Harold of Wessex marches from Gloucester and burns the ships and residence of King Gruffydd ap Llywelyn of Gwynedd (the scribe describes him as "king over the whole of Wales") at Rhuddlan in Denbighshire; and defeats the Welsh. Around Rogationtide (end of April) Earl Harold sails from Bristol, Gloucestershire and he and his fleet sail around Wales. The Welsh make peace with him and provide hostages (no further information provided). Meanwhile Earl Tostig of Northumbria marches into Wales with land levies. On 5 August King Gruffydd is killed by his own men. King Gruffydd's head is taken to Earl Harold who then takes it, the figure-head of King Gruffydd's ship, and "the adornments with it (no further

Manuscript "A" (Winchester or Parker): Trebuchet.
Manuscript "C" (Abingdon II): 18thCentury.
Manuscript "D" (Worcester): Swiss 721 Hv BT.
Manuscript "E" (Peterborough or Laud): Courier New.
Manuscript "F" (Canterbury): Alexa.
Manuscript "H" (Winchester): Calligraphic.

details provided) to King Edward the Confessor of England. King Edward appoints two brothers of King Gruffydd, Bleddyn and Rhiwallon, to rule Wales. These two brothers give hostages to both King Edward and Earl Harold and swear oaths of loyalty to the king; they agree to provide the same tribute to King Edward as they had done to King Gruffydd.

1065 – Before 1 August Earl Harold of Wessex gathers his wealth in Wales and starts to build a residence at Portskewett, Monmouthshire in Wales; he proposes to invite King Edward the Confessor of England to visit for the hunting. Caradog, son of King Gruffydd ap Llywelyn of Gwynedd, gathers as large a force as he can. On the 24 August Caradog attacks and kills most of the workforce at Portskewett when building is nearly complete; he takes away all the portable possessions he can. All the Yorkshire **and Northumberland** thanes meet in York **and outlaw Earl Tostig of Northumbria**. They kill all the housecarles/**all the retainers whether English or Dane**, of Earl Tostig who they can find and seize all his **stock of weapons, his gold and silver and** treasure **they can find** in York. The Northumbrians appoint Morcar, son of Earl Aelfgar of Mercia, as their Earl **who marches south with all the men of Yorkshire together with the men from Nottinghamshire, Derbyshire and Lincolnshire. At Northampton he is joined by his brother Earl Edwin of Mercia with the men from his earldom and many Welshmen**. Whilst this is happening Earl Tostig is with King Edward at Britford in Wiltshire. Very soon thereafter a great council is held at Northampton **where Earl Harold meets the Northumbrians and Mercians who ask him to request King Edward appoint Morcar as their earl; they send messengers to accompany Earl Harold on this mission.** Another great council is held at Oxford (on 25 September). Earl Harold tries to get an agreement but fails. All the men in Earl Tostig's earldom want him removed; they outlaw him and all his followers who they accuse of promoting injustice through robbing the Church and ruining the lives of his people and their property. **King Edward agrees to the Northumbrian's requests and sends Earl Harold to Northampton to inform them accordingly; which he does on the 27 October. In addition King Edward agrees to re-enact the laws of King Cnut of England, Denmark and Norway. Whilst waiting for the return of Earl Harold the northerners do much damage around Northampton, killing men, burning houses and corn, and seizing thousands of livestock and taking hundreds of captives when they return home; Northamptonshire and other neighbouring shires are the poorer for many years as a result.** Earl Tostig and his wife Judith **and all his supporters** flee to the court of Count Baldwin V of Flanders (her half brother) at Saint Omer in France where they stay over the winter. At Christmas King Edward goes to Westminster, London, and has the abbey church of Saint Peter (Westminster Abbey) consecrated on 28 December.

1066 – King Edward the Confessor of England dies and is buried in the Abbey Church of Saint Peter's, Westminster, London on 6 January. (There then follows a eulogy to King Edward.) Earl Harold of Wessex becomes King and is consecrated King of England (on 6 January; it is likely that Archbishop Ealdred of York crowned Harold king, and not Archbishop Stigand of Canterbury) "as the king granted it to him and as he was elected thereto" and rules for forty weeks and a day, but was not to "enjoy a tranquil reign". In this year Duke William of Normandy conquers England.

King Harold II of England travels from York to Westminster, London and arrives for Easter on 16 April. On 18/24 April a comet appears, and every night for a week, the "long-haired star" is seen (Halley's Comet as depicted in the Bayeux Tapestry) throughout England "a portent such as men had never seen before". Soon

---

Manuscript "A" (Winchester or Parker): Trebuchet.

Manuscript "C" (Abingdon II): 18thCentury.

Manuscript "D" (Worcester): Swiss 721 Hv BT.

Manuscript "E" (Peterborough or Laud): Courier New.

Manuscript "H" (Winchester): Calligraphic.

afterwards Earl Tostig, former Earl of Northumbria, with as many of his household troops as he can muster, raids the Isle of Wight where he receives money and provisions. He raids along the south coast up to Sandwich in Kent. When King Harold hears of this he gathers the largest naval and land levies ever known in England and heads for Sandwich. The King had been "credibly" informed that Duke William/**William the Bastard** was about to invade England. When Earl Tostig hears of his brothers intent he leaves Sandwich taking with him both willing and unwilling sailors from the town. He sails north raiding and sailing on to the River Humber (separating Yorkshire from Lincolnshire) **with sixty ships** where he raids Lindsey (Lincolnshire) killing many men. He is forced to flee by the forces of Earl Edwin of Mercia and Earl Morcar of Northumbria (Tostig's replacement as earl) **and the shipmen desert him**. Earl Tostig sails **with twelve small vessels** to Scotland: where King Malcolm III of Scotland offers him protection and provides him with provisions; he stays in Scotland all summer **where he is met by King Harald III of Norway with three hundred ships. Together they sail to the River Humber and then to York. (Both Manuscripts D and** E **record this sequence of events.)**

Meanwhile King Harold II of England arrives in Sandwich and waits for his household troops to gather; their mobilisation takes a "long time". When they assemble he sails to the Isle of Wight and waits there all summer and autumn; he stations his levies "everywhere" along the south coast "although in the end it was all to no purpose". King Harold "sailed out against William with a naval force". On 8 September provisions run out and consequently the levies are given permission to return home. King Harold rides to London and his ships sail to London although many are lost before they arrive.

Whilst King Harold is in London, King Harald III of Norway sails into the River Tyne (Tyne and Wear, bordering Northumberland and County Durham) with a fleet of 300 ships and, as had previously been agreed (no further information given, but according to King Harald's Saga Tostig had visited Norway and persuaded King Harald to invade England) he is joined by Earl Tostig with as many forces he can muster. The combined forces of King Harald and Earl Tostig sail up the River Ouse in Yorkshire where they land near York (at Riccall, Yorkshire, where they leave their ships). Meanwhile King Harold II of England is informed of these events when he comes ashore from his ships at London. King Harold then marches north by day and night as quickly as he can assemble his levies.

Before King Harold II of England arrives, Earl Edwin of Mercia and Earl Morcar of Northumbria assemble as great a force they can from their earldoms and fight the combined forces of Earl Tostig and King Harald III of Norway on Wednesday 20 September (at Fulford, on the outskirts of York). Although a great number of Norwegians are killed in the battle King Harald III of Norway and Earl Tostig are victorious. Many of the English are killed in battle or drown, others flee. Afterwards King Harald III of Norway and Earl Tostig enter York with "as great a force as to them seemed necessary"; they receive hostages and provisions. They offer the citizens of York "abiding peace" provided they all march south with them to conquer England.

King Harold II of England arrives with all his levies at Tadcaster in Yorkshire on Sunday 24 September, and draws up his household troops in battle order. On Monday 25 September King Harold II of England marches through York. King Harald III of Norway and Earl Tostig meanwhile leave their ships at Riccall in North Yorkshire and base themselves at Stamford Bridge, east of York, awaiting the promised hostages from York. At Stamford Bridge, King Harold II of England comes upon them "unawares beyond the bridge". The ensuing battle is fierce and lasts until late in the day; King Harald III of Norway and Earl Tostig are killed with "countless" men on both sides – English and Norwegian. **The English pursue the Norwegians until they reach their**

Manuscript "A" (Winchester or Parker): Trebuchet.

Manuscript "C" (Abingdon II): 18thCentury.

Manuscript "D" (Worcester): Swiss 721 Hv BT.

Manuscript "E" (Peterborough or Laud): Courier New.

Manuscript "H" (Winchester): Calligraphic.

ships; some Norwegians are drowned some are burnt to death; there are few survivors.

Manuscript C ends in 1066.

(Manuscript C ends in 1066 with the incomplete reference to the Battle of Stamford Bridge. It ends with the words "The Norwegians". A twelfth century scribe then adds the twelfth century Icelandic saga writer Snorri Sturluson story about the lone Norwegian on the bridge and King Harold II of England allowing King Harald III's son Olaf to return to Norway.)

King Harold gives quarter to Olaf, son of King Harald of Norway, "to their bishop" (no further information readily available), and to the Jarl of Orkney (Paul Thorfinnsson and Erlend Thorfinnsson ruled together as Jarls/Earls of Orkney) provided they maintain peace with England – King Harold allows them and their surviving men to board the twenty-four ships needed to take them home. The two pitched battles of Fulford and Stamford Bridge were fought within five days.

Duke William sails from Normandy into Pevensey in Sussex on 28 September (Manuscript E says he landed at Hastings in Sussex on 29 September) **and constructs a castle at Hastings as soon as his men are fit for service. On hearing this news King Harold marches south and assembles his forces at "the grey apple-tree". On 14 October William comes upon King Harold "unexpectedly" before his army is ready. Many are killed on both sides including King Harold, his brothers Earl Leofwine (Earl of Kent, Essex, Middlesex, Hertford, Surrey and probably Buckinghamshire) and Earl Gurth (Earl of East Anglia, Cambridgeshire and Oxfordshire) and many good men. "The French had possession of the place of slaughter, as God granted them because of the nation's sins."**

Archbishop Ealdred of York and the citizens of London wish to have Prince Edgar (the aetheling, a male of royal blood, the heir apparent, great nephew of King Edward the Confessor of England) as king as is his birthright; Earl Edwin and Earl Morcar promise to fight for him. However, whenever "some initiative should have been shown there was delay from day to day until matters went from bad to worse, as everything did in the end." Duke William returns to Hastings to await surrender. No surrender occurs and so with the remains of his host and some reinforcements he marches inland to Berkhamsted, Hertfordshire ravaging the countryside on the way. There he is met by Archbishop Ealdred, Prince Edgar, Earls Edwin and Morcar and the best men of London who submit to him "from force of circumstances, but only when the depredation was complete". (The scribe in Manuscript D comments) "It was great folly that they had not done so (submit) sooner when God would not remedy matters because of our sins." William promises to be a "gracious lord" but his forces harry everywhere they go.

Christ Church Canterbury is burnt **down on 6 December (Manuscripts D and E attribute this to 1067).**

Manuscript "A" (Winchester or Parker): Trebuchet.
Manuscript "C" (Abingdon II): 18thCentury.
Manuscript "D" (Worcester): Swiss 721 Hv BT.
Manuscript "E" (Peterborough or Laud): Courier New.
Manuscript "H" (Winchester): Calligraphic.

On Christmas Day William is crowned king in Westminster by Archbishop Ealdred and agrees to govern according to the best practices of his predecessors if the English would be loyal to him. Men pay King William tribute and give him hostages and redeem their lands from him. **King William imposes a very heavy tax on the country.**

(The remaining text for this entry from Manuscript E is thought to have been added sometime onwards from the early twelfth century.)

"Leofric, abbot of Peterborough, took part in this campaign, and there fell ill and returned home; he died soon afterwards on the eve of All Saints" (31 October). Leofric was the nephew of Earl Leofric of Coventry (Lady Godiva was his aunt). King Edward the Confessor of England had given to him the monastery of Peterborough, the abbacies which Earl Leofric had founded at Burton-on-Trent, Staffordshire, and Coventry, Warwickshire and the abbeys of Crowland, Lincolnshire and Thorney, Cambridgeshire. "More than any man before or since he enriched the abbey of Peterborough with gold and silver, with vestments and land. Then "Golden Borough" (see **1052** above) became the "Wretched Borough". The monks chose Brand the provost to succeed Leofric as abbot and sent him to Prince Edgar "because the people of that district thought he ought to be king", who consented to Brand's appointment. When King William hears of this he becomes angry but is reconciled by the intervention of good men (no further information readily available) and the payment by Brand of forty marks of gold. Abbot Brand lives for three years after his appointment, "Thereafter all manner of calamities and evils befell the monastery".

1067 – In the spring King William I of England, Duke of Normandy takes with him to Normandy Archbishop Stigand of Canterbury, Abbot Aethelnoth of Glastonbury in Somerset, Prince Edgar (the aetheling – a male of royal blood, the heir apparent – great nephew of King Edward the Confessor of England), Earl Edwin of Mercia, Earl Morcar of Northumbria, Earl Waltheof of Northamptonshire and Huntingdonshire, and many others (no further information provided). Bishop Odo of Bayeux in Normandy and Earl William of Hereford were left in charge in England and "built castles far and wide throughout the land, oppressing the unhappy people, and things went from bad to worse". King William returns to England on 6 December "he gave away every man's land". **Bishop Wulfwig dies and is buried at his Episcopal see at Dorchester-on-Thames in Oxfordshire.**

Eadric the Wild (a Herefordshire thane who might have been "Edric the Steersman", Bishop Wulfstan of Worcester's former military commander. He was also known as "the Forester", "the Outlaw", "Silvaticus (Salvagius)" and "Salvage"(in French); surnamed "the Woodsman") and the Welsh (no further information readily available) attack the Norman garrison at Hereford castle and cause many casualties.

Manuscript "A" (Winchester or Parker): Trebuchet.
Manuscript "D" (Worcester): Swiss 721 Hv BT.
Manuscript "E" (Peterborough or Laud): Courier New.
Manuscript "H" (Winchester): Calligraphic.

King William imposes a "heavy tax upon the unhappy people of the country", notwithstanding this he allows his men to "harry wherever they came". King William marches into Devonshire and besieges Exeter (Gytha, mother of King Harold II of England, is in the city) for eighteen days which surrenders because the thanes desert the town. Although a great part of his host is destroyed King William makes promises to the citizens which are "badly kept".

In the summer Prince Edgar, his mother Agatha and his sisters Margaret and Christina, and Maerleswin (no further information readily available) and his followers go to Scotland and take refuge with King Malcolm III of Scotland. King Malcolm wishes to marry Prince Edgar's sister Margaret but both Prince Edgar and his men oppose this as does Margaret herself who prefers to go to a nunnery. Eventually Prince Edgar gives way to the demands of King Malcolm and agrees to the marriage, "he dared not do otherwise". (In 1070) Margaret marries King Malcolm "against her will" (this information is included in the entry for 1067).

Gytha, mother of King Harold II of England, and the wives of other men stay on the island of Flatholm in the Bristol Channel for some while and then go to Saint Omer in France.

1068 – On 23 March, at Easter, King William I of England, Duke of Normandy, goes to Winchester in Hampshire. Matilda of Flanders, wife of King William, comes to England and is consecrated queen by Archbishop Ealdred of York at Westminster in London on Whit Sunday.

King William hears that the people of the north are in revolt. He marches north building castles at Nottingham, Lincoln and two in York, and in many other places in that part of the country (no further information readily available). Earl Gospatric of Northumbria and the "best men" go to Scotland (no further information readily available).

Godwin and Edmund, the sons of King Harold II of England, come unexpectedly with a pirate host from Ireland. They sail into the mouth of the River Avon in Somerset plundering the surrounding countryside. They attempt to capture Bristol, Gloucestershire but the citizens resist them. They sail to Somerset where Eadnoth, the Staller (someone with duties in the royal court), with the men of Somerset oppose them; Eadnoth is killed along with many men on both sides. King Harold's sons return to Ireland.

King William appoints Robert, Earl of Northumberland.

1069 – Inside the borough of Durham, Earl Robert of Northumberland and nine hundred of his men are killed in a local uprising. Immediately Prince Edgar (the aetheling, a male of royal blood, the heir apparent, great nephew of King Edward the Confessor of England), with the Northumbrians go to York where the citizens come to terms with him. Unexpectedly King William arrives from the south with an

Manuscript "A" (Winchester or Parker): Trebuchet.
Manuscript "D" (Worcester): Swiss 721 Hv BT.
Manuscript "E" (Peterborough or Laud): Courier New.
Manuscript "H" (Winchester): Calligraphic.

overwhelming force and routs the Northumbrians; he kills several hundred who could not escape. He plunders York and makes St Peter's Church (present day York Minster) "an object of scorn" (no further information readily available). He plunders and humiliates all others. Prince Edgar returns to Scotland.

Godwin and Edmund, the sons of King Harold II of England, come from Ireland to the mouth of the River Taw in Devon. Earl Brian (no further information readily available) with a considerable force surprises them killing many of their best troops, a few survivors escape to their ships. Godwin and Edmund return again to Ireland.

On 11 September Archbishop Ealdred of York dies and is buried at York.

Between 15 August and 8 September, **three sons of King Swein (Sweyn II Estridsson) of Denmark and Jarl Osbern** his brother, **with Jarl Thurkill come from Denmark with two hundred and forty**/three hundred **ships to the River Humber separating Yorkshire from Lincolnshire. The Danes are joined ashore by Prince Edgar, Earl Waltheof of Northamptonshire and Huntingdonshire, Maerleswein (no further information readily available), Earl Gospatric of Northumbria with the Northumbrians and all the people of the country**/many hundreds of men join these troops **march on York. Before they arrive, the Frenchmen burn York to the ground including St Peter's Church (present day York Minster). The Northumbrians and Danes take York, destroy the castle, kill many hundreds of Frenchmen, seize innumerable treasures and prisoners** from the leading citizens of York **and take them to their ships. The Danes stay with their ships all winter in the River Humber,** between its confluence with the River Ouse, Yorkshire and its confluence with the River Trent, Lincolnshire **where King William cannot reach them. When King William learns of this he musters as many levies as he can and marches northwards plundering and laying waste Yorkshire. King William stays in York at Christmas and stays in the north all winter returning to Winchester in Hampshire for Easter 1070.**

On 27 November Abbot Brand of Peterborough dies (see **1066** above).

Bishop Aethelric (formerly Bishop of Durham who had resigned his see and retired to Peterborough Abbey where he had been a monk) is accused (allegedly he had appropriated a treasure hoard discovered when replacing the existing church at Chester-le-Street in County Durham) and taken to Westminster in London along with his (successor and) brother Bishop Aethelwine of Durham; both are outlawed (allegedly he had helped his brother appropriate the treasure; Aethelwine also tried to flee to the Holy Island of Lindisfarne in Northumberland with Northumbrian treasures including the body of Saint Cuthbert during the "Harrying of the North".)

1070 – Abbot Lanfranc of Caen in Normandy comes to England and in a few days is appointed Archbishop of Canterbury; he is consecrated on 29 August by eight (no further information readily available) of his suffragans (those bishops he can summon to assist); those suffragans not present explain the reasons for their absence by letter or messenger. Thomas of Bayeux

---

Manuscript "A" (Winchester or Parker): Trebuchet.
Manuscript "D" (Worcester): Swiss 721 Hv BT.
Manuscript "E" (Peterborough or Laud): Courier New.
Manuscript "H" (Winchester): Calligraphic.

in France who had been elected Archbishop of York comes to Canterbury to be consecrated. Archbishop Lanfranc demands that Archbishop Thomas swear obedience to him, this Thomas refuses on the basis that he was under no obligation to give it. Archbishop Lanfranc becomes "very angry" and the service is abandoned without Archbishop Thomas being consecrated. Archbishop Lanfranc and Archbishop Thomas go to Rome together and they present their case to Pope Alexander and the whole council; Archbishop Lanfranc gets his way. On their return Archbishop Thomas goes to Canterbury swears his allegiance and is consecrated.

Manuscript A of the Chronicle ends in 1070.

(Manuscript A of the Chronicle ends in 1070 with an account in Latin about Archbishop Lanfranc of Canterbury and the consecration of his successor Archbishop Anselm.)

Earl Waltheof of Northamptonshire and Huntingdonshire makes peace with King William I of England, Duke of Normandy. King William plunders all the monasteries in England. There is a great famine.

King Swein (Sweyn II Estridsson) of Denmark sails into the River Humber separating Yorkshire from Lincolnshire and the people of the surrounding countryside submit to him "thinking that he was sure to conquer the whole country". The Danish Bishop Christian (no further information readily available), Jarl Osbern (brother of King Sweyn II) and Danish housecarles go to Ely in Cambridgeshire and are joined by all the Englishmen in the fenlands "thinking they were sure to conquer the whole land". The monks at Peterborough heard it said that their own men "namely Hereward and his band" wished to plunder their monastery because they had heard that King William had given the abbacy of Peterborough to a French Abbot Turold of Malmesbury, Wiltshire, "a very ferocious man" who had arrived at Stamford, Lincolnshire with all his French followers. Yware, the monastic sacristan (the custodian of vestments, sacred vessels and other valuable property), acting on the advice of the monks, one night stole all he could including gospels, chasubles, copes, and albs and "immediately before dawn" took them to Abbot Turold seeking his protection and informing him that the outlaws intended to go to Peterborough.

The monastery at Peterborough is plundered. In the morning all the outlaws (presumably both the Danes and Hereward and his band) came in many boats intending to enter the monastery at Peterborough, but the monks resisted and so the outlaws burn down all the monastic buildings and the entire town except for one house. Through the use of fire the outlaws force an entrance at "Bolhithe Gate" (near the east end of the abbey), the monks request they be spared but are ignored. The outlaws climb "up to the holy cross and took the diadem all of pure gold from our Lord's head, then took the foot-support made entirely of

Manuscript "A" (Winchester or Parker): Trebuchet.
Manuscript "D" (Worcester): Swiss 721 Hv BT.
Manuscript "E" (Peterborough or Laud): Courier New.
Manuscript "H" (Winchester): Calligraphic.

red gold which was underneath His feet. They climbed up to the tower, and brought down the altar frontal made entirely of gold and silver that was hidden there. They seized there two golden and nine silver shrines, and fifteen great crosses made both of gold and silver. It is impossible for anyone to estimate how much gold and silver they took from there and what riches, whether in money, vestments, or books." The outlaws said that they took this action out of loyalty to the monastery; they then return to their ships and go to Ely where they hand over all the treasures. The Danes then decide that they can defeat the French so they expel all the monks apart from one Leofwine the Tall who lies sick in the infirmary. On 2 June Abbot Turold arrives at Peterborough with one hundred and sixty full armed Frenchmen and finds the monastic buildings are all destroyed by fire apart from the church but by this time the outlaws are on their ships.

King William and King Swein come to terms and the Danes leave Ely taking with them all the treasures they had stolen from Peterborough. Whilst at sea on the way to Norway, Denmark and Ireland a great storm occurs scattering the Danish ships with the treasure (from Peterborough). In Denmark the altar-frontal, some shrines and crosses and many of the other treasures are taken to a royal manor (there is a space in the manuscript for the place to be identified) and placed in a church. However, one night through carelessness or drunkenness this church is burnt down consuming all the treasures it contained. Divine services resume at Peterborough after a gap of a week. When Bishop Aethelric (formerly Bishop of Durham who had resigned his see and retired to Peterborough Abbey where he had been a monk) hears of these events he excommunicates all those involved. **(Manuscript D refers to the Bishop having excommunicated these men earlier "because they had carried off everything he possessed".)**

In the summer the Danes sail from the River Humber **into the River Thames and stay for two days before returning to Denmark. Count Baldwin VI of Flanders dies and is succeeded by his son Arnulf III; King Philip I of France and Earl William FitzOsbern of Hereford are appointed his guardians. Robert (Curthose, eldest son of King William I of England, Duke of Normandy) goes to Flanders and at the battle of Cassel in Flanders kills his nephew Count Arnulf III and Earl William FitzOsbern of Hereford, and defeats the army of King Philip I of France killing many thousands of his men.**

1071 – Earl Edwin of Mercia and Earl Morcar of Northumbria flee across country and through woodland until Earl Edwin is killed/"basely slain" **by his own men; Earl Morcar goes by ship to Ely in Cambridgeshire as do Bishop Aethelwine of Durham and Siward Barn (a northern thane and landowner) and many hundreds of men with them. King William I of England, Duke of Normandy, orders out naval and land levies who surround the district, builds a causeway/**building a causeway as he advanced deeper into the fens **and conducts naval patrols out to sea. Ely**

Manuscript "D" (Worcester): Swiss 721 Hv BT.
Manuscript "E" (Peterborough or Laud): Courier New.
Manuscript "H" (Winchester): Calligraphic.

surrenders including Bishop Aethelwine and Earl Morcar and all their followers. Hereward (the Outlaw, or the Exile, often referred to as "Hereward the Wake") "courageously" leads the escape of his followers. King William seizes the English ships, treasure and weapons and deals with those he captures as he pleases; he sends Bishop Aethelwine to Abingdon in Oxfordshire where the bishop dies in the winter time.

1072 – King William I of England, Duke of Normandy, leads naval and land levies against Scotland and blockades the country. King William leads his forces over the River Forth but gains no advantage. King Malcolm III of Scotland makes peace with King William and becomes his vassal and gives him hostages (no further information readily available). King William returns home with all his levies. Bishop Aethelric dies (former Bishop of Durham – see 1069 above). (The scribe in Manuscript D comments) that although Aethelric had been consecrated Archbishop of York, he was unjustly deprived of his see and given the bishopric of Durham which he held for as long as he wished. Aethelric then resigned to retire to St Peter's Church, Peterborough Abbey, where he lived as a monk for twelve years before King William has him taken to Westminster in London where he dies in captivity on 15 October; he is buried in the chapel of St Nicholas in Westminster Abbey in London.

1073 – King William I of England, Duke of Normandy leads English and French levies overseas and conquers the French province of Maine. "The English laid it completely waste; they destroyed the vineyards, burnt down the towns, and completely devastated the countryside, and brought it all into subjection to the king". They then return home.

1074 – King William I of England, Duke of Normandy goes to Normandy in France. On 8 July Prince Edgar the aetheling, (a male of royal blood, the heir apparent, great nephew of King Edward the Confessor of England) travels from Flanders to Scotland where he is received in great ceremony (no location is indicated) by his sister Queen Margaret of Scotland and her husband King Malcolm III of Scotland. At this "ceremony" King Philip I of France sends a letter inviting Prince Edgar to come to France where he will give him the castle of Montreuil (Montreuil-Bellay), in France so that he can "daily work mischief" on his enemies. King Malcolm and Queen Margaret give Prince Edgar and all his men great gifts and precious things: "skins covered with rich purple cloth, pelisses of marten-skin, miniver and ermine, robes of costly purple, and golden and silver vessels". Prince Edgar and his sailors set out from Scotland "in great state". Whilst at sea very rough weather occurs; raging seas and violent gales. All their ships are driven ashore (on the French coastline) and smashed to pieces and almost all their treasures are lost. Some of Prince Edgar's men are seized by the French but Prince Edgar and those of his men who are able return to Scotland, "some pitiably walking on foot, others wretchedly mounted". King Malcolm advises Prince Edgar to make his peace with King William; this Prince Edgar does. King Malcolm and Queen Margaret again give "countless treasure" to Prince Edgar and his men and once more they set out from Scotland "in great state" to meet King William. The sheriff of York (Hugh, son of Baldic) meets Prince Edgar at Durham and accompanies him, arranging food and

---

Manuscript "D" (Worcester): Swiss 721 Hv BT.
Manuscript "E" (Peterborough or Laud): Courier New.
Manuscript "H" (Winchester): Calligraphic.

fodder at each castle on the way until they go to King William in Normandy. **King William receives Prince Edgar with great ceremony** and revokes the sentence of outlawry against the Prince and all his men; **Prince Edgar stays at the king's court and accepts the privileges (no further information readily available) granted to him.**

1075 – King William I of England, Duke of Normandy, gives in marriage Emma the daughter of the late Earl William FitzOsbern of Hereford to Ralph who was born in Norfolk; his mother was a Breton and his father was English. On account of his parents and birth King William makes Ralph Earl of Norfolk and Suffolk. Earl Ralph and his wife Emma go to Norwich in Norfolk. Earl Roger of Shrewsbury, Shropshire and Earl Waltheof of Northamptonshire and Huntingdonshire, as well as bishops and abbots (no further information readily available) attend the wedding (at Norwich) where they plot to overthrow King William.

King William becomes aware of this plot whilst in Normandy. Earl Ralph and Earl Roger are identified as the leaders of this "foolish" **plot. They obtain the support of the Bretons and send to Denmark for a pirate host. Both Earl Ralph and Earl Roger go to their respective earldoms where they gather their supporters. Earl Ralph takes to the field but the garrisons of the Norman castles together with the inhabitants of the country oppose and hinder him so he achieves nothing and is glad to escape to his ships. His wife remains in Norwich Castle in Norfolk until she makes terms (no further information readily available) and leaves England with all her followers who wish to accompany her. King William returns to England and has Earl Roger imprisoned. Earl Waltheof of Northamptonshire and Huntingdonshire goes overseas (no further information readily available) and confesses to his "treachery"; he asks for pardon and offers treasures in return. King William makes light of Earl Waltheof's offence until he returns to England; Waltheof is then imprisoned.**

Two hundred ships from Denmark commanded by Cnut, son of King Swein II of Denmark, and Jarl Hakon (no further information readily available) arrive in English waters – they "durst not join battle with King William" but instead go to Flanders/ **sack York, including St Peter's Church (present day York Minster) but Jarl Hakon and all others who take part die (no further information readily available).**

Seven days before Christmas Queen Edith, wife of King Edward the Confessor of England, dies and is buried at Westminster Abbey beside him. King William spends Christmas at Westminster in London and decides the punishment for all the Bretons (the plotters) who attended the wedding of Emma and Earl Ralph of Norfolk and Suffolk. Some he has blinded, others are banished.

1076 – King Swein (Sweyn II Estridsson) of Denmark dies and is succeeded by his son Harald. King William I of England, Duke of Normandy, appoints the monk Vitalis (the former Abbot of Bernay in France) as Abbot of Westminster in London. On 31 May Earl Waltheof of Northamptonshire and Huntingdonshire is beheaded at Winchester in Hampshire and is buried at Crowland Abbey in Lincolnshire.

Manuscript "D" (Worcester): Swiss 721 Hv BT.
Manuscript "E" (Peterborough or Laud): Courier New.
Manuscript "H" (Winchester): Calligraphic.

King William leads his levies in Brittany in France and besieges the castle at Dôl where the garrison hold out until relieved by King Philip I of France. King William retreats and loses men, horses and countless treasure.

1077 – King William I of England, Duke of Normandy, and King Philip I of France come to an agreement (no further information readily available) but it is short-lived. On 13 August London suffers fire damage which is more extensive than ever before.

1078 – **Three days before 30 January there is an eclipse of the moon. On 16 February Abbot Aethelwig of Evesham in Worcestershire, "who was wise in secular affairs", dies; he is succeeded by Walter (the first Norman abbot).** On 20 February **Bishop Hereman of Berkshire, Wiltshire and Dorset (Bishop of Sherborne, Dorset) dies.**

King Malcolm III of Scotland captures the mother (no further information readily available) of Maelslaehta (son of King Lulach of Moray) and all his best men, livestock and treasures. Maelslaehta himself only escapes with difficulty. (This entry is incomplete as there are blank lines on the original manuscript.)

A dry summer with wildfire spreading into many shires burning down both villages and boroughs (no further information readily available).

1079 – Between 15 August and 8 September, King Malcolm III of Scotland with great levies plunders Northumbria as far south as the River Tyne, killing hundreds, taking home much money and treasure and captives.

Robert Curthose (Duke Robert II), the eldest son of King William I of England, flees from his father because he would not let him govern his earldom (dukedom). King William had given Robert his dukedom of Normandy with the consent of King Philip I of France; the leading men of the country had sworn oaths to Robert and accepted him as their lord. Duke Robert goes to Flanders to his maternal uncle Count Robert I of Flanders. Duke Robert and King William gather their forces and a battle ensues near the castle of Gerberoy in Normandy. **Duke Robert wounds his father in the hand; King William's horse is killed under him. Toki, son of Wigod, who brings up a replacement horse for King William which is immediately killed by a bolt from a crossbow.** William (William Rufus, the future King William II of England) is wounded. **Many at this battle are killed or taken prisoner. Duke Robert returns to Flanders. (The scribe in Manuscript D then comments) "We do not wish, however, to chronicle here more of the harm which he (did to) his father".**

1080 – In May Bishop Walcher of Durham a native of Lorraine in France, and a hundred French and Flemings with him are killed by the Northumbrians (after failing to bring to justice the murderers of the Saxon nobleman Ligulf, Bishop Walcher and his men are killed outside St Mary's Church, now Gateshead Heritage(Visitor) Centre, Gateshead, Tyne and Wear.)

Manuscript "D" (Worcester): Swiss 721 Hv BT.
Manuscript "E" (Peterborough or Laud): Courier New.
Manuscript "H" (Winchester): Calligraphic.

Angus, Earl of Moray, is killed by an army of the Scots and in the battle there is great slaughter. (The scribe in Manuscript D then comments) "God's justice was vindicated by his death, because he was utterly foresworn".

Manuscript D of the Chronicle ends in 1080.

(Manuscript D of the Chronicle ends in 1080. For reasons of palaeography and spelling it is considered that the entry included in 1080 was added much later. The events relate to 1130.)

1081 – King William I of England leads his levies into Wales and frees many hundreds of captives (no further information readily available).

1082 – King William I of England has Bishop Odo of Bayeux in Normandy arrested (for planning a military campaign in Italy, possibly to make himself Pope. He loses his English estates and is removed as Earl of Kent but he is not deposed as Bishop of Bayeux.) There is a great famine (no further information readily available).

1083 – Abbot Thurstan of Glastonbury Abbey, Somerset sends armed Frenchmen to force their way into the monastic church to bring the recalcitrant monks back to his rule (they objected to his insisting that the ceremonies and chants from Dijon in France be substituted for their Gregorian traditions). Arrows are shot into the church and three monks are killed and eighteen wounded. Arrows strike the cross which stands above the altar and blood runs down from the altar on to the steps below and on to the floor. On 2 November Matilda, wife of King William I of England, dies.

After Christmas King William imposes severe taxes on the whole of England amounting to seventy-two pence for every "hide" (the amount of land which could be tilled with one plough in a year to support one family and its dependants) of land.

1084 – On the 19 April Abbot Wulfwold of Chertsey, Surrey, dies.

1085 – It is reported that King Cnut IV of Denmark with the help of Robert I of Flanders – Cnut had married Robert's daughter Adela – intended to conquer England (he was grand nephew of King Cnut of England, Denmark and Norway 1016-1035). When King William I of England hears this he returns from Normandy to England with a vast host greater than ever before of horse and foot from France and Brittany. King William quarters this host throughout the land with each of his vassals providing billets for the numbers that the produce of their estates can support. King William causes much hardship by ordering

---

Manuscript "D" (Worcester): Swiss 721 Hv BT.
Manuscript "E" (Peterborough or Laud): Courier New.
Manuscript "H" (Winchester): Calligraphic.

coastal districts to be laid waste to deprive the enemy of any provisions should they land. When King William discovers the invasion has been postponed he sends half his host home to their own country whilst retaining the other half in England. (King Cnut calls off the invasion because his province of Schleswig is being threatened by the forces of Henry IV the Holy Roman Emperor.)

King William spends Christmas with his councillors at Gloucester holding a court for five days followed by a three-day synod with the Archbishop (presumably Lanfranc of Canterbury rather than Archbishop Thomas I of York?) and the clergy. At this synod three chaplains to the king are elected bishops; Maurice became Bishop of London, William Bishop of Norfolk and Robert Bishop of Cheshire.

King William then has "exhaustive discussions with his council" about "this land, how it was peopled, and with what sort of men". He commissions a survey (which soon becomes known as the "Domesday Book"). He requires his surveyors go into every part of the country in each shire and ascertain the amount and value of the land and its assets (at the time of King Edward the Confessor of England and) at the present time. The information requires, in addition to the king's own holdings, the identity of the landholders, their tenants, the amount of land they own and their livestock (the survey includes how many people occupy the land and whether they are villagers, smallholders, freemen or slaves; the amount of woodland, meadows, animals, fish and ploughs for the land; the number of churches, castles, mills and salt houses). "So very thoroughly did he have the inquiry carried out that there was not a single "hide" (the amount of land which could be tilled with one plough in a year to support one family and its dependants), not one virgate of land, not even – it is shameful to record it, but it did not seem shameful to him to do – not even one ox, nor one cow, nor one pig, which escaped notice in his survey." When the surveyors have completed their task they are to bring back their work to King William.

1086 – King William I of England "wore his crown" and held his court at Winchester, Hampshire at Easter. He then journeys to Westminster in London where his son Henry (later King Henry I of England) is made a knight. King William travels around the country and reaches Salisbury, Wiltshire by 1 August where he is met by his council and all the landowners of any account throughout England; they all swear him oaths of allegiance. He then goes to the Isle of Wight on his way to Normandy. Before leaving England "he did as he was wont, he levied very heavy taxes on his subjects, upon any pretext, whether justly or unjustly."

Prince Edgar (the aetheling, a male of royal blood, the heir apparent, great nephew of King Edward the Confessor of England) leaves the court

Manuscript "E" (Peterborough or Laud): Courier New.
Manuscript "H" (Winchester): Calligraphic.

of King William because "he had little honour from him"; Christina, Prince Edgar's sister, becomes a nun at Romsey in Hampshire.

This year is "very disastrous" because of the weather with pestilence amongst the livestock and corn and fruits "at a standstill"; the thunder and lightning is so violent that many are killed. "Things steadily went from bad to worse for everybody."

1087 – A very "disastrous and pestilential year", diseases, hunger and storms kill hundreds of people. The problems are attributed to the nation's sins. (The scribe in Manuscript E comments) "The king and the leading men were fond, yea, too fond, of avarice: they coveted gold and silver, and did not care how sinfully it was obtained, as long as it came to them."; "the louder the talk of law and justice, the greater the injustices committed". Fires consume much of London, St Paul's and other churches are burnt to the ground. Nearly every other important town in England is also burnt down.

On 15 August King William I of England makes war against "his own lord" King Philip I of France invading France from Normandy. King William's forces kill many men and burn down the town of Mantes in France including the churches; two "holy men" are burnt to death in an anchorite's cell. King William returns to Normandy where he falls sick and suffers "terribly", dying on the 9 September. He is buried at the Abbey of Saint Stephen in Caen which he had founded.

(The scribe then records a lengthy obituary which offers a commentary on King William's character, stratagems and achievements. The scribe) "then we shall write of him as we have known him, who have ourselves seen him and at one time dwelt in his court". King William "was a man of great wisdom and power, and surpassed in honour and in strength all those who had gone before him. Though stern beyond measure to those who opposed his will, he was kind to those good men who loved God". He records the foundation of Battle Abbey in Sussex, the building of a new Canterbury Cathedral, Benedictine monks filling the land and opportunities for anyone regardless of rank to become a monk, the imprisonment of his brother Bishop Odo of Bayeux in Normandy, the "Domesday" survey and the introduction of a "vast deer preserve" and the laws connected with it. He records that King William wore his royal crown as often as he could in England with all the great men of England assembled around him; at Winchester in Hampshire at Easter, at Westminster in London at Whitsun and at Gloucester at Christmas. King William subjugated Wales, Scotland and Maine in France as well as ruling Normandy; (the scribe asserts that) had he lived two more years he would also have subjugated Ireland. "Assuredly in his time men suffered grievous oppression and manifold injuries".

King Cnut IV of Denmark is "basely" killed by his own people in a

Manuscript "E" (Peterborough or Laud): Courier New.
Manuscript "H" (Winchester): Calligraphic.

church (Saint Alban's Priory in Odense in Denmark). In Spain the heathen conquer much of the country but the Christian King Alfonso VI of Spain (self-styled Emperor of Spain) with help and assistance from every Christian country re-conquers the territories seized.

Bishop Stigand of Chichester, Sussex, Abbot Scotland (Scoland) of St Augustine's Abbey in Canterbury, Abbot Aelfsige of Bath in Somerset, Abbot Thurstan of Pershore in Worcestershire, die.

King William's eldest son Robert Curthose becomes (he had already been appointed Duke by his father King William, see **1079** above) Duke of Normandy, (Duke Robert II) and his third son Henry – later Henry I of England – is bequeathed innumerable treasures. His second son becomes King William II of England and is crowned by Archbishop Lanfranc of Canterbury on 26 September at Westminster Abbey in London. After his coronation he goes to Winchester in Hampshire to inspect the treasury and the wealth his father has accumulated. In accordance with his father's wishes and for the benefit of his father's soul, King William distributes money to the monasteries, churches and the poor people in the shires. Before King William I died he commanded that all those in captivity should be freed. King William II goes to London.

1088 – A plot led by Bishop Odo of Bayeux, Bishop Geoffrey (the uncle of Earl Robert of Northumbria), Bishop William of Durham, Earl Roger of Norfolk, with very many others "all Frenchmen" forms to replace William II with Duke Robert II of Normandy. At Easter the plotters lay waste the king's farms and the lands of all those who owe allegiance to him and man and provision their own castles. Bishop Geoffrey and Earl Robert go to Bristol, Gloucestershire and plunder Somerset, including Bath and Gloucestershire including the district of Berkeley Harness. Worcestershire is burnt by the men of Herefordshire, Shropshire and Wales but Worcester itself is saved by the forces of Bishop Wulfstan (the last Anglo-Saxon bishop) of Worcester who kill and capture five hundred men and put the others to flight. The Bishop of Durham does as much damage as he can in the north, Earl Roger of Norfolk acts similarly in the east "no one behaved worse than he" and then returns to his castle in Norwich, Norfolk. Hugh (no further information readily available) does "nothing to improve matters" in Leicestershire or Northampton. Bishop Odo goes to his (former – see **1082** above) earldom of Kent and causes much damage in the county laying waste the lands of both the king and the lands of Archbishop Lanfranc of Canterbury; Odo takes his booty to his castle at Rochester, Kent.

King William II of England requests the assistance of the English, "promising them the best law there had ever been in this land; he prohibited every unjust tax, and granted men their woods and hunting rights; but his promises were short-lived". Despite this the English assist King William and make for Rochester in Kent and Bishop Odo. On

Manuscript "E" (Peterborough or Laud): Courier New.
Manuscript "H" (Winchester): Calligraphic.

the way they capture the castle at Tonbridge, Kent from Bishop Odo's knights who then make their peace with the King. King William too goes to Rochester where he expects to find Bishop Odo but learns he has gone to Pevensey in Sussex. King William and his forces besiege Pevensey Castle for six weeks until the food runs out in the castle forcing Bishop Odo to surrender; he promises to leave England and surrender his castle at Rochester. Within Pevensey Castle there are some "very good knights" including Eustace the Young (no further information readily available) and the three sons of Earl Roger (it is not clear whether this refers to Earl Roger Bigod of Norfolk or Earl Roger Montgomery of Shrewsbury) as well as "all the best born men".

In the meantime, Duke Robert of Normandy assembles a "very great force" and sends some of his men to England ahead of him, but "the Englishmen who guarded the sea captured some of these men and slew them, and drowned more than anyone could reckon".

After his success at Pevensey King William appeals to all in England, to "every honest man, whether French or English, to rally to him, from town and country"; as a result of their help he captures Rochester Castle (despite Bishop Odo agreeing to surrender this castle when he was captured at Pevensey). Bishop Odo and his men go overseas. King William then sends a host to Durham to besiege the castle which Bishop William surrenders; Bishop William then goes to Normandy. Many Frenchmen (no further information readily available) surrender their lands and go overseas. King William rewards those (no further information readily available) faithful to him with lands.

1089 – Archbishop Lanfranc of Canterbury dies. On the 11 August there is a great earthquake "over all" England. "A very backward year for corn and produce of every kind" resulting in the corn being harvested about the 11 November and even later.

1090 – King William II of England considers how he can take vengeance on his brother Duke Robert II of Normandy and deprive him of his dukedom. In Normandy King William takes the castle and harbour of St Valéry, the castle of Aumale, and seizes more castles (no further information readily available), garrisoning them with his knights; his forces despoil the countryside. Duke Robert seeks the assistance of King Philip I of France who comes to Normandy with a great host and helps the Duke besieging a castle (possibly Aumale, it is not specifically identified) held by King William's men. King William then contacts King Philip and either for the "love of him, or on account of his great costly gifts" abandons his vassal Duke Robert and returns to France. Whilst these events are occurring England is "utterly ruined by unjust taxation, and by many other misfortunes".

1091 – (This year begins at Christmas 1090.) King William II of England holds his court at Christmas at Westminster in London. After 2 February he goes to Normandy. King William and Duke Robert II of Normandy are reconciled and agree a treaty which is witnessed by twelve nobles from each side. Under this treaty the Duke surrenders to King William in France, Fécamp, the county of Eu and Cherbourg; he agrees to King William retaining those castles the King had captured. King William agrees to assist Duke Robert in re-conquering the province of Maine which was in revolt; he also agrees to restore lands to Duke Robert's followers in England. They both agree that if either die without an heir the other will inherit their domain.

Prince Edgar (the aetheling, a male of royal blood, the heir apparent, great nephew of King Edward the Confessor of England) loses lands in Normandy because of this treaty. As a result he leaves Normandy and goes to Scotland to his sister Queen Margaret and her husband King Malcolm III of Scotland. Whilst King William is away from England King Malcolm invades. King William and Duke Robert call out their land and sea levies. Despite losing most of their fleet four days before Michaelmas King William and Duke Robert march on Scotland with their land levies. When King Malcolm hears this "he left Scotland and went into Lothian in England with his levies and there waited". Duke Robert and Prince Edgar intervene and peace is agreed between the two kings with King Malcolm swearing an oath of obedience to King William. Prince Edgar is also reconciled with King William. Duke Robert remains in England with King William almost until Christmas discovering there was little good faith in their agreement". Two days before Christmas Duke Robert and Prince Edgar go to the Isle of Wight and then on to Normandy.

1092 – King William II of England goes to Carlisle in Cumbria, restores the town and builds a castle; he drives out Dolfin (son of Earl Gospatrick of Northumbria) who had formerly ruled the district. King William sends "very many" peasants, their families and livestock to settle in the Carlisle area.

1093 – King William II of England is taken seriously ill in March at Gloucester; he is reported dead "everywhere". During his illness he undertakes to lead a righteous life, to protect churches "and never again to sell them for money", and to maintain just laws for his people. He appoints Abbot Anselm of Bec in France as Archbishop of Canterbury and appoints his chancellor Robert as Bishop of Lincoln. He makes grants of lands to many monasteries which he withdraws when he recovers and abolishes "all the good laws he had promised us earlier".

King William summons King Malcolm III of Scotland to him at Gloucester providing him with hostages to ensure his safe return and sends Prince Edgar(the aetheling, a male of royal blood, the heir apparent, great nephew of King Edward the Confessor of England) to him in Scotland.

Manuscript "E" (Peterborough or Laud): Courier New.
Manuscript "H" (Winchester): Calligraphic.

When King Malcolm arrives King William decides not to grant him an audience; the two kings part in "great enmity". King Malcolm returns to Scotland, gathers his levies, and invades England "harrying with great recklessness". Earl Robert of Northumbria and his men surprise King Malcolm; the earl's steward, Morel of Bamburgh in Northumberland, kills the king. King Malcolm's son Edward is also killed. The Scots elect Donald, brother of King Malcolm, king and he evicts all the English who had been with King Malcolm. When King Malcolm's son Duncan, who is a hostage at King William's court, hears of this, he agrees to King William's terms so that he can return to Scotland. With French and English assistance Duncan overthrows Donald and is accepted as king. Soon afterwards some Scots kill most of King Duncan's supporters. On condition that King Duncan doesn't introduce Englishmen or Frenchmen into the country the Scots agree to his retaining the kingship.

1094 – (This year begins at Christmas 1093.) King William II of England holds his court at Gloucester over Christmas. He learns that his brother Duke Robert II of Normandy has renounced the treaty between them agreed in 1091 (see **1091** above). On 2 February King William goes to Hastings in Sussex and whilst waiting for favourable winds to enable his ships to sail, he has Battle Abbey in Sussex consecrated. He also deprives Bishop Herbert Losanga of Thetford in Norfolk of his pastoral staff (no further information readily available. Bishop Herbert moves the cathedral of the diocese to Norwich in Norfolk.)

King William travels to Normandy and meets Duke Robert with the guarantors of the treaty of 1091. King William is blamed for the breach of this treaty but he does not accept the verdict; the two brothers depart with ill-feeling. King William seizes the castle of Bures in Suffolk and takes prisoner some of Duke Robert's men (no further information readily available). In retaliation Duke Robert, with the support of King Philip I of France, takes the castle of Argentan in France and captures Roger of Poitou plus seven hundred of King William's knights who were with him; Duke Robert also captures the castle at Le Houlme in France. Both King William and Duke Robert burn each other's towns and take prisoners.

King William calls up twenty thousand Englishmen to go to his assistance in Normandy. He sends them back after getting them to return "the ten shillings each man had taken with him for the campaign". Duke Robert with the assistance of King Philip go to Eu in France intending to besiege King William who is in residence but when they get to Longueville King Philip has to retire because of "intrigue"; as a result the campaign peters out. King William sends ships for his brother Henry (later Henry I of England) who is in the castle of Domfront in France and Earl Hugh of Chester – they could not travel overland. Instead of joining King William in Eu in France Prince Henry and Earl Hugh sail to England and land at Southampton, Hampshire on

---

Manuscript "E" (Peterborough or Laud): Courier New.
Manuscript "H" (Winchester): Calligraphic.

31 October; at Christmas they are in London.

The Welsh campaign against the Frenchmen who have taken their lands in Wales, destroying castles and killing the garrisons. Earl Hugh of Shropshire defeats some of the Welsh; others continue with their attacks. King Duncan II of Scotland is killed through the betrayal of his paternal uncle Donald who then becomes King Donald III of Scotland.

1095 – (This year begins at Christmas 1094.) For the first four days of Christmas King William II of England is in Wissant in France, he then sails to England and lands at Dover in Kent. King William's brother Henry (later Henry I of England) "with great treasures as the king's deputy" campaigns in Normandy against Duke Robert II of Normandy inflicting severe losses.

During the night of the 3 April many stars are seen falling from heaven almost everywhere in the country.

Earl Robert of Northumbria refuses to attend King William's court at Winchester in Hampshire at Easter on 25 March. He also fails to attend the king's court at Whitsun at Windsor in Berkshire because the King will not guarantee his safety. As a result King William leads the levies into Northumbria and takes Tynemouth Castle, Tyne and Wear, taking prisoner the earl's brother (no further information readily available) and all those with him. King William then goes to besiege Earl Robert in his castle at Bamburgh in Northumberland. When King William sees that he cannot take the castle he orders another castle be built in front of it which he garrisons; this new castle is called "Malueisin" in the king's language and "Evil Neighbour" in English. King William goes south and on learning this Earl Robert sails one night for Tynemouth. But King William's men in the new castle (Malueisin) are forewarned and capture him, wounding him, and capture or kill some of his followers.

King William hears that the Welsh have destroyed the castle at Montgomery in Wales and have killed the garrison of Earl Hugh of Shropshire. He orders up more levies and invades Wales in October dividing his army into a number of detachments which all converge on Snowden in Wales on 1 November. The Welsh evade his army so King William turns homewards because he realises nothing can be done in the winter.

King William has Earl Robert brought to Bamburgh and orders that both his eyes be put out unless the castle surrenders. The castle is garrisoned by Earl Robert's wife Matilda and Morel, his steward and nephew; the castle surrenders. Morel joins King William's retinue and identifies ecclesiastics and laymen who have been involved in the conspiracy against the king. King William issues a proclamation that all those who hold land from the king and wish to have his protection must attend his court at the appointed time. King William retains Earl Robert as a captive in Windsor Castle in Berkshire.

Towards Easter Pope Urban II's legate Bishop Walter from Albano in Italy arrives in England and stays for most of the year. He provides Archbishop Anselm of Canterbury with his pallium (vestment of office, a cloak). On his return to Rome he takes with him "Peter's Pence" (a tribute or "tax" levied on households with a value of thirty pence or over – originally paid to support the School of the English in Rome – see **817** above) which has not been given for many years.

The weather is very unseasonable and consequently the crops are poor throughout the country.

1096 – (This year begins at Christmas 1095.) King William II of England holds his court at Christmas at Windsor in Berkshire. On New Year's Day Bishop William of Durham dies. On 13 January King William and his councillors are in Salisbury, Wiltshire where Geoffrey Bainard, Sheriff of York accuses William of Eu in France, the king's kinsman, of treason; his accusation is "maintained" through his success in trial by combat. The King orders William of Eu's eyes be put and that he be castrated. He also orders the hanging of his steward William the son of his mother's sister (no further information readily available). At Salisbury King William deprives Count Odo of Champagne in France and many others of their lands (no further information readily available), others, (no further information readily available) are taken to London and mutilated.

Pope Urban II launches the "First Crusade"; a "countless number" of people in England and on the Continent wish to take part. As a result King William and Duke Robert II of Normandy are reconciled; King William relinquishes his claim on Normandy on payment of a sum of money (no further information readily available) and Duke Robert then sets out on crusade in the company of Count Robert II of Flanders and Count Eustace III of Boulogne in France. Duke Robert spends the winter in Apulia in Italy; many thousands on crusade who go through Hungary die and many "miserable and hunger-bitten" return on the approach of winter.

A disastrous year in England due to the imposition of numerous taxes and the very serious famine. During the year levies are sent into Wales frequently but they achieve nothing other than losing men and wasting money.

1097 – (This year begins at Christmas 1096.) King William II of England spends Christmas in Normandy in France. He intends to return to Winchester, Hampshire to hold his court at Easter but bad weather delays his return and he lands at Arundel in Sussex and holds his

---

Manuscript "E" (Peterborough or Laud): Courier New.
Manuscript "H" (Winchester): Calligraphic.

court at Windsor in Berkshire. King William, with a great host and with Welsh guides, goes deep into Wales and stays there nearly to August; he suffers great losses in men and horses. The Welsh overthrow their king (no further information readily available) and replace him with Cadwgen (the second son of Bleddyn ap Cynfyn, King of Powys and Gwynedd; his uncle is King Gruffydd ap Cynan of Gwynedd). King William returns and has castles built along the marches between England and Wales.

In the evening of 4 October and for nearly a week a strange comet appears in the south-west of the country with a very long trail of light shining towards the south-east.

Archbishop Anselm of Canterbury receives King William's permission to go overseas, despite the King's displeasure. In the Archbishop's opinion "little was done lawfully in this land or as he (the archbishop) directed".

Whilst waiting for favourable winds to sail to Normandy the retinue of King William plunder the shires (no further information readily available) where they are billeted.

The weather is bad when the land had to be tilled and when crops had to be harvested. Men from many shires fulfil their labour service to the City of London by building the wall around the Tower of London, repairing the bridge which had nearly all been carried away, and constructing the king's hall at Westminster. Many are oppressed and there is no relief from excessive taxation.

Prince Edgar (the aetheling, a male of royal blood, the heir apparent, great nephew of King Edward the Confessor of England), with King William's support, invades Scotland and drives out King Donald III of Scotland and replaces him with Edgar, a kinsman, the son of King Malcolm and Queen Margaret. Prince Edgar returns to England.

1098 – (This year begins at Christmas 1097.) King William II of England spends Christmas in Normandy in France. Bishop Walchelin of Winchester, Hampshire and Abbot Baldwin of Bury St Edmunds, Suffolk die during the Christmas festival. Abbot Turold of Peterborough dies. In the summer a pool bubbles up blood at Finchampstead in Berkshire.

Earl Hugh of Shropshire is killed in Anglesey in Wales by "pirates" (led by Magnus Bareleg, King of Norway, son of King Harald III of Norway and Harold, son of King Harold II of England. A union of the sons of the victor and the vanquished at the battle of Stamford Bridge in 1066.)

In the autumn the whole night sky appears as though it is on fire. Heavy rains occur throughout the year ruining all the cultivated lands in low-lying areas; there is excessive taxation.

1099 – (This year begins at Christmas 1098.) King William II of England spends Christmas in Normandy and returns to England at Easter. At Whitsun he holds his court at his new hall in Westminster, London for the first time. His chaplain Rannulf, who formerly "directed and superintended all the king's councils throughout all England", is made Bishop of Durham. King William goes to France subjugating Maine and expelling its count Helias de la Flèche. King William returns to England.

In November the incoming tide is stronger than anyone can remember and there is much damage as a result; on the same day there is a new moon. In December Bishop Osmund of Salisbury, Wiltshire dies.

1100 – (This year begins at Christmas 1099.) King William II of England holds his court at Christmas at Gloucester, at Easter at Winchester, Hampshire, and at Whitsun at Westminster, London. On Whit Sunday at a village in Berkshire (presumably Finchampstead again – see **1098** above) blood is seen bubbling from the ground.

On Thursday 2 August King William is killed by an arrow shot by one of his men (whether it was Walter Tyrell or Tirel, Lord of Poix in France, is a matter of debate) while out hunting in the New Forest in Hampshire. He is buried the next morning.

The scribe then records an obituary which offers a commentary on King William whom he describes as "very harsh and fierce in his rule over his realm, and towards his followers and to all his neighbours, and very terrifying". He was advised by "evil councillors", he was covetous and imposed "unjust taxes". He oppressed the church, sold bishoprics and abbacies for money or rent when their incumbents died, "he claimed to be the heir of every man, cleric or lay". When he died he was receiving the revenues due to the continued vacancies in the posts of the Archbishop of Canterbury, the bishops of Winchester, Hampshire and Salisbury, Wiltshire and eleven abbacies. "Everything that was hateful to God and righteous men was the daily practice in this land during his reign" and King William was "hated by almost all his people and abhorrent to God".

The councillors elect King William's brother Henry king. Straightaway he appoints William Gifford as Bishop of Winchester. Henry goes to London and on the following Sunday at Westminster Abbey he is crowned king by Bishop Maurice of London. Henry promises to abolish all the injustices of his brother's reign and "to maintain the best laws which had stood in the time of his predecessors". Following the advice of his councillors King Henry has Bishop Rannulf of Durham arrested and imprisoned in the Tower of London. King Henry summons Archbishop Anselm of Canterbury who returns to England before the autumn. He had left England because of the "great injustice" King William II had done to him (see **1097** above).

At Westminster Abbey in London Archbishop Anselm officiates at the marriage of King Henry and Matilda (born and named "Edith" but crowned and named "Matilda"), daughter of King Malcolm III of Scotland and Queen Margaret "King Edward's (King Edward "the Confessor" of England) kinswoman, of the rightful royal house of England". The Archbishop consecrates Matilda queen. Archbishop Thomas of York dies. Duke Robert II of Normandy, Count Robert II of Flanders, and Count Eustace III of Boulogne in France return from Jerusalem. Duke Robert is welcomed by all those in his dukedom apart from those supporters of King Henry with whom he has many battles (no further information readily available.)

1101 – (This year begins at Christmas 1100.) King Henry I of England holds his court at Christmas at Westminster, London and at Easter at Winchester, Hampshire.

Bishop Rannulf of Durham escapes one night in February from the Tower of London and goes to Normandy. Through Bishop Rannulf's scheming Duke Robert II of Normandy decides to invade England. King Henry sends ships to intercept Duke Robert's forces but some of their crews desert and join Duke Robert. At midsummer King Henry goes to Pevensey in Sussex to await the invasion of Duke Robert. Duke Robert lands at Portsmouth in Hampshire in late July and King Henry marches his levies to oppose him. The two brothers are reconciled because of the intercession of "persons of high rank" (no further information readily available). They make an agreement (known as the Treaty of Alton" in Hampshire) that King Henry relinquish all he has in Normandy, that the Duke's supporters in England should have their lands restored, Count Eustace of Boulogne in France should have restored all the lands in England his father owned, and that Duke Robert should receive three thousand marks of silver a year from England. They both agree that if either dies without an heir the other will inherit their domain. This agreement is ratified by twelve men of high rank on each side (no further information readily available). The Duke stays in England until the autumn and his men do much damage wherever they go.

1102 – (This year begins at Christmas 1101.) King Henry I of England holds his court at Christmas at Westminster, London and at Easter at Winchester, Hampshire. A dispute arises between King Henry and Robert of Bellême, Earl of Shrewsbury. King Henry with his levies besiege Arundel Castle in Sussex but is unable to capture it quickly so he builds castles "before it" and garrisons them. King Henry goes with all his levies to Bridgnorth in Shropshire and captures the castle. King Henry deprives Earl Robert of his lands and everything he possesses in

England. Earl Robert goes overseas and King Henry's levies return home.

Late in the autumn King Henry holds a council at Westminster in London involving ecclesiastics and laymen. Archbishop Anselm of Canterbury holds a synod of the clergy resulting in many English and French ecclesiastics losing their offices which they had acquired "unjustly or had occupied in perversity of life".

At Whitsun "thieves" from Auvergne and other unnamed places in France and from Flanders break into the monastery at Peterborough and steal gold and silver crosses, chalices and candlesticks.

1103 – (This year begins at Christmas 1102.) King Henry I of England holds his court at Christmas at Westminster, London. Soon afterwards William Giffard, former Lord Chancellor and Bishop of Winchester, Hampshire, leaves the country because he refuses "to act uncanonically and accept consecration from Archbishop Gerard of York". At Easter King Henry holds his court at Winchester and Archbishop Anselm of Canterbury goes to Rome as he and the king had agreed. Duke Robert II of Normandy comes to England and receives the agreed sum of three thousand marks as set out in the "Treaty of Alton" (see **1101** above).

Blood is seen coming out of the ground at Finchampstead in Berkshire (see **1098** and **1100** above). A disastrous year on account of the numerous taxes, the murrain (cattle plague) and the ruin of the corn and fruit tree harvests. Unlike anything before, the wind does great damage to the crops on 10 August.

On 21 October Abbot Mathias of Peterborough dies in Gloucester and is buried there.

1104 – (This year begins at Christmas 1103.) King Henry I of England holds his court at Christmas at Westminster, London, at Easter at Winchester, Hampshire, and at Whitsun at Westminster. At noon on the Tuesday following 5 June "there appeared four intersecting halos around the sun, white in colour, and looking as if they had been painted". No one who saw it has seen anything like it before.

Duke Robert II of Normandy and Robert of Bellême, Earl of Shrewsbury are reconciled and as a result Duke Robert and King Henry are at variance. King Henry sends his "officers" into Normandy where the leading men receive them into their castles "acting treacherously to their lord the duke"; they harry and burn the Duke's lands. Count William of Mortain in France flees England for Normandy and there he conspires against King Henry; as a result the king deprives him of all the possessions and lands he has in England.

England suffers "manifold injustices" with no lessening of taxes and wherever the king went his "wretched subjects suffered from the wholesale depredations of his retinue, very often including arson and manslaughter".

1105 – (This year begins at Christmas 1104.) King Henry I of England holds his court at Christmas at Windsor in Berkshire and in the spring goes to Normandy to wage war against his brother Duke Robert II of Normandy capturing Caen and Bayeux and almost all the castles; the leading men submit to him. King Henry returns to England in the autumn. Normandy remains peaceful and within his control apart from those who live anywhere near the Count William of Mortain who frequently harasses them because of his loss of lands in England. Robert of Bellême, Earl of Shrewsbury comes to King Henry in England.

A very disastrous year because of the destruction of crops and the numerous taxes.

1106 – (This year begins at Christmas 1105.) King Henry I of England holds his court at Christmas at Westminster in London. At the same time Robert of Bellême, Earl of Shrewsbury, is unable to resolve his differences with King Henry and so goes to Normandy. Whilst King Henry is in Northampton Duke Robert II of Normandy joins him and asks him to restore the lands the king has taken from him in Normandy. The king refuses, "they part with enmity", and Duke Robert returns to Normandy.

In the evening of Friday 16 February and for a while each evening thereafter, a strange small and dark star appears in the sky in the south-west with a bright light forming a beam shining north-east; one evening it appears that the beam is flashing in the opposite direction to the star. Some say that they have seen other unknown stars around this time "but we cannot speak about these without reservation, because we did not ourselves see them". On the Thursday before Easter two moons, one to the east and one to the west are seen in the sky before daylight; the moon is a fortnight old at this point.

At Easter King Henry is at Bath in Somerset and at Whitsun at Salisbury in Wiltshire. Before August King Henry goes to Normandy and receives the submission of everyone apart from Robert of Bellême, Earl of Shrewsbury, Count William of Mortain in France and the few other leading men who support Duke Robert II of Normandy. Whilst besieging Tinchebrai castle in Normandy belonging to Count William, King Henry and his forces are attacked by Duke Robert, Robert of Bellême and Count William and their forces. King Henry wins the ensuing battle capturing Duke Robert, Count William and Robert of Estouteville in France who are then imprisoned in England. William Crispin (a nobleman with lands in Normandy) and many others are taken prisoner; Robert of Bellême escapes. Prince Edgar (the aetheling, a male of royal blood, the heir apparent, great nephew of King Edward the Confessor of England) who had shortly before sided with Duke Robert, is also captured but King

---

Manuscript "E" (Peterborough or Laud): Courier New.
Manuscript "H" (Winchester): Calligraphic.

Henry releases him. King Henry then conquers the whole of Normandy.

At the same time there is conflict between the Holy Roman Emperor Henry IV of Germany and his son Henry; the father dies and is succeeded by his son who becomes Henry V Holy Roman Emperor.

1107 – (This year begins at Christmas 1106.) King Henry I of England, Duke of Normandy, is in Normandy at Christmas to bring the land and administration under his control. He returns to England in March and holds his court at Easter at Windsor in Berkshire and at Whitsun at Westminster in London. At the beginning of August he is in Westminster and appoints many bishops and abbots in vacancies in England and Normandy –"there was nobody who remembered so many being given together". Prior Ernulf of Canterbury is appointed Abbot of Peterborough. Many people say they saw "various portents in the moon during the year, and its light waxing and waning contrary to nature." Bishop Maurice of London, Abbot Robert of Bury St Edmunds, Suffolk, and Abbot Richard of Ely, Cambridgeshire die. On 13 January King Edgar of Scotland dies and is succeeded by his brother Alexander I.

1108 – (This year begins at Christmas 1107.) King Henry I of England holds his court at Christmas at Westminster in London and at Easter at Winchester in Hampshire; he returns to Westminster at Whitsun. Before August he goes to Normandy. King Philip I of France dies on 5 August and is succeeded by his son Louis VI of France; constant warfare occurs between France and England whilst King Henry stays in Normandy. Archbishop Gerard of York dies before Whitsun and is succeeded by Thomas ("Thomas II" or "Thomas the Younger" former provost of Beverly Abbey, Yorkshire).

1109 – (This year begins at Christmas 1108.) King Henry I of England, Duke of Normandy, is in Normandy at Christmas and at Easter and before Whitsun he returns to England and holds his court at Westminster, London where the contract for the marriage of his daughter Matilda to the Holy Roman Emperor Henry V is completed. There are many terrifying thunderstorms during the year. On 22 March Archbishop Anselm of Canterbury dies.

1110 – (This year begins at Christmas 1109.) King Henry I of England, Duke of Normandy, holds his court at Christmas at Westminster in London and at Easter he is at Marlborough, Wiltshire. At Whitsun he holds his court for the first time at New Windsor, Berkshire. King Henry sends his daughter Matilda with "innumerable treasures" overseas to marry Henry V, the Holy Roman Emperor (see **1109** above).

On the 5 May the moon shines brightly in the evening but gradually dims until it seems to be extinguished. At daybreak it appears fully and shining brightly; on this day the moon is a fortnight old. All night the sky is very clear and the stars can clearly be seen but the fruit on the trees is damaged by the frost. For many nights in June a star appears in the north-east, its rays shining south-west; when it rises higher in the sky it moves in a north-west direction.

Philip de Braose (with lands in Sussex and the Welsh Marches), William Malet (with lands in Eye in Suffolk), William Bainert (no further information readily available) are deprived of their lands. Count Helias de la Flèche of Maine in France who recognised King Henry's overlordship, dies. Count Fulk V of Anjou in France (later King of Jerusalem) succeeds to Maine and holds it against King Henry.

A disastrous year because of the monies levied by King Henry for the marriage of his daughter Matilda and the Holy Roman Emperor and the bad weather which resulted in the crops being damaged and the fruit harvest nearly all ruined. Work begins on the new abbey church at Chertsey in Surrey.

1111 – (This year begins at Christmas 1110). King Henry I of England, Duke of Normandy does not "wear his crown" at Christmas, Easter or Whitsun. In August he goes to Normandy to counteract the hostility of the French and in particular Count Fulk V of Anjou in France (later King of Jerusalem), who holds the province of Maine against King Henry. The two sides carry out many "cruel raids" against each other. Count Robert II of Flanders dies and is succeeded by his son Count Baldwin VII. A severe and long winter with severe damage to crops as a result; the worst murrain (cattle plague) in living memory.

1112 – King Henry I of England, Duke of Normandy remains in Normandy all year on account of the hostilities with France and the Count of Anjou, Fulk V (later King of Jerusalem). King Henry deprives the Count of Evreux (no further information readily available) and William Crispin (see **1106** above) of their lands and restores Philip de Braose his lands in Sussex and the Welsh Marches. King Henry has Robert of Bellême, Earl of Shrewsbury, put in prison. This year was very productive in woods and open country but there is a "fearful pestilence".

1113 – (This year begins at Christmas 1112.)King Henry I of England, Duke of Normandy, spends Christmas, Easter and Whitsun in Normandy. King Henry sends Robert of Bellême, Earl of Shrewsbury to prison in the castle at Wareham in Dorset. Soon after, King Henry returns to England. **On 17 July Abbot Peter of Gloucester dies and William, a monk at Gloucester, is appointed as his successor on 5 October by King Henry.**

1114 – (This year begins at Christmas 1113.) King Henry I of England, Duke of Normandy, holds his court at Christmas at Windsor in Berkshire; he does not hold court again this year. **At Windsor King Henry appoints**

his chaplain Theobald as Bishop of Worcester. Rainald, a monk from Caen in France, is appointed Abbot of Ramsey in Cambridgeshire. Richard, a monk from York, is appointed Abbot of York. Robert, a monk at St Evroul in France, is appointed Abbot of Thorney near Peterborough. David, the brother of Queen Matilda (wife of King Henry I) is appointed Earl of Northampton. Archbishop Thomas of York dies on 17 February. William, a monk from Caen in France, is appointed Abbot of Cerne Abbas in Dorset.

King Henry spends Easter at Kingsthorpe near Northampton. After Easter King Henry appoints Bishop Ralph of Rochester, Kent as Archbishop of Canterbury who "took office on 24 February" (this seems to be a mistake in the sequence of dates, unless the new Archbishop did not take up his post until the following February). ✗ ?

On 3 May Abbot Nigel of Burton-on-Trent in Staffordshire dies. On 5 May Chichester in Sussex is burnt down (no further information readily available), including the Cathedral.

Near the end of May for many nights a strange star is seen with a long trail of light. One day an ebb tide is so low that people are able to walk and ride across the River Thames to the east of London Bridge.

King Henry spends Whit Sunday at St Albans in Hertfordshire. At midsummer King Henry leads his levies into Wales, the Welsh make peace, and King Henry then has castles built in Wales.

Archbishop Thomas ("Thomas II" or "Thomas the Younger") of York dies and King Henry's chaplain Thurstan succeeds him; King Henry makes the appointment whilst at Winchester in Hampshire. On 16 August King Henry appoints Albold, a monk from Bec in France, as Abbot of Bury St Edmunds in Suffolk.

On 14 September King Henry appoints Ealdwulf, a monk at Muchelney in Somerset, as Abbot of Muchelney Abbey. Geoffrey, a monk in the Old Minster in Winchester, Hampshire, is appointed Abbot of Burton-on-Trent in Staffordshire.

King Henry commands Abbot Ernulf of Peterborough to come to him whilst he waits to cross the sea to the Continent. They meet on 15 September at Westbourne in Sussex, and with the support of all the ecclesiastics and the laity, King Henry tries to persuade Ernulf to become Bishop of Rochester, Kent. He orders ✗ Archbishop Ralph of Canterbury to take Ernulf to Canterbury and consecrate him bishop "willy nilly". When the monks at Peterborough hear the news they are overcome with grief as Ernulf is a "very good and kind man and did much good both inside and outside the monastery whilst he was there".

Manuscript H ends in 1114.

(Manuscript H ends in 1114 with an incomplete reference to Archbishop Ralph giving the bishopric of Rochester......It survives as a single leaf and records entries relating to 1113 and 1114 only.)

Manuscript "E" (Peterborough or Laud): Courier New.
Manuscript "H" (Winchester): Calligraphic.

Whilst at Rowner in Hampshire, on 21 September, King Henry appoints John, a monk from Séez in France, as the new abbot of Peterborough at the behest of Archbishop Ralph. Abbot John goes to Rome to obtain Archbishop Ralph's pallium (vestment of office, a cloak), he is accompanied by Warner, a monk and also by Archdeacon John of Canterbury, the Archbishop's nephew; the visit is a success. The same day King Henry boards a ship at Portsmouth in Hampshire and goes to Normandy in September.

There are strong winds in October and the 18 November is a particularly violent night with a trail of damage everywhere in woods and villages.

1115 – (This year begins at Christmas 1114.) King Henry I of England, Duke of Normandy, spends Christmas in Normandy and whilst there makes the leading men swear allegiance to his son William Adelin. King Henry returns to England in July.

The winter is the worst in living memory with frost and snow which results in a "fearful pestilence among cattle". Pope Paschal II sends the pallium (vestment of office, a cloak) for Archbishop Ralph of Canterbury; it was brought to England by Abbot Anselm, nephew of Archbishop Anselm (see **1109** above), and by Abbot John of Peterborough.

1116 – (This year begins at Christmas 1115.) King Henry I of England, Duke of Normandy, spends Christmas in St Albans in Hertfordshire for the consecration of the Abbey Church. He spends Easter at Odiham in Hampshire.

After Easter King Henry goes to Normandy and "in the numerous cruel raids and forays between France and Normandy many castles were taken". The main cause of the fighting is the support given by King Henry to his nephew Count Theobald of Blois who is at war with his overlord King Louis VI of France."

"A very hard year". Before August and up to February (the following year) very heavy rain causes disaster to the crops. There is a shortage of mast (the fruits of the forest trees including beech, oak and chestnut – food for pigs) in both England and Wales. The people suffer through the taxes levied by King Henry "within boroughs and without" (King Henry was the instigator of a number of financial and taxation reforms).

On Friday 4 August the monastery at Peterborough is completely destroyed by fire apart from the chapter house and dormitory; most of the town is also burned down.

1117 – King Henry I of England, Duke of Normandy, spends the whole year in Normandy because of the hostility of King Louis VI of France and his neighbours. During the summer the forces of King Louis and Count Baldwin VII Hapkin of Flanders enter Normandy for one night but retire the following morning before any fighting commences. Normandy suffers both from taxation and the forces gathered by King Henry to defend it; England too suffers through numerous taxes.

In England on 1 December there are violent storms with thunder, lightning, rain and hail. For most of the night of the 11 December the moon appears to turn bloody and is later eclipsed. On the night of 16 December the sky is very red "as if there were a conflagration in the sky". The rains hardly stop all year and as a result grain production suffers. On 6 December Abbot Gilbert of Westminster Abbey and on 23 February Abbot Faircius of Abingdon Abbey, Oxfordshire, die.

On 3 January there is a great earthquake in Lombardy in Italy resulting in the collapse of many churches, towers and houses and causing havoc among the people.

1118 – King Henry I of England, Duke of Normandy, spends the whole year in Normandy because of the wars with King Louis VI of France, Count Fulk V of Anjou in France (later King of Jerusalem) and Count Baldwin VII Hapkin of Flanders. Count Baldwin is wounded in Normandy and so returns to Flanders. Due to these wars King Henry suffers many problems including a great loss of property and lands, but his greatest problem is the desertion of his men to the enemy with the attendant surrender of their castles.

England pays for all this through numerous taxes. One night early in the year there is severe lightning and thunder. On 1 May Queen Matilda (born and named "Edith" but crowned and named "Matilda") dies at Westminster in London where she is then buried. Count Robert of Meulan in France dies. On 21 December there is an exceptionally high wind more violent than any in living memory; houses and trees everywhere suffer. Pope Paschal II dies and is succeeded by Pope Gelasius II.

1119 – King Henry I of England, Duke of Normandy, spends the whole year in Normandy because of the wars with King Louis VI of France and the desertions of his own men to the enemy. A battle (no further information readily available) is fought between the two kings in Normandy; King Henry is victorious and takes many of the leading Frenchmen prisoners. As a result some of King Henry's subjects who had opposed him in their castles restored their allegiance to him; other castles he takes by force. William Adelin, son of King Henry and Queen Matilda (born and named "Edith" but crowned and named "Matilda") goes to his father in Normandy and marries Matilda (also called Isabella), daughter of Count Fulk V of Anjou in France (later King of Jerusalem).

On 28 September a great earthquake occurs in England; it is most severe in Gloucestershire and Worcestershire. Pope Gelasius II dies "on this side of the Alps" and is buried at Cluny in France. Calixtus, Archbishop of Vienne in France succeeds as pope.

Manuscript "E" (Peterborough or Laud): Courier New.

On 18 October Pope Calixtus II holds a council in Rheims in France. Archbishop Thurstan of York attends (despite King Henry failing to give him permission), to resolve the question of his consecration as Archbishop of York and refusal to recognise the supremacy of Canterbury (requiring a profession of obedience) as demanded by Archbishop Ralph of Canterbury who is supported by King Henry. Thurstan loses his archbishopric. (At the Council of Salisbury in 1116 King Henry orders Thurston to submit to Canterbury, he refuses and publically resigns. Subsequently Thurstan receives a letter from Pope Paschal II supporting him. Pope Paschal also sends a letter to Archbishop Ralph ordering him to consecrate Thurston. When Pope Paschal's letters become public Thurstan's letter of resignation is set aside. Thurstan's case is supported by three popes, Pope Paschal II, Pope Gelasius II, Calixtus II. In 1119 Thurstan is consecrated by Pope Calixtus in Rheims in France despite the Pope's promise not to consecrate him without King Henry's permission. Enraged, King Henry bans Thurstan from returning to England. Pope Calixtus issues two bulls, one releasing York from Canterbury's supremacy forever and the other demanding King Henry allow Thurstan to return to York.)

Count Baldwin VII Hapkin of Flanders dies from the wounds he received in Normandy (see **1118** above) – he is succeeded by Charles I, "the Good", his father's sister's son, the son of Saint Cnut, King (Canute IV) of Denmark.

1120 – King Henry I of England, Duke of Normandy, King Louis VI of France, Count William III of Ponthieu in France, Count Charles I of Flanders, and King Henry's subjects in Normandy are all reconciled. King Henry puts into place the arrangements he considers necessary for the administration of his castles and lands in Normandy. Before the end of November King Henry returns to England.

(On the night of the 25 November in the English Channel off Barfleur in Normandy) the vessel (known as the "White Ship") carrying King Henry's only legitimate son William Adelin is lost; one of his illegitimate sons Richard is also drowned. Earl Richard of Chester and his brother Ottuel, and a great many of the king's household and other "outstanding men" also drowned; few of the bodies are recovered.

Through the intervention of Pope Calixtus II, Archbishop Thurstan of York returns to England, and is reconciled with King Henry and resumes his duties in York; Archbishop Ralph of Canterbury is "very much displeased" (see **1119** above).

1121 – (This year begins at Christmas 1120.) King Henry I of England, Duke of Normandy, spends Christmas at Brampton in Huntingdonshire. Before 2 February King Henry marries Adeliza at Windsor in Berkshire; thereafter she is consecrated queen. (Adeliza is the daughter of Godfrey I, Landgrave of Brabant in the Low Countries, and Count of Brussels and Leuven or Louvain in Belgium and from 1106 Duke of Lower

Lorraine in France and Margrave of Antwerp in Belgium.)

There is an eclipse of the moon on 4 April. King Henry spends Easter at Berkley in Gloucestershire and on Whit Sunday he holds a court at Westminster in London. Later in the year King Henry leads the levies into Wales; the Welsh meet him and agree his terms.

Count Fulk V of Anjou (later King of Jerusalem), returns from Jerusalem to Anjou in France; he sends to England for his widowed daughter Matilda (also called Isabella who was married to King Henry's only legitimate son William Adelin who drowned with the "White Ship" – see **1120** above). Just before Christmas there is a very violent wind over all of England; its effects are "very noticeable".

1122 – (This year begins at Christmas 1121.) King Henry I of England, Duke of Normandy, spends Christmas at Norwich in Norfolk and Easter at Northampton.

On the 8 March the monastery at Gloucester and the borough are burnt down. The monks were singing mass when the fire started in the upper tower; many of the monastery's treasures are lost.

On 21 March there is a violent wind after which numerous portents and illusions appear throughout England. On the night of the 25 July there is a very great earthquake throughout Somerset and Gloucestershire.

On 8 September a violent wind occurs from morning until it becomes dark. On 20 October Archbishop Ralph of Canterbury dies. On 7 December sailors report they see a "great and extensive fire near the ground in the north-east" which increases in size as it rises up to the sky, the sky opens into four parts; this lasts from dawn until full daylight (it is now presumed to have been the "aurora borealis").

1123 – (This year begins at Christmas 1122.) King Henry I of England, Duke of Normandy, spends Christmas at Dunstable in Bedfordshire where he is visited by messengers from Count Fulk V of Anjou in France (later King of Jerusalem). They fail to come to an agreement with King Henry. (The messengers had requested the return of the dowry provided by Count Fulk for his daughter Matilda – also called Isabella – when she married King Henry's legitimate son William Adelin who drowned with the "White Ship"; see **1120** above).

King Henry and his court then go to Woodstock in Oxfordshire. On Wednesday 10 January whilst riding in his deer park accompanied by Bishop Roger of Salisbury, Wiltshire and Bishop Robert Bloet of Lincoln, King Henry dismounts and catches Bishop Robert as he dies in the saddle. Bishop Robert is buried in front of St Mary's altar in Lincoln by Bishop Robert Pecceth of Chester.

King Henry holds a meeting of his council on 2 February at Gloucester and invites them to choose an Archbishop of Canterbury (Archbishop Ralph died the previous year - see **1122** above). The council agree not to appoint someone from the monastic orders ever again and wish to appoint someone from the secular clergy. Bishop Roger and the late Bishop Robert were the main supporters of this proposal because "they had never had any love for the monastic rule, but were ever in opposition to monks and their rule". Canon William Curbeil of St Osyth's, Essex, a member of the secular clergy, is chosen. King Henry appoints William Archbishop of Canterbury supported by the bishops but the monks, earls and almost all the thanes oppose the appointment.

The legate of Pope Calixtus II, Abbot Henry of St Jean d'Angély in France, comes to England about the payment of "Peter's Pence" (a tribute or "tax" levied on households with a value of thirty pence or over - originally paid to support the School of the English in Rome; see **817** above). Abbot Henry informs King Henry that it is unlawful for a member of the secular clergy to be responsible for monks especially when the canons have already chosen a suitable candidate (no further information readily available) from within their number. Despite this King Henry does not change his mind and so William Curbeil is consecrated Archbishop of Canterbury by Bishop Richard de Beaumis I of London, Bishop Ernulf of Rochester in Kent, Bishop William Giffard of Winchester in Hampshire, Bishop Bernard of St David's in Pembrokeshire, and Bishop Roger of Salisbury, Wiltshire.

In the spring Archbishop William travels to Rome to receive his pallium (vestment of office, a cloak) accompanied by Bishop Bernard, Abbot Sigefrith of Glastonbury, Somerset, Abbot Anselm of Bury St Edmunds, Suffolk, Archdeacon John of Canterbury and the king's court chaplain Gifford. Three days before Archbishop William arrives in Rome, Archbishop Thurstan of York arrives as commanded by Pope Calixtus. A week goes by before Archbishop William sees Pope Calixtus who considers he has been appointed in opposition to those in monastic orders, but "Rome, like the rest of the world, was won over by gold and silver". Pope Calixtus gives Archbishop William his pallium and sends him home with his blessing.

On 25 March at Woodstock Godfrey, Queen Adeliza's chancellor is appointed Bishop of Bath in Somerset; he was born in Louvain in Belgium. King Henry goes to Winchester in Hampshire for Easter, and appoints as Bishop of Lincoln a cleric Alexander, a "nephew" of Bishop Roger of Salisbury.

At Whitsun King Henry goes to Portsmouth in Hampshire and awaits favourable winds so that he can sail to Normandy. King Henry entrusts England to Bishop Roger in his absence. King Henry sails to Normandy and remains there for the rest of the year. In Normandy many desert King Henry including Count Waleran of Meulan in France and Earl of Worcester, Almaric (Amaury III of Montfort, Count of Évreux in France), Hugh (Lord) of Montfort in France, William of Roumare (Lord of Bréval in France). In the ensuing fighting King Henry captures the castle of Pont Audemer from Count Waleran and the castle of Montfort from Hugh; the longer the fighting goes on the more successes King Henry achieves. Before Bishop Alexander arrives in his bishopric, on the 19 May, almost all of Lincoln is destroyed by fire and countless people are burned to death.

1124 – King Henry I of England, Duke of Normandy, spends the whole year in Normandy because of the wars with King Louis VI of France and Count Fulk V of Anjou (later King of Jerusalem) "but most of all against his own subjects".

On 25 March Count Waleran of Meulan in France and Earl of Worcester goes from his castle at Beaumont-le-Roger in France to Vatteville in France accompanied by Almaric (Amaury III of Montfort, Count of Évreux in France), the seneschal of King Louis (i.e. the administrator of justice and controller of domestic arrangements in the king's household), and by Hugh Fitz Gervase, Hugh (Lord) of Montfort in France, and many other knights.

A battle is fought and King Henry's forces are victorious. Count Waleran, Hugh Fitz Gervase of Châteauneuf-en-Thymerais in France, Hugh (Lord) of Montfort and twenty-five other knights are captured and brought before King Henry who has Count Waleran and Hugh Fitz Gervase imprisoned in Rouen in France and Hugh (Lord) of Montfort imprisoned in Gloucester Castle in England; others are dispersed and imprisoned in his (unnamed) castles.

King Henry then captures or receives the submission of all the castles of Count Waleran in Normandy and all other castles held by his enemies. All this fighting is due to William ("Clito" the Latin equivalent of aetheling – a male of royal blood, the heir apparent), the son of Duke Robert II of Normandy. William had married Sibylla the younger daughter of Count Fulk V of Anjou in France, and as a consequence had the support of King Louis and the French nobility. The French consider it is wrong for King Henry to hold in captivity Duke Robert (held in England – see **1106** above) and unjustly banish his son William Clito from Normandy (this is the first mention of the banishment).

Grain and crop failures in England result in "two seed-lips (the basket containing the seed to be sown by hand) of seed required to sow an acre of wheat cost six shillings, and the three seed-lips for an acre of barley cost six shillings, while the four seed-lips for an acre of oats cost four shillings". The shortage of grain results in debasement of the coinage.

On 15 March Bishop Ernwulf of Rochester dies. On 23 April King Alexander I of Scotland dies and is succeeded by his brother King David I who is also Earl of Northamptonshire. On 14 December Pope Calixtus II dies in Rome and is succeeded by Pope Honorius II.

Manuscript "E" (Peterborough or Laud): Courier New.

On 30 November Ralph Basset (an itinerant royal justice) holds a (circuit) court of the king's thanes at Cossington in Leicestershire where more thieves "than ever before" are hung; forty-four are hung and six have their eyes put out and are castrated.

This is a "very distressful year" whoever has money loses it through extortion or the actions of the courts, those who have no money die of hunger.

1125– (This year begins at Christmas 1124.) King Henry I of England, Duke of Normandy, is in Normandy and before Christmas issues instructions that all moneyers in England should lose their right hand and be castrated because a pound is not worth a penny at market. Bishop Roger of Salisbury of Wiltshire carries out these instructions at Christmas at Winchester in Hampshire. (The scribe comments) that this is entirely justified because the moneyers had "ruined the whole country".

Pope Honorius II sends Cardinal John of Crema in France to King Henry in Normandy. King Henry has Archbishop William of Canterbury accompany Cardinal John to Canterbury. Cardinal John goes to all the bishoprics and abbacies in the country and receives "great and splendid gifts". On the 8 September Cardinal John holds a three-day council of all the ecclesiastics and laity in London at which he reiterates the laws laid down by Archbishop Anselm of Canterbury (see the relevant entries for the years **1095–1109** above) and others, "though little came of it". Cardinal John goes to Rome accompanied by Archbishop William of Canterbury, Archbishop Thurstan of York, Bishop Alexander of Lincoln, Bishop John of Lothian(Glasgow), Scotland and Abbot Geoffrey of St Albans, Hertfordshire, where they are received by Pope Honorius; they stay all winter.

On 10 August many villages are flooded, many people drown, bridges and crops are destroyed. This results in hunger and death to the human and the animal population; "there was more unseasonableness in crops of every kind than in many years past". On 14 October Abbot John of Peterborough dies.

1126 – King Henry I of England, Duke of Normandy, spends most of the year in Normandy, he returns to England in the autumn with Queen Adeliza and his daughter Aethelic who had been married to the Holy Roman Emperor Henry V, King of Germany (he died in 1125). King Henry is also accompanied by Count Waleran of Meulan in France and Earl of Worcester whom he sends into captivity at Bridgnorth in Shropshire and then on to Wallingford in Oxfordshire. King Henry sends Hugh Fitz Gervase into captivity "in strict confinement" in Windsor in Berkshire.

King David I of Scotland and Earl of Northamptonshire comes to England and is received by King Henry with "great ceremony"; King David stays a year in England. On the advice of King Henry's daughter Matilda and King David, Earl Robert of Gloucester, (an illegitimate son of King Henry) becomes the custodian at his castle in Bristol in Gloucestershire of Duke Robert II of Normandy, replacing as custodian Bishop Roger of Salisbury, Wiltshire.

1127 – (This year begins at Christmas 1126.) King Henry I of England, Duke of Normandy, holds his court at Christmas at Windsor in Berkshire. King David I of Scotland, Earl of Northamptonshire, is present as are all the important ecclesiastics and laymen in England. King Henry gets them all to swear an oath that on his death his daughter Aethelic (the Empress Matilda, also known as Adeliza, widow of the Holy Roman Emperor Henry V, King of Germany) would inherit both England and Normandy. King Henry then sends Aethelic to Normandy with her half brother Earl Robert of Gloucester and Brian son of Count Alan Fergant (Alan IV Duke of Brittany; but there is no record of a son called Brian). Aethelic is married to Geoffrey Martel (Geoffrey Plantagenet who later becomes Count Geoffrey V of Anjou) son of Count Fulk V of Anjou in France. The marriage "gave as much offence" to the French as the English. King Henry wants the friendship of the Count of Anjou to secure his help against his nephew William Clito ("Clito" the Latin equivalent of aetheling – a male of royal blood, the heir apparent) the son of Duke Robert II of Normandy.

In the spring Count Charles I of Flanders is killed by his own men whilst praying in church. William Clito is appointed as his replacement by King Louis VI of France. (The scribe recalls) that William Clito had been married to Sibylla the younger daughter of Count Fulk V of Anjou and that the marriage had been dissolved "entirely" at the behest of King Henry on the grounds of consanguinity. William Clito had afterwards married Joanna of Montferrat in France the half-sister of Queen Lucienne de Rochefort of France and as a result had been given Flanders.

King Henry appoints as Abbot of Peterborough, Abbot Henry of Poitou in France who also holds the abbacy of St Jean d'Angély in France. Archbishop William of Canterbury and the bishops object to the appointment on the grounds that an individual should not have charge of two abbeys. King Henry believes that Abbot Henry had left the Abbey of St Jean d'Angély because of the wars in France and on the advice and with the permission of Pope Honorious II and Abbot Peter of Cluny in France. In addition Abbot Henry had been appointed the Pope's legate (see **1123** above) to collect "Peter's Pence" (a tribute or "tax" levied on households with a value of thirty pence or over – originally paid to support the School of the English in Rome – see **817** above).

The scribe then relates the various machinations of Abbot Henry regarding a number of church appointments in France. In London, following special pleading by Abbot Henry, King Henry confirms the appointment as Abbot of Peterborough – because he was his kinsman and had been the chief witness to the required oath associated with the dissolution of the marriage of William Clito and Sibylla. Abbot

Henry accompanies King Henry to Winchester, Hampshire and then goes to Peterborough. On taking up his appointment Abbot Henry removed "everything that he could take, from within the monastery or outside it, from ecclesiastics and laymen, he sent oversea. He did nothing for the monastery's welfare and left nothing of value untouched." On Sunday 6 February immediately after Abbot Henry arrives the spectre of twenty or thirty huntsmen and hounds (the "Wild Hunt") is seen in the deer park in Peterborough stretching to Stamford in Lincolnshire. "This was seen and heard from the time of his arrival all through Lent and up to Easter."

1128 – King Henry I of England, Duke of Normandy, spends all year in Normandy because of his conflict with Count William I Clito of Flanders son of Duke Robert II of Normandy. Count William is wounded at the siege (of Aalst in Belgium) by a foot soldier and retires to the monastery of St Bertin at St Omer in France and "straightway became a monk" but he lives for only five days and dies on 27 July; he is buried in the monastery. Bishop Rannulf Flambard of Durham dies and is buried at Durham on 5 September.

Abbot Henry of both St Jean d'Angély in France and Peterborough, with the permission of King Henry, returns to his French monastery to relinquish his abbacy and then return to Peterborough. The scribe comments that Abbot Henry wished to remain in France for twelve months or more before returning to England (see **1127** above).

Hugh of the Knights Templar from Jerusalem visits King Henry in Normandy who provides him with treasures. King Henry sends him on to England and Scotland where he is given "treasures by all" and recruits many people for a Crusade in the Holy Land. It had been declared that a decisive battle was imminent "but, when all those multitudes (more than those involved in the First Crusade) got there (Jerusalem), they were pitiably duped to find it was nothing but lies".

1129 – In Normandy King Henry I of England, Duke of Normandy, gives hostages and sends for Count Waleran of Meulan in France and Earl of Worcester, who is restored all his lands with the exception of his castle at Beaumont-le-Roger in France. Count Waleran remains with King Henry, and accompanies him to England; they become "good friends as they had previously been foes". Hugh Fitz Gervase of Châteauneuf-en-Thymerais in France is allowed to return to his lands.

At King Henry's suggestion, Archbishop William of Canterbury summons all ecclesiastics in England to an assembly in London in the autumn where they discuss "all the rights of the church". Despite lasting five days, this assembly discusses only the order to archdeacons and priests to "put away" their wives by the 30 November. They decide that anyone who does not comply should lose all claims to church, house and glebe. Archbishop William issues the requisite decree which is ignored "they all kept their wives by the king's permission, as they had formerly done". Bishop William Gifford of Winchester in Hampshire dies and is buried at Winchester on 25 January. King Henry appoints his nephew Abbot Henry of Glastonbury in Somerset as Bishop of Winchester; Henry is consecrated by Archbishop William of Canterbury on 17 November.

Pope Honorius II dies; two popes are elected. One is Peter, a monk from Cluny in France, who is from one of the richest families in Rome and is supported by Rome and by Duke Roger II of Sicily. The other is Gregory, a secular clerk of Rome, supported by the Holy Roman Emperor Lothair III, King Louis IV of France, King Henry of England, and by "all on this side of the Alps". "Now more heresies were rife in Christendom than ever before."

Before dawn on 6 December there is a great earthquake.

1130 – On 4 May the cathedral church at Canterbury is consecrated by Archbishop William of Canterbury, attended by Bishop John of Rochester, Kent, Bishop Gilbert of London, Bishop Henry of Winchester, Hampshire, Bishop Alexander of Lincoln, Bishop Roger of Salisbury, Wiltshire, Bishop Simon of Worcester, Bishop Roger of Coventry, Warwickshire, Bishop Godfrey of Bath, Somerset, Bishop Everard of Norwich, Norfolk, Bishop Sigefrith of Chichester, Sussex, Bishop Bernard of St David's, Pembrokeshire, Bishop Audoenus of Evreux in Normandy and Bishop John of Séez in France. Archbishop William attended by these bishops then consecrates St Andrew's Cathedral in St Andrews in Scotland.

King Henry I of England, Duke of Normandy, is in Rochester in Kent when the borough is almost burnt down. In the autumn King Henry goes to Normandy.

After Easter Abbot Henry of both St Jean d'Angély in France and Peterborough (see **1127** and **1128** above) returns to Peterborough saying he has entirely relinquished the monastery of St Jean d'Angély. Abbot Peter of Cluny in France comes to England with King Henry's permission and is welcomed wherever he goes. At Peterborough Abbot Henry tries to enlist his support by promising that the Abbey of Peterborough would become subject to the Abbey of Cluny; Abbot Peter returns to France.

1131 – (This year begins at Christmas 1130.) On the evening of Sunday 11 January, "just after bedtime", the northern sky appears like a blazing fire terrifying all those who see it. Throughout England there are diseases among cattle (murrain) and pigs worse than in any living memory. In villages where there are ten or twelve ploughs the disease leaves none working and where a man had owned two or three hundred pigs he found he had none. Hens die, meat, cheese and butter are in short supply.

Before Easter Abbot Henry of both St Jean d'Angély in France and Peterborough (see **1127**, **1128** and **1130** above) goes to King Henry I of England, Duke of Normandy, in Normandy. He reports that Abbot Peter of Cluny in France has ordered him to report and hand over the Abbey of St Jean d'Angély. Abbot Henry proposes, and King Henry agrees, that he should take this action and then return to England. Abbot Henry goes to the Abbey of St Jean d'Angély and remains there, but on the 25 June the monks choose a new abbot (no further information readily available). Duke William X of Aquitaine and "all the leading men and monks" expel Abbot Henry from the monastery. Abbot Henry then goes to the Abbey at Cluny and promises to give Abbot Peter "complete control of both the internal and external affairs of the monastery" of Peterborough. Abbot Henry stays in France for a year.

King Henry comes to England sometime between 29 June and the autumn.

1132 – King Henry I of England, Duke of Normandy, returns to England (the entry for 1131 does not record his departure from England sometime in the autumn). Abbot Henry (former Abbot of St Jean d'Angély in France) of Peterborough (see **1127**, **1128**, **1130** and **1131** above) goes to King Henry and makes accusations about the monks at Peterborough; he wants to make their monastery subject to Cluny Abbey in France (see **1131** above). Through the advice of Bishop Roger of Salisbury, Wiltshire, Bishop Alexander of Lincoln, and other leading men, King Henry hears that Abbot Henry is "acting treacherously". King Henry sends for Abbot Henry and deprives him of the Abbey of Peterborough and makes him leave England. King Henry appoints Prior Martin of St Neot's in Cambridgeshire as Abbot. He arrives at Peterborough on 20 June.

1135 – On 1 August King Henry I of England, Duke of Normandy, sails to Normandy and on the following day, whilst he slept on board ship, there is an eclipse of the sun with stars around it at midday; this is considered a portent of some important event. King Henry dies in Normandy on 30 November and is buried at Reading in Berkshire. As a consequence of his death "every man who could was quick to rob his neighbour". The scribe then records a brief obituary; King Henry "was a good man, and was held in great awe. In his days no man dared to wrong another."

King Henry's nephew, Stephen of Blois and Count of Boulogne in France, comes to London and is consecrated king by Archbishop William of Curbail of Canterbury on Christmas day. (The scribe comments that) In the days of King Stephen "there was nothing but strife, evil, and robbery, for quickly the great men who were traitors rose against him".

1136 – Baldwin de Redvers (he later becomes Earl of Devon) holds Exeter in Devon against King Stephen, who successfully besieges the town and they come to terms. Others (no further information readily available) man and hold their castles against King Stephen. King David I of Scotland joins in the fighting against King Stephen until the two kings meet and are reconciled "but it was to little purpose".

Manuscript "E" (Peterborough or Laud): Courier New.

Archbishop William of Canterbury dies (the archbishopric of Canterbury is vacant until 1139, see **1139** below).

1137 – King Stephen of England and Count of Boulogne in France goes to Normandy where he is welcomed because he has the royal treasury "but he gave it away and squandered it foolishly". King Stephen holds a council at Oxford and arrests Bishop Roger of Salisbury, Wiltshire, Bishop Alexander of Lincoln and the Lord Chancellor Roger le Poer, and has them put in prison until they surrender their castles. "When the traitors saw that (King) Stephen was a good-humoured, kindly, and easy-going man who inflicted no punishment, then they committed all manner of horrible crimes." The leading men of the country break their oaths of allegiance to King Stephen and build many castles with forced labour to hold against him. These castles they fill "with devils and wicked men" who torture and rob people; all manner of atrocities are described and many thousands are starved to death. In addition King Stephen raises at regular intervals a tax known as "tenserie" (protection money) on villages. King Stephen's forces plunder and ruin the land, sparing nothing or no one, including the church and ecclesiastics. "Never did a country endure greater misery."

The scribe records that Abbot Martin of Peterborough takes good care of the monastery, its fabric and its monks, despite the vicissitudes; the monks enter the "new" church on 29 June. Abbot Martin goes to Rome and is well-received by Pope Eugenius III (but he was not recorded as elected until 1145). Abbot Martin recovers lands in Northamptonshire at Cottingham and Easton Maudit from William Mauldit who held the castle at Rockingham in Northamptonshire. Also in Northamptonshire, Abbot Martin recovers lands at Irthlingborough and Stanwick and a yearly rent of sixty shillings from Aldwinkle from Hugh of Waterville (Northamptonshire). Abbot Martin "admitted many monks and planted vineyards, and built many domestic buildings, and changed the site of the town to a better position than formerly".

The scribe records the story of the Jews in Norwich in Norfolk torturing, hanging and burying a Christian child (a twelve year old boy called William) before Easter. The monks in Norwich take William's body to their monastic church where he is buried (William was accorded the status of a saint and miracles are attributed to him.)

King Stephen fails to capture Earl Robert of Gloucester (half brother of Aethelic, the Empress Matilda, also known as Adeliza, the widow of the Holy Roman Emperor Henry V, King of Germany and daughter of King Henry I of England who was also Duke of Normandy; she is now Countess of Anjou in France and married to Count Geoffrey V Plantagenet of Anjou – see **1127** above) because the Earl receives prior warning.

1138 – King David I of Scotland invades England "with immense levies, determined to conquer it". He is defeated by the forces of William le Gros, Earl of Aumale, (Albemarle, Earl of Yorkshire, and Lord of

Manuscript "E" (Peterborough or Laud): Courier New.

Holderness) to whom King Stephen had entrusted the city of York, at the "Battle of the Standard" (north of Northallerton, North Yorkshire); a great number of Scots are killed.

NOTE: THE DATING OF THE ENTRIES AFTER 1138 IS CONFUSING, WITH SOME DATES AND EVENTS OUT OF SEQUENCE.

1139 – Abbot Theobald of Bec in France is appointed Archbishop of Canterbury. Aethelic/the Empress Matilda (see **1127** and **1137** above) comes to London.

1140 – On 20 March an eclipse occurs whilst men are eating around noon, they light candles so they can continue eating.

Earl Rannulf of Chester and his half-brother William de Roumare (Lord of Roumare in Normandy, who circa 1143 becomes Earl of Lincoln) hold Lincoln Castle against King Stephen. Earl Rannulf leaves the castle to gain reinforcements and returns with the additional help of Earl Robert of Gloucester (half brother of Aethelic, the Empress Matilda – see **1127** and **1137** above) with "great levies".

Eustace (he becomes Count Eustace IV of Boulogne in 1146), the son of King Stephen, goes to France and marries Constance, a "good woman", the sister of King Louis VII of France. He intends to acquire Normandy but has little success. He is described as an "evil man" robbing lands and raising heavy taxes. He brings Constance to Canterbury Castle. In this entry the scribe refers to the deaths of Eustace (1153) and his mother Matilda of Boulogne (1152).

1141 – On 2 February the Earl Rannulf of Chester and his half-brother William de Roumare (Lord of Roumare in Normandy, who circa 1143 becomes Earl of Lincoln) fight a battle outside Lincoln with King Stephen of England and Count of Boulogne in France. They capture King Stephen after his men betray him and imprison him in fetters in Bristol in Gloucestershire.

The people of London try to make prisoner Aethelic/the Empress Matilda (see **1127** and **1137** above); she flees but suffers "great loss".

"The Empress" (this descriptor is used rather than Aethelic or "the daughter of King Henry") is "given" the city of Oxford by those who consider King Stephen will never be allowed his freedom.

Following discussions, Bishop Henry of Winchester in Hampshire, the brother of King Stephen, decides to support the Empress and Earl Robert of Gloucester (half brother the Empress) promising to surrender Winchester to them; Earl Robert and the Empress then travel to the city. Whilst in Winchester the Empress and Earl Robert are besieged by the forces of Queen Matilda (consort of King Stephen and the daughter of Count Eustace III of Boulogne in France), the city starves

Manuscript "E" (Peterborough or Laud): Courier New.

and whilst trying to escape, Earl Robert is captured and imprisoned in Rochester Castle in Kent; the Empress escapes to a monastery (no further information readily available). The prisoners King Stephen and Earl Robert are later exchanged for each other.

1141–4 – The people in Normandy change their allegiance from King Stephen of England and Count of Boulogne in France to Count Geoffrey V Plantagenet of Anjou (husband of Aethelic/the Empress Matilda see **1127** and **1137** above); some by force of arms, some willingly – they receive no help from King Stephen.

1142 – On his release from prison King Stephen of England and Count of Boulogne in France and Earl Rannulf of Chester are reconciled at Stamford in Lincolnshire. King Stephen besieges the Empress (Aethelic/the Empress Matilda – see **1127** and **1137** above) at Oxford. She escapes by night, let down from a tower in the castle by ropes, and goes on foot to Wallingford in Oxfordshire.

1146 – Acting on bad advice King Stephen of England has Earl Rannulf of Chester arrested in Northampton (this could be Southampton in Hampshire instead) but then lets him go providing he surrenders all his castles to the king; he surrenders some but not all.

1147 – The Empress (Aethelic/the Empress Matilda – see **1127** and **1137** above) goes oversea.

1151 – Count Geoffrey V Plantagenet of Anjou in France dies and is succeeded by his son Henry (the future King Henry II of England. His mother is Aethelic, the Empress Matilda, see **1127** and **1137** above).

1152 – The marriage between Eleanor of Aquitaine, Queen of France, and King Louis VII of France is annulled. She marries Count Henry of Anjou (the future King Henry II of England) at Poitou in France; she brings "all Poitou with her".

1153 – Count Henry of Anjou (the future King Henry II of England) lands and campaigns in England. The superior forces of King Stephen of England confront those of Count Henry (at Wallingford in Oxfordshire) but no battle takes place. Through the intercession of Archbishop Theobald of Canterbury and wise men (no further information readily available) it is agreed King Stephen will reign in England and that on his death he will be succeeded as king by Count Henry. Count Henry goes to Winchester in Hampshire and London. A "good and lasting peace" is established. Count Henry goes oversea.

1154 – King Stephen of England dies and is buried with his wife Matilda and their son Count Eustace IV of Boulogne in France at the monastery at Faversham in Kent which they had founded. Count Henry of Anjou (the future King Henry II of England) is overseas when King Stephen dies but "no man dared do other than good, for he was held in great awe".

Manuscript "E" (Peterborough or Laud): Courier New.

On Sunday 19 December Count Henry is consecrated King of England in London; he holds there a "great court".

On 2 January Abbot Martin of Peterborough dies and is buried in the monastery. The Peterborough monks choose as his successor a monk from among their number, William de Warterville. Abbot William goes to Oxford to have his appointment confirmed by King Henry; he is subsequently consecrated at Lincoln. Abbot William is "received with ceremony at Peterborough and with solemn procession" and likewise at the abbeys of Ramsey in Cambridgeshire, Thorney near Peterborough, Crowland and Spalding in Lincolnshire, and St Albans in Hertfordshire.

Manuscript E of the Chronicle ends in 1154.